CARL AND KARIN LARSSON
CREATORS OF THE SWEDISH STYLE

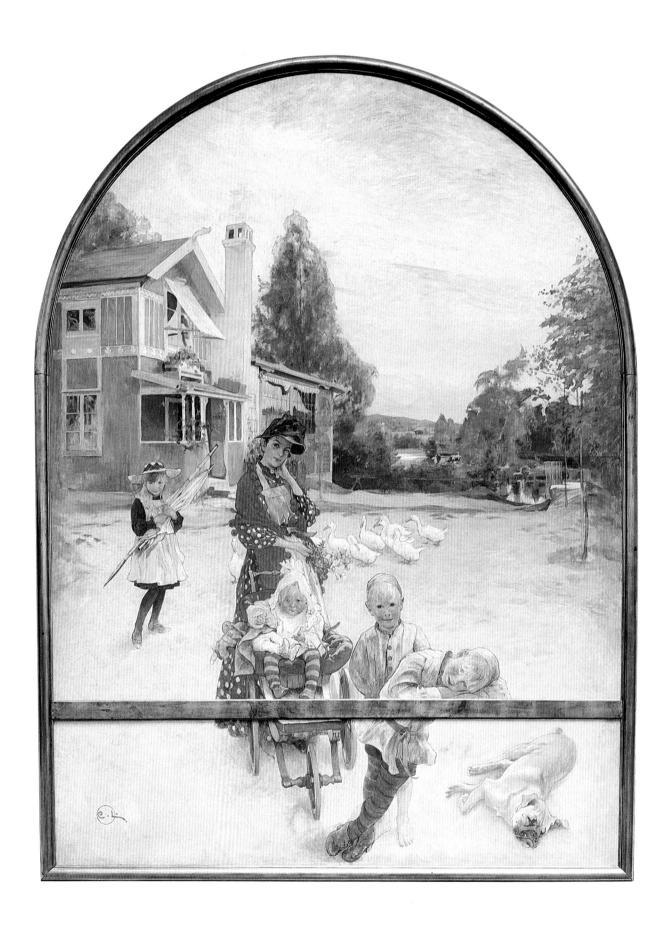

CARL AND KARIN LARSSON
CREATORS OF THE SWEDISH STYLE

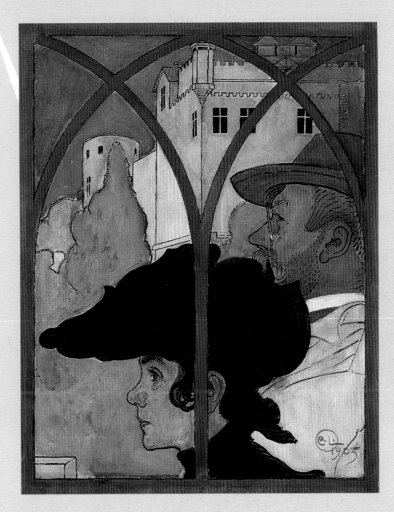

EDITED BY MICHAEL SNODIN AND ELISABET STAVENOW-HIDEMARK

A Bulfinch Press Book

LITTLE, BROWN AND COMPANY

BOSTON   NEW YORK   LONDON

Carl and Karin Larsson's home, now called Carl Larsson-gården, is situated in the village of Sundborn, 13 km northeast of Falun, about 3 hours' drive north of Stockholm. The property belongs to the Carl and Karin Larsson Family Association. It is open to the public every day from May 1 to September 30, from 10 am to 5 pm. Visits at other times can be arranged by telephoning (46) 23 600 69.

Copyright © 1997 by The Board of Trustees of the Victoria and Albert Museum

First U.S. Edition
First published in Great Britain by V&A Publications, 1997
Fourth printing, 2001. First paperback printing, 2001

(Numbers in square brackets after the figure numbers refer to the List of Exhibits on pages 237–239.)

Front jacket: Suzanne and Another, *1901. Watercolor.*
Back jacket: *Lilla Hyttnäs. The porch and part of the west front.*
Frontispiece: *Carl Larsson. De Mina (My Loved Ones, 1892).*
The house at Lilla Hyttnäs is as much part of the subject matter as the family (from right to left): Ulf, Pontus, Lisbeth, Karin, and Suzanne. This great painting, 3.6 meters high, was eventually installed as the centerpiece of a Stockholm villa designed in 1905 by Ragnar Östberg for Larsson's patron, Thorsten Laurin.

Library of Congress Cataloging-in-Publication Data

Carl and Karin Larsson: creators of the Swedish style/edited by
Michael Snodin and Elisabet Stavenow-Hidemark.
    p.   cm.
    Catalog of an exhibition held at the Victoria and Albert Museum,
London, fall 1997.
    Includes bibliographical references.
    ISBN 0-8212-2481-6 HC ISBN 0-8212-2713-0 PB
    1. Larsson, Carl, 1853–1919 — Exhibitions. 2. Larsson, Karin —
Exhibitions. 3. Decoration and ornament, Rustic — Sweden —
Exhibitions. 4. Interior decoration — Sweden — History — 19th
century — Exhibitions. 5. Carl Larsson-gården (Sundborn, Sweden) —
Exhibitions. I. Larsson, Carl, 1853–1919. II. Larsson, Karin.
III. Snodin, Michael. IV. Stavenow-Hidemark, Elisabet. V. Victoria
and Albert Museum.
NK2061. Z9L373   1998
747.2 — dc21   97-19666

Designed by Janet James

Chapters 1, 2, 3, 6, 7, 8, 9, and 10 translated from the Swedish by Janet Cole

Bulfinch Press is an imprint and trademark of
Little, Brown and Company (Inc.)

PRINTED IN ITALY

CONTENTS

FOREWORD

The major autumn and winter exhibition for 1997-8 at the Victoria and Albert Museum is truly made in the spirit of the Museum's founder. The Prince Consort strove for light and air, solid craftsmanship, and the coming together of the arts, institutions and nations. To a considerable degree the exhibition, and this accompanying book, have been prompted by the Prince's values. The Victoria and Albert Museum, the Nordic Museum (the Swedish National Museum of Cultural History), the Carl and Karin Larsson Family Association, the Nationalmuseum (the Swedish National Museum of Fine Arts), the Gothenburg Art Museum, and many other Swedish institutions and private lenders have worked together to show and describe Carl and Karin Larsson's lives and home. No major exhibition can take place without generous external support, and I can think of no more appropriate sponsor than IKEA, with its mission to spread Swedish design around the world. Together everyone has worked to present a central part of Sweden's cultural heritage and a beautiful expression of Sweden's soul.

Carl and Karin Larsson were children of the nineteenth century, the century of utopias. It was Britain that led the way in recognising the great change wrought by industry, and in struggling against the monster of technology. The town had become a living thing, tearing Western man away from the soil that had been the basis of life. The Larssons, in their own utopia, created a permanent dream picture of Sweden and Swedishness, of a country idyll bathed in Nordic light.

Certain artists have the ability to spread gold dust on the wintry path of life. The Larssons were such artists. Their vision of Swedishness is more firmly embedded in the national psyche even than the Swedish sense of community. To have a lilac-embowered cottage in the country, in your family's place of origin, that is the Swedish dream. To have it light and white, clean and airy, like a summer meadow sprinkled with ox-eye daisies, is the very essence of that dream.

All countries need their story-tellers and their myth-makers. The years around 1900 in Sweden were filled with such figures, including the authors Selma Lagerlöf and August Strindberg, the reformer Ellen Key, and the museum man Artur Hazelius, who strove to preserve the story of ordinary people and of everyday things. Carl Larsson and his wife gave shape and colour to this period of change. But they also created a symbol of the happy home with the family and children at its heart, not rituals and restraint. Ellen Key proclaimed the new century, now almost over, as the 'century of the child'. As an expression of this culture of childhood the Larssons and their home have gained a permanent place in Swedish family life.

Anders Clason
Cultural Counsellor
Embassy of Sweden

ACKNOWLEDGEMENTS

This book, and the major exhibition it accompanies, has been the result of complex international cooperation on a remarkable scale, arranged by the Victoria and Albert Museum in collaboration with the Nordic Museum, Stockholm. From its inception the exhibition has been magnificently supported by the Swedish Government and by the Embassy of Sweden in Great Britain. We are particularly indebted to the Swedish Ministry for Foreign Affairs, the Swedish Ministry of Culture, and the Swedish Ministry of Defence (through its Air Force). We owe very special thanks to Anders Clason, Cultural Counsellor at the Embassy, without whose active involvement the project could not have been realised. The Board of Trustees of the Victoria and Albert Museum is most grateful to the exhibition sponsors: IKEA, Ericsson, Skandinaviska Enskilda Banken, and Skanska AB. The official carrier for the Carl and Karin Larsson exhibition is SAS, Scandinavian Airlines.

Special thanks for loans are due to the Carl and Karin Larsson Family Association, the Nationalmuseum, The Gothenburg Art Museum, the Nordic Museum, Malmö Art Museum, Prince Eugen's Waldemarsudde, The Bonniers Portrait Collection, Falu Kommun, Stiftelsen SAF, the British Museum, Helsingborg Museum, the Östergötland County Museum, the Zorn Collections, Mora, Gothenburg University, Gothenburg University Library, the Pro Arte Foundation, Stockholm, the Swedish Church, London, and many private owners.

Both book and exhibition have greatly benefited from the assistance and advice of a large number of scholars, curators, administrators and owners of Larsson works both in Sweden and Britain, to all of whom we extend our thanks. The Carl and Karin Larsson Family Association, under its President Göran Ranström, has been unwaveringly enthusiastic about the project since it was first suggested. The curator at Sundborn, Marianne Nilsson, together with Birgitta Daun and Lars and Gunborg Larsson-Hytte, have been unstintingly helpful, patiently bearing numerous requests and intrusions, and extending to their British and Swedish guests a warm hospitality and a direct experience of the Larsson home that can never be repaid. Among the many invaluable contacts with the Larsson family we owe a special debt to Ulwa Neergaard, who unselfishly shared with us her profound knowledge of Lilla Hyttnäs and of her grandfather's paintings. At the Nationalmuseum, so notably generous in its loans, we owe special thanks to Torsten Gunnarsson, who went far beyond his brief as an author in this book to help us with numerous questions concerning works of art and practical matters.

As editors and exhibition curators we would also particularly like to thank for assistance either practical or scholarly, or both, Stikkan Anderson, Monica Boman, Frances Carey, Görel Cavalli-Björkman, Barbro Edwards, Barbro Ek, Anders Eriksson, Michelle Facos, Jonas Gavel, Jan and Erica Govella, Bo Grandien, Bengt and Agneta Heinö, Jacob Hidemark, Anne Hobbs, Lillie Johansson, Nina Linde, Åke Livstedt, Charles Newton, Bengt Nyström, Magnus Olausson, Nisse Peterson, Berit Rönnstedt, Rickard Sangwill, Katarina Sjöström, Anna Brita Snodin, Martin Stintzing, Maria Wistrand and Ola Henriksson, and the staff at Christies, Sothebys, Nordéns and Bukowskis. We would also like to thank especially Denise Hagströmer, Guest Curator of the final section of the exhibition, for her skilful telling of the complex story of the Larsson legacy. We extend our thanks to the lenders to this section, many of whom cannot be named at the time of writing.

The exhibition has been staged by the Exhibitions Department under Linda LLoyd Jones, and has been the special responsibility of Tina Manoli, ably assisted by Anna Gustavsson (who also contributed to this book) and Suzanne Fagence, with conservation matters headed by Nicola Costaras.

The exhibition has been designed by Sharon Beard, with graphics by Richard Cottingham. Ruth Thackeray has played a key role as publisher's editor. Our final thanks must go to Mary Butler, Head of V&A Publications, for guiding the book to its successful completion with a firm but ever tactful hand.

Michael Snodin
Elisabet Stavenow-Hidemark
March 1997

LILLA HYTTNÄS

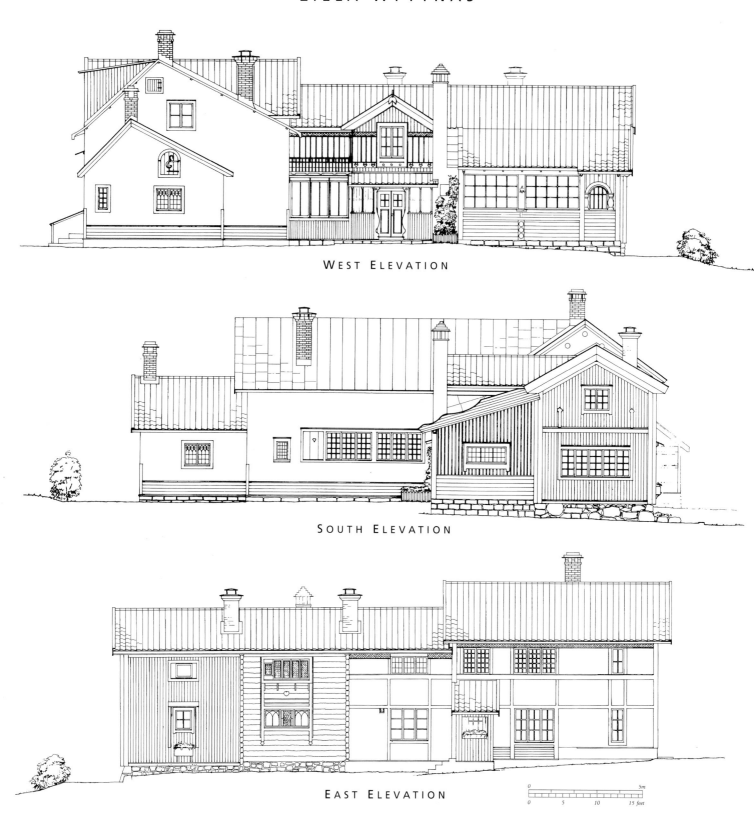

WEST ELEVATION

SOUTH ELEVATION

EAST ELEVATION

Elevations and plans surveyed and drawn by Jacob Hidemark and Martin Stintzing

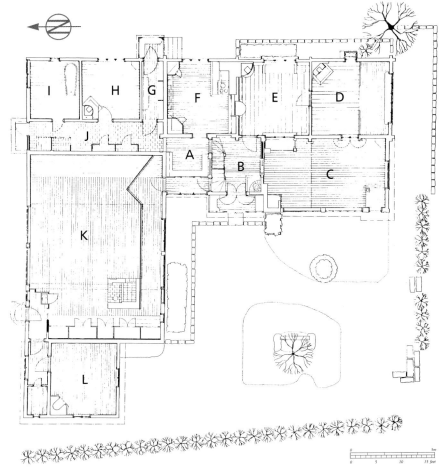

GROUND FLOOR PLAN

KEY

A: Scullery

B: Staircase hall

C: Workshop (former studio)

D: Drawing-room

E: Dining-room

F: Kitchen

G: Larder

H: Maids' room

I: Bathroom (as in 1909, formerly boys' room)

J: Kitchen corridor

K: Studio

L: Little Aspeboda room (Mine-shareholder's cottage)

M: Karin's writing room

N: Sleeping space

O: Karin's bedroom

P: Carl's bedroom

Q: Library (former small studio)

R: Old Room

S: Suzanne's room

T: Upper Dovecote (girls' bedroom)

U: Lower Dovecote (girls' bedroom)

V: Staircase hall

W: Store

X: Kitchen (stove later)

Y: Room (former living-room)

Z: Drawing-room (former bedroom)

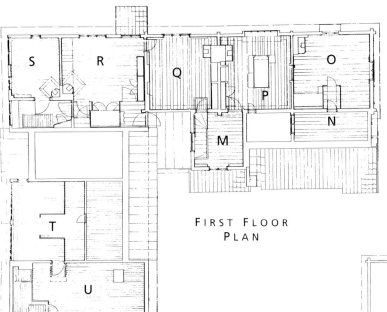

FIRST FLOOR PLAN

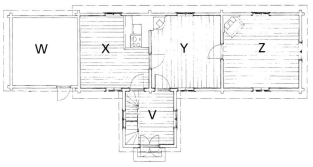

GROUND FLOOR PLAN IN 1888

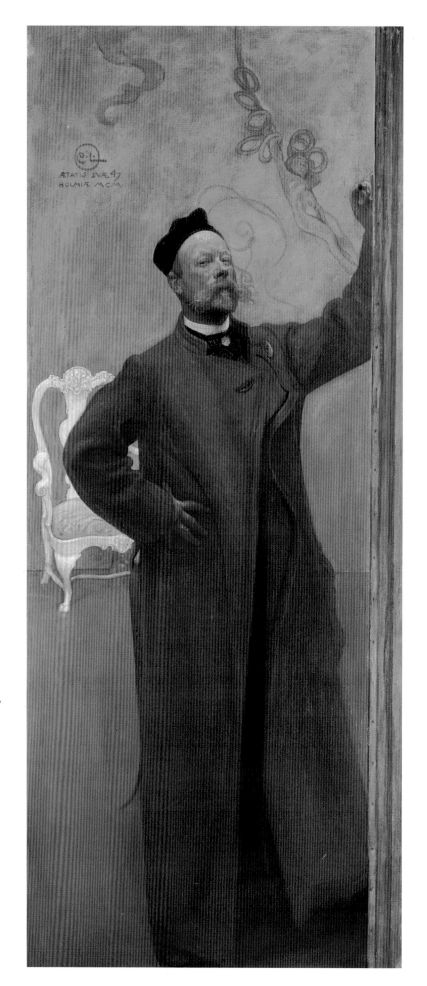

1.[1] Carl Larsson. Before the Mirror
(Self-portrait in a Red Dressing-gown),
1900. Oil on canvas. Reproduced in
Larssons, *1902.*
This supremely self-confident yet slightly
ironical portrait was painted when
Larsson was at the peak of his career
and established as a monumental mural
painter: in the background is the
cartoon for his decorations at the
Stockholm Opera House. In its
composition, colouring and content the
painting clearly shows the chief
elements which lay behind his pictorial
style, namely the Rococo of the
18th century, Japanese prints and Art
Nouveau.

INTRODUCTION
Michael Snodin

Should I die, which, strangely enough, could happen, I believe that the home will carry on just as well as it has always done, although not just in the same way. But then it wasn't the same yesterday as today. A home is not dead but living, and like all living things must obey the laws of nature by constantly changing. At least it can have a long life before finally coming to an end. I would like to think of my home passing through the generations; perhaps my great-grandchildren will write a book about it. That book you should buy, for you, dear reader, must never die, never disappear![1]

The artist Carl Larsson wrote these words about his home at Lilla Hyttnäs in the village of Sundborn, in the book *Åt solsidan* (On the Sunny Side) in 1910. They were more prophetic than he knew, for not only has he never lacked readers (and admirers as Sweden's most popular artist), but the home he created with his wife Karin has since become a model for Swedish domestic design, spread in its turn through the international success of the Swedish style. The particular interest that this is now inspiring is perhaps a result of the increasing appreciation of different local and national styles as well as that accorded to the concept of regionalism. This book (even if not written by his great-grandchildren) is the deepest exploration so far of the Larssons, their home and its contribution to Swedish design, and it has certainly gained immensely from the fact that the Larsson house is no dead thing but a living home still within the family.

If Carl Larsson had not been an artist, it is possible that his house would now be forgotten, and certain that it would have had no effect on Swedish design and national consciousness. For it was not through the house itself, but through reproductions of Carl Larsson's pictures of it and his family, actively promoted through a series of illustrated books, that the Larsson message reached the world.[2] The first and most important of these books was *Ett hem* (A Home), published in 1899, in which a set of twenty-four watercolours reproduced in full colour take us around the house and through it room by room. In his accompanying text, its passion leavened by humour, Larsson portrays his house as an ideal home and his own family as a model for a happy life.

Like all great ideas, the *Ett hem* series (and the book) seems at first to spring from a brilliantly simple concept. Why not just set out to draw your own home peopled with your family, especially if you believe that you have found the secret to happiness? Larsson's story of simply picking up his pencil was of course a gross simplification, for the Sundborn pictures were the result of an extraordinary coming together of different factors, including the particular circumstances of his life and artistic development, as well as the influence of international and national movements in art, design and culture at the end of the nineteenth century.

The powerful appeal of the pictures themselves, an important element in the story, derives from their perfect conjunction of style and content combined with a certain detachment. Descriptive yet highly decorative, intimate yet generalized, they invite us to project our own families and children *we* know into their scenes of a hundred years ago. We are presented with an instantly accessible and intense reality that nevertheless remains a dream. The Larsson images were strong enough not only to survive new or altered texts in foreign languages, beginning in Germany with *Das Haus in der Sonne* (The House in the Sun, 1909), but to work with undiminished effect on their own, whether hung as reproductions in

2. [161] Carl Larsson. Nameday Congratulations. *1900. Watercolour. Namedays were much celebrated at Lilla Hyttnäs. Here Karin's, which fell on 2nd August, is being marked by a very early morning visit from the water sprite and his two daughters.*

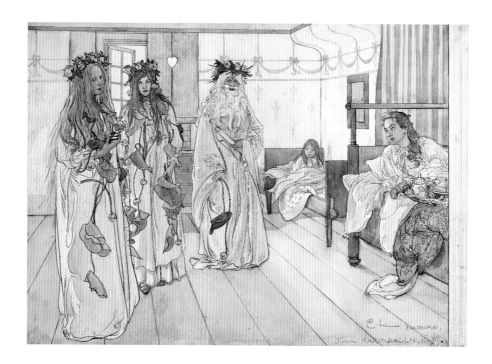

the home (in Sweden and elsewhere) or being disseminated through advertising and merchandising. Visitors to the Larsson house itself, one of Sweden's top tourist attractions, now inevitably view it through Carl Larsson's own eyes.

Carl Larsson's early years, during which he struggled to overcome the difficulties of a Stockholm slum childhood while supporting himself through his artistic talents alone, profoundly affected his character and ambitions; they also played a vital role in the conception, formation and recording of the home in Sundborn. In 1871, aged eighteen, he began working as an illustrator, a form of employment which provided his bread-and-butter for the next twenty years. As a painter he had an eclectic talent, and tried a number of dead-ends before discovering *plein-air* watercolour in France in 1882. This moment coincided with his engagement to the artist Karin Bergöö, six years his junior. Blessed with sudden success and recognition, he now also had a wife prepared to carry him through the darker moments of his outwardly sunny nature. It was the classic story of the poor boy with no permanent home marrying a sensitive girl from the secure propertied bourgeoisie.

In 1885 the Larssons moved definitively back to Sweden. Carl Larsson's delight in his young family was becoming evident in the ever-increasing number of child and family portraits (figs 3, 4). The precious sense of stability which came with Karin culminated in 1888 with the gift to the Larssons of the property of Lilla Hyttnäs. It came to absorb far more energy than the Larssons' flats in Gothenburg or Stockholm, both Carl and Karin revelling in a rural life in the picturesque province of Dalarna, an area supremely rich in surviving folklore and customs. The old plain house was turned into an elaborately designed and decorated summer retreat redolent of the virtuous (and pre-industrial) Swedish past, its style combining elements of folk and 'Viking' design with the more elegant Gustavian taste of the late eighteenth century while also being completely modern. In 1901 the family left Stockholm to settle in Sundborn. But Lilla Hyttnäs was more than just architecture and decoration, it was a whole way of life, informal and family centred. For this the Larssons consciously created a middle-class town-dweller's idyll of the healthy country life: they took up a number of local customs, like boating and crayfishing, and added some of their own, like habitually eating outside. After the publication of the *Ett hem* watercolours the Larssons' vision of summer came to be adopted by the whole of Sweden.

3. *[24] Carl Larsson.* Brita and I, *1895.*
Watercolour.
Larsson described the difficulty of holding
this pose with his lively two-year-old daughter
on his shoulders; in reality it would have
taxed even his abilities, although he could
turn out a watercolour portrait in half an
hour. Painted in the studio-cum-dining-room
at the Larssons' Stockholm flat, this portrait
is among the earliest examples of the linear
style which established him as a popular
watercolourist.

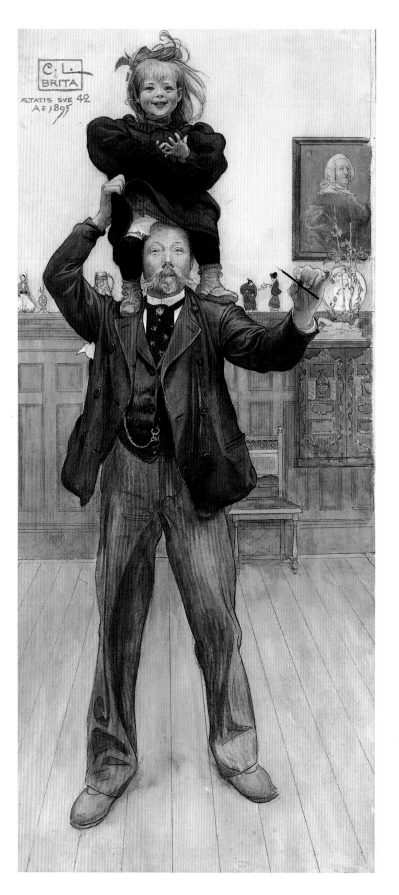

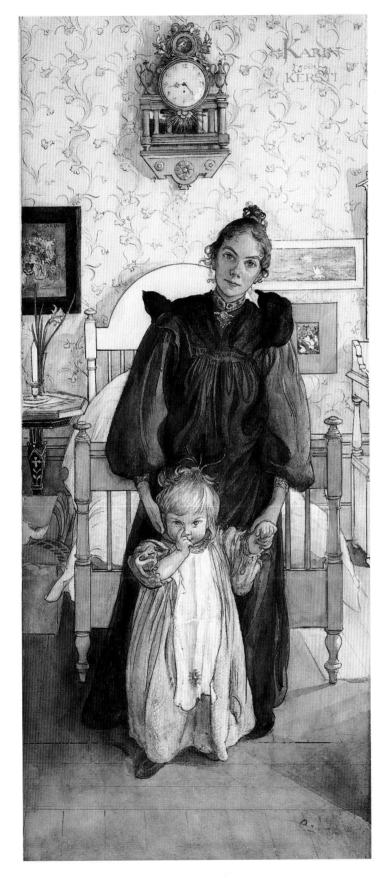

4.[25] *Carl Larsson.* Karin and Kersti, *1898.*
Watercolour.
Painted to match the self-portrait with Brita,
Karin is shown with a new two-year-old in
the bedroom of the Stockholm flat. Karin
wears one of the loose aesthetic-style dresses
she designed and made herself.

At Lilla Hyttnäs the Larssons employed no architect or other designer and for its execution relied entirely on local labour. In public Carl played down Karin's role in its creation, in a manner characteristic of the era and of his attitude towards her (the house was always his house, and she an idealized angel in it). Karin had given up painting after marrying Carl (who in any case did not believe women should be painters) and thereafter devoted most of her time to homemaking and bringing up seven children, born over a span of sixteen years from 1884.[3] This did not, however, prevent her from continuing to exercise her creative abilities; there can be no doubt that Lilla Hyttnäs was the result of an intimate aesthetic partnership, in which Karin's remarkable textiles combined perfectly with Carl's painted decorations. It will probably never be possible to untangle the full story of their individual contributions.

Such a sudden development as Lilla Hyttnäs could not of course have sprung from nothing, however strong Carl Larsson's urge to set down roots. The immediate chronology is certainly suggestive. Carl's interest in ornamental design was definitively shown in the *japoniste*-style frames designed by January 1889 for a triptych for Pontus Fürstenberg, the forms

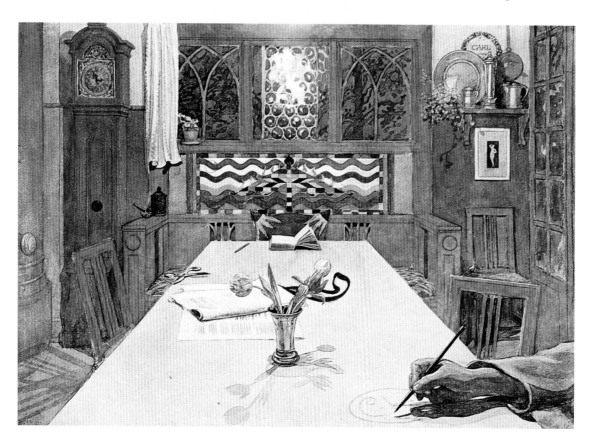

5. *Carl Larsson. It is Evening, Good Night, c. 1910. Reproduction of a watercolour in Åt solsidan, 1910. At the end of Åt solsidan Carl Larsson signed off with this mysterious picture of the dining-room at Lilla Hyttnäs. Carl's and Karin's partnership, symbolised in the book and pencil and cloth and scissors, is also reflected in the room: the cushion and other textiles are by her and the design of the bench is by him.*

of which were to influence the façade of Lilla Hyttnäs. In June 1889 he painted walls, doors and furniture with ornament and figurative scenes in the Bergöös' new house at Hallsberg. Further indications of a new all-encompassing approach to the applied arts and craft (and homemaking) appear in a letter of 1889, written in Amsterdam after the first summer at Sundborn, in which Carl passionately attacks the money wasted on academic teaching in the art schools, urging artists to go out and convert people rich and poor to 'a yearning for attractive colours and graceful forms'. The artists themselves were entreated to 'carve tankards, doors and cupboards, storm the porcelain factories ... and teach them to love the wonderful medium, blow glass into fantastic forms, scrawl on the walls and wake up those engineers hypnotized by the academy, who are called architects. Yes, build your own houses, you painters who have not already had your imaginations killed.'[4]

In February 1890, with the dining-room of the house decorated and the rest of the work about to start, Carl and Karin made a visit to Bingsjö in Dalarna, in the celebrated Rättvik folklore area. Although both were already familiar with folk art, this seems to have been a decisive experience, Carl admiring the craft and wall painting, and Karin being taught to weave. Early in 1890, while Carl was preparing to design the new additions to the house, a further awareness of ornament was prompted by the commission to decorate a school in Gothenburg in a range of historical styles, including motifs close to those used at Sundborn. Finally, in 1891, Carl was given an eighteenth-century decorator's pattern book from which the Gustavian scheme of the drawing-room was devised.

What was happening at Lilla Hyttnäs was in one sense not unique. All over Europe artists and architects were developing the idea of the 'artistic house', first conceived by William Morris at Red House in 1860, and which by the 1870s was prompting English writers of the aesthetic movement to claim that 'art and artistic feeling are as much shown in the design of furniture and other accessories as in what have hitherto been considered the higher of "fine" arts of sculpture and painting'.[5] The Larssons, from their years abroad, would of course already have been aware of such ideas and others linking art, design and social reform which were sweeping Europe. Lilla Hyttnäs, both an artist's house and an artistic house, inevitably became a visual expression of these ideas, which appeared in written form in the text of *Ett hem*.

In other respects, however, Lilla Hyttnäs was very different from other artistic houses. For while it bears traces of the Larssons' foreign experiences, including *japonisme*, the English Arts and Crafts movement and Queen Anne style, in overall effect the Larssons' retreat from urbanism was a distillation of Swedishness, in line with the national romantic movement and the linked drive to preserve a rapidly disappearing folk culture. The result, as Carl Larsson himself agreed, was certainly idiosyncratic and in social terms not a little revolutionary. The room arrangements, furnishings and decoration consciously set out to break down previous distinctions of function and status, while the contents, whether new or antique, were (like those of William Morris) valued on grounds of use or beauty alone.

The Larssons, however, while being extremely adept at combining practicality with stylish design and valuing and promoting the hand-made, were not whole-hearted believers in the well-made. This divergence from the tenets of Morris and his followers was as evident in Karin's textiles (often experimental in technique) as in the manner in which existing pieces of furniture were knocked up into new ones. This attitude was also reflected in Carl's published writings, in which he casually underplayed the scale of the work at Lilla Hyttnäs. From his more private observations it is clear that the slum child in him was constantly amazed by his good fortune and that he believed everybody to be capable of achieving similar success and happiness.

The central role of Lilla Hyttnäs as a family idyll was first displayed publicly in *De mina* (My Loved Ones), a huge work painted in the summer of 1892, in which the house almost as much as the family was the subject of the picture (see Frontispiece). When shown in America the next year, it was praised as 'a joyous cantata to sunlight, life, and love': Carl Larsson had arrived.[6] In 1895 the picture was featured in a book of the same title incorporating many of Larsson's earlier cartoon stories of family life (fig. 6). When the *Ett hem* series of watercolours was displayed at the Stockholm exhibition of Art and Industry in 1897, it was approvingly described by the social reformer Ellen Key, thus taking Lilla Hyttnäs (and the Larssons) a step further towards the full limelight of the *Ett hem* book, published two years later.

Thereafter, Lilla Hyttnäs rapidly turned into Sweden's most famous house and the Larssons into its best-known family. By 1913 Swedish commentators could look back on the Larsson watercolours as having played a key role in the design-reform battle, by then effectively won among the Swedish bourgeoisie if not yet among the working classes. In a broader sense, although depicting a particular and rather idiosyncratic house, they had succeeded in expressing in visual terms a sense of national identity, both in the style of the interiors and in their concentration on a special relationship to nature, which was at that very moment emerging as an element of nationalism. Their social message, descending from the sunny vision of a family life without hierarchy, continued to play a vital role, especially after the Second World War, when Sweden's economy improved and thousands were rehoused in small modern flats and houses built to standard formats.

The Larsson ideal, unpretentious and family centred, and carried out in small light rooms economically furnished, was now found to fit exactly the needs and conditions of modern life. At the same time the real house at Sundborn began to be re-examined and was seen to contain many practical ideas, related by commentators to the functionalism which had dominated Swedish design since the 1930s. With the advent in the 1960s of mass producers of good design, notably IKEA, the Larsson model was inevitably among those selected and has since reached a world market through that firm's international success. The beginnings of this last phase coincided with the flood of Larsson images in contexts appropriate and inappropriate, which came with the ending of copyright in 1969. In spite of this last cheapening process, and the negative reactions it produced, the power of Lilla Hyttnäs and Carl Larsson's images of it is such that they continue to set the agenda, more or less overtly, for designers, decorators and homemakers in Sweden and beyond.

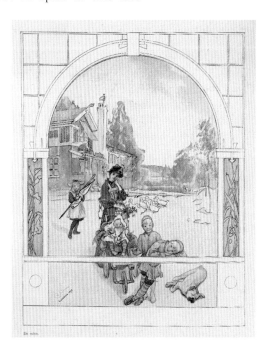

6. Carl Larsson. De mina, *1893. Reproduction of a watercolour, forming the frontispiece of* De mina *(1919 edition). For the coloured frontispiece of the first book on his family Carl Larsson redrew* De mina *and showed it in the japoniste-style frame for which the picture had originally been painted, and which had been intended for the triptych painted for Pontus Fürstenberg in 1889. When the painting was installed in the Laurin villa the* japoniste *frame was replaced by one in plain bronze, the picture widened, and some details, like the palette-shaped windvane painted out.*

1

SWEDEN
IN THE 1890s

Eva Eriksson

Snow has just fallen on Norrbro in the centre of Stockholm, some time in the early 1890s (fig. 7). Perhaps it is Saturday. The flags are flying, and a lot of people are about. Two trams have just passed each other at the passing loop. The town's communications are mainly horse-drawn, although there are a couple of steam trams at work on the steep slopes in the south. Electric trams will not appear until after the turn of the century, but electric light has begun to spread over the dark, wintry town, and a tower for telephone wires rises high above the roofs, like a knight's castle of iron. It is a proud testimony to the dawning of a new age. Wires radiate in all directions. You can already make calls to Malmö and Gothenburg. In fact, in 1885, Stockholm had more telephones than any other town in the world, both in relation to population and in total number. Compared with London, where the first electric underground railway started running in 1890, it is otherwise a fairly backward, small town.

But this is a town in the process of transformation.[1] The old eighteenth-century opera house has just been demolished, and a new one will soon be built behind the curtain of trees in the picture. Carl Larsson will then be commissioned to decorate the ceiling and lunettes in the foyer. In the square in the background, there is a row of mid-nineteenth-century houses, which will be replaced within twenty years by palatial new banks on a quite different scale. The building to the left, with the noticeable doorway, is the famous Hotel Rydberg, the rendezvous of the middle classes, writers and artists, which Carl Larsson often goes past. The Academy of Fine Arts is situated slightly to the west, the National Museum a few blocks to the east. The opera house is being built here, and it is not far to the spot where the Royal Dramatic Theatre is to be built, where Larsson will also be given a commission.

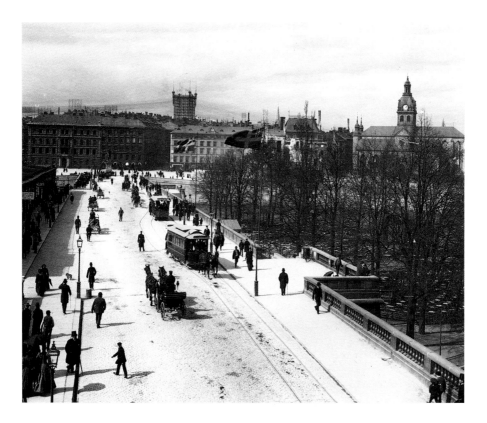

7. Norrbro (the North Bridge), Stockholm, seen from the Royal Palace, 1890s.
Photograph by Hans Klemming.

Above all, Sweden's financial centre is now being established in this district. The town's middle-class drawing-rooms are being taken over by the banks, with their key role in the industrialization of the period. The transformation, which is expressed all over the country in smoking chimneys, is manifest here in expensive stone and increasing building heights. Hotel Rydberg will be demolished to make way for one of the banks.

The low row of stalls (fig. 7, left-hand corner) will also disappear soon and be replaced by a new Parliament building and national bank. Like the banks, the representative assembly will thus acquire a new monumental expression. Placed right in front of the Royal Palace, the traditional seat of royal power (behind the photographer's back), it can perhaps be seen as a sign of the times. It is not a question of a truly democratic parliament, but rather of the power of money. As yet, only those with sufficient wealth have the right to vote; the ordinary working poor do not have the vote, neither do women.

But the struggle for the right to vote is intensifying. At the same moment as the photographer takes his picture of Norrbro, a meeting is perhaps being held somewhere else with different flags, where the right to vote is being discussed. The labour movement is being organized in Sweden. The Social Democratic party had been founded in 1889, and the demand for universal and equal suffrage is the first item on its agenda. Before the end of the century, the labour movement will begin to build its own 'People's House' at Norra Bantorget in Stockholm. This will be a symbolic place for many future meetings.

The gap between rich and poor is large in Stockholm in the 1890s. Most working-class families live in overcrowded conditions. The usual dwelling consists of one room and kitchen, or just one room with a tiled stove. They are often forced to take in lodgers as well, in order to pay the rent. Statistics illustrating the conditions begin to be available to contemporary society. By the turn of the century Stockholm will have about 300,000 inhabitants, about a quarter of whom will live in one room and kitchen. On average they will share this accommodation with three or four others.[2]

Building is going on everywhere. Stockholm is like two interwoven towns. The new city, with its wide avenues and high buildings, is developing amidst the remains of the Old Town, with its untidy mix of low wooden houses, picturesque streets and small workshops. Carl Larsson grew up on the seamy side of town, among the ordinary people in the poor district of Ladugårdslandet to the east. In the 1890s this is being transformed into Stockholm's most exclusive district. A great many large flats are being built here, with plenty of room even for the servants.

High-class residential suburbs outside the town are now also beginning to develop. In 1895 the first electrified railway in Sweden is built to Djursholm, which was to become Stockholm's most exclusive residential suburb. Djursholm has a certain intellectual character from the start; the cultural élite are in the process of adopting a new lifestyle, with a more relaxed life close to nature. In the summer, middle-class families take the steamer to their 'summer houses', a new concept in itself. Large wooden houses with glass verandas are spreading along the shores and among the islands of the Stockholm archipelago.

In 1897 an Art and Industry Exhibition is organized in Stockholm along the lines of those abroad. The official reason is the celebration of the twenty-fifth anniversary of Oscar II's accession to the throne. The main

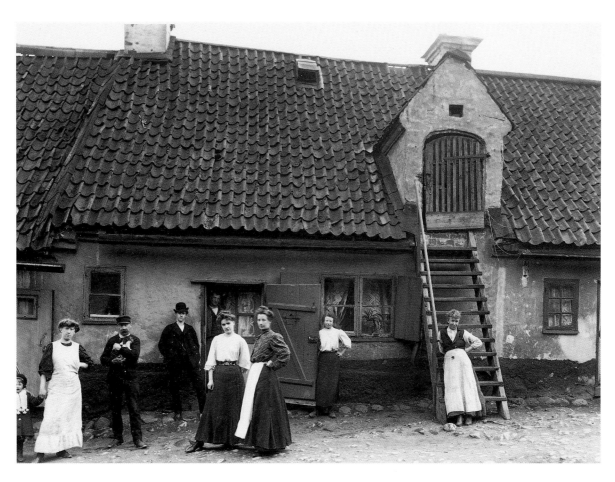

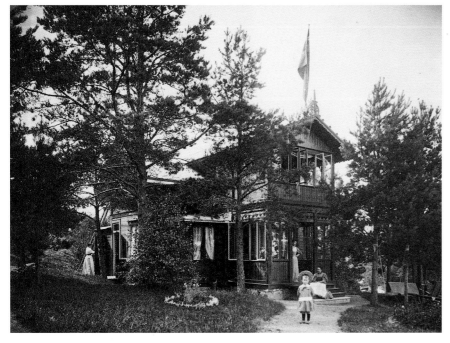

8. *Workers' houses in Fatbursgatan,*
Stockholm, at the turn of the century.
The buildings date from the 18th century.
Photograph by Oskar Heimer.

9. *A summer house in the Uppland*
archipelago, 1890s.
When steamers opened up the islands of the
Stockholm archipelago to the middle classes,
summer houses with glazed verandas and
elaborate woodwork spread rapidly along
the shores. They soon became an established
part of middle-class life. Photograph by
K.J. Olsson.

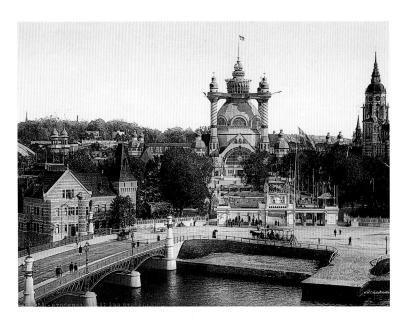

10. The Art and Industry Exhibition, Stockholm, 1897.
In the centre is the domed hall of industry designed by Ferdinand Boberg and Fredrik Liljekvist. The exhibition was a demonstration of Sweden's rapid industrial expansion at the turn of the century. In the art section Carl Larsson was represented by the painting De mina *(My Loved Ones) and the series of watercolours exhibited under the title* A Home in Dalarna, *all showing the Larssons' house at Sundborn. Hand-coloured photograph.*

reason is in fact to display the recent progress in industry and technology, both to the surrounding world and to the Swedish people. The exhibition gives a great boost to national self-esteem. The many Swedish visitors are impressed by the 'accumulation of national strength and national intelligence shown in the fields of major industry and inventions', as one of Sweden's leading intellectuals of the period, Ellen Key, expresses it.[3] But the exhibition is also an important artistic manifestation. The turn-of-the-century generation of Nordic artists make a convincing showing. Among the works exhibited is Carl Larsson's painting *De mina* (My Loved Ones), as well as twenty watercolours of the Larssons' house at Sundborn in Dalarna, in their first public display in Sweden.

The exhibition is typical of the period in its split between optimism about progress in industry and technology on the one hand, and an awareness of tradition and an interest in nature within the arts on the other. While middle-class circles feel a certain nostalgia for the past, the labour movement is more whole-heartedly positive to some of the technical advances. Attitudes to electric light may be seen as symbolic of this divide. Well-to-do families had previously gathered around the oil lamp for reading aloud in the evening. The lamp spread a magic circle of togetherness during dark winter evenings. In the case of poor, working-class families in cramped backyard flats, which the faint rays of daylight scarcely reach, reading – and consequently knowledge – is still restricted by the price of oil.[4] As time goes by, electricity illuminates Sweden in more ways than one.

Historical conditions

In the 1890s Sweden was a peripheral country in the north, in the process of being transformed into a modern industrial nation. Since time immemorial it had been a sparsely populated agrarian society in which farmers owned their land. The bulk of the population lived in the country; the towns functioned solely as small centres for trade and crafts.

People's conditions had been determined by the forces of nature. The relationship between man and nature is central to Nordic myths and fairy tales, in which the forest is full of supernatural beings: elves, trolls, wood sirens and water sprites. The annual festivals and traditions also follow the rhythmic changes of nature. Spring is still welcomed today with enormous bonfires on 30 April, and midsummer is celebrated with dancing around maypoles adorned with flowers.

But this farming nation also had a very long history of industrial production for export. Copper and iron had been mined since the Middle Ages. The export trade had increased greatly in the seventeenth century, when the Dutchman Louis de Geer established a Swedish iron industry of world renown, with the aid of Walloon smiths from his own country. In the early eighteenth century Sweden produced a third of Europe's iron (about 65 per cent of Swedish exports went to England at that time).

Even the production of iron was linked to the countryside. It had developed where there was ore, and required access to forest for charcoal and to watercourses for energy. Small industrial communities grew like islands in the countryside. They were beautifully designed environments, in which each individual house, from manor house to workman's cottage, formed part of a unified whole. They were also communities with their own social pattern and a strict hierarchy. Everyone knew his place, but there was also a certain social security. Those who became ill or frail were taken care of at the expense of the ironworks.

Rural Sweden had changed during the nineteenth century due to a rapid increase in the population, which had resulted in a reduction in the proportion of land-owning farmers to those without land. This led to migration, emigration and urbanization. Those without land tended to move to the towns in search of work. But the manor-house tradition lived on to a certain extent. A network of manor houses acted as centres of culture and a meeting place for social life, reading and music. The majority of the best-known Swedish authors of the 1890s came from a manor-house milieu. Country life was therefore reflected naturally in literature, and nature was the great source of inspiration for the cultural élite of the period.

Looking back and looking forward

Artists and authors in peripheral regions have naturally always been keen to absorb ideas from abroad, and the Nordic countries were no exception. In the late nineteenth century a period abroad had been a standard part of cultural education. But in the 1890s many Nordic writers and artists returned home again. They had imbibed the criticism of Western civilization and the *fin-de-siècle* atmosphere of the period in Paris and Berlin. They were looking for an alternative, and many Swedes found it in their sparsely populated and recently industrialized homeland. Sweden offered a wealth of unspoiled nature with changing emotional moods: dark and mysterious pine forests, smiling silver birches; glittering lakes, sea and mountains, desolate wide open spaces; and of course the long, light, Nordic summer nights. The still unbroken rural traditions symbolized something fresh and natural for the people of the period.

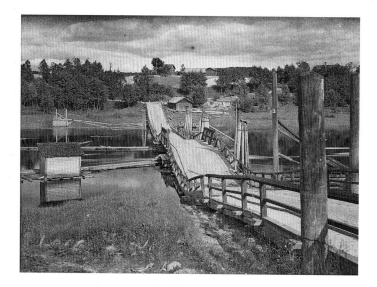

11. A bridge over the Österdalälven at Djurås, Dalarna, 1910.
Dalarna, the most tradition-rich of all Swedish provinces, had a special appeal for Swedish artists. Carl Larsson was among those to settle there. Autochrome photograph by August Leon.

The new railways had made even the most remote areas of the country accessible. Not only artists but a growing middle class set out for new tourist destinations. Groups of young people made walking tours, armed with rucksacks and walking-sticks, particularly to areas where they could find a genuine and original culture. They found surviving traditions and unspoiled villages in Dalarna, endless forests in Värmland, and an exotic mountain world in Norrland, where they climbed the summits and stayed in Lapp tents. But guesthouses and hotels were now also being built in

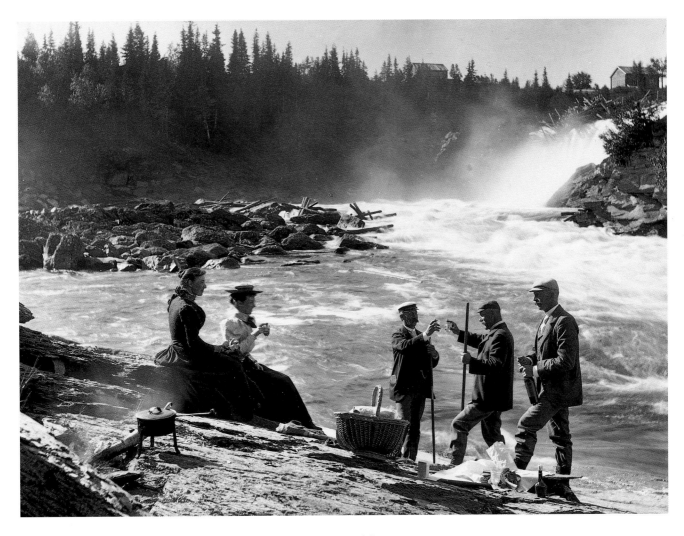

12. Tourists by a waterfall, 1890s.
Tourism in Sweden became an increasingly popular pursuit at the end of the
nineteenth century. Not only artists but the wider middle classes went ever further
in search of undisturbed nature. Here the river is being used to float timber.

attractive tourist resorts. This made it possible to visit previously
uninhabited countryside without great difficulty: tourism made its first
breakthrough. For Swedish artists the 1890s involved a rediscovery of their
own country, the Nordic light and landscape, and the various regions with
their different traditions. A study of the subjects of their paintings alone
might give the impression that Sweden was a beautiful, but fairly stagnant
idyll (figs. 49-51).

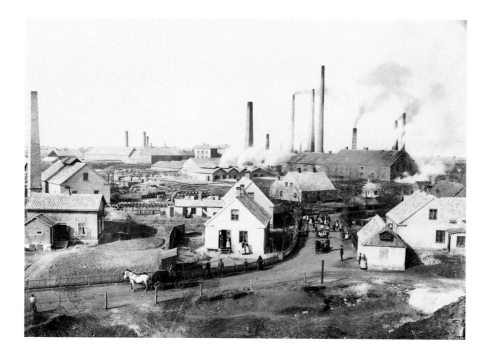

13. The brick and ceramic factory of the Höganäs company, 1895.
The smoke from the many factory chimneys was a characteristic sign of Sweden's
new industrialization. Photograph by Peter P. Lundh.

The process of change had in fact never been more violent. Industrialization came late but was all the more rapid for that[5]. It began with the breakthrough of steam power in the 1860s. At first the most exciting developments were in the timber industry, centred on the coast of Norrland, where the timber was floated down from the forest areas of the interior to a large number of new sawmills. At the same time, iron production began to be consolidated and rationalized.[6] Engineering workshops were now also established for the production of various types of machinery, particularly for agriculture. Where agriculture could be intensified and made more efficient, the surpluses increased. (At one time Sweden was an important exporter of oats for London's tram horses.) Communications were also revolutionized at this time. Steamboats and trains linked up the country, and the towns began to grow increasingly rapidly. But it was not all progress. The bad harvests of the late 1860s had been a setback, and were followed by a wave of emigration. Between 1868 and 1872 around 125,000 people emigrated, mostly to the USA. Some golden years in the early 1870s had been followed by a new recession and a second wave of emigration in the 1880s. Counteracting emigration became an important political goal in late nineteenth-century Sweden.

The boom of the 1890s, however, was to last for an unusually long time. Swedish industrialization entered a new phase, and the age of steam was succeeded by the age of electricity. In Europe the market for Swedish raw materials grew: much iron was needed for all the new machinery. New mining methods suddenly made it profitable to exploit the large iron deposits in the north of Sweden. In the 1890s a railway was built, through endless wilderness, to a spot north of the Arctic circle, which was to become the new mining town of Kiruna. The timber industry was still thriving, but exports shifted increasingly towards wood pulp. The demand for paper and newsprint in particular was insatiable in Europe. Raw materials were also increasingly being processed within Sweden; the engineering industry was growing fast.

Several Swedish inventions were a great financial success, and gave rise to the term 'genius industry'. These included Gustav De Laval's milk separators and steam turbines. Also in the 1890s the engineer Jonas Wenström, at the small company ASEA in Västerås, solved one of the key problems in the electrical engineering industry, that is the transmission of electric power over long distances without losses of current. As a result a couple of waterfalls in Sweden could supply industries throughout the country with electric power. A world market for electrical engineering products opened up simultaneously, and ASEA grew into a global company within a couple of decades.

This industrial progress breathed optimism. The future belonged to the engineer, and there was great confidence in science. Alfred Nobel's legacy was a manifestation not only of one man's ideas but also of the spirit of the age. He had made his fortune from the invention of dynamite, and he now wanted the money to be used in the service of mankind, by furthering scientific development, peace and literature. Technical progress was thus central for Nobel, but was to be balanced by cultural achievements, a division characteristic of the period.

The nationalistic undercurrents of the time expressed themselves in Sweden through industrial progress, a struggle against emigration and the rediscovery of traditional values. During the upheavals of 1905, when Norway was pushing towards a dissolution of the union with Sweden, expressions of nationalism could become quite chauvinistic, but artists and intellectuals tended to remain basically sympathetic towards the Norwegian cause and therefore towards nationalism in general.

The 1890s were marked by great individualism and a growing respect for the individual's creative talent in various cultural spheres. Artistic genius drew ever greater regard. Sheer talent became a means for a poor person to achieve a respected position in the upper echelons of society. Carl Larsson was one of those who succeeded in doing so. Another was the architect Ferdinand Boberg, who rose from the humblest beginnings to the highest position in his profession at the turn of the century. Both were active in a period when Stockholm, like other Swedish towns, was undergoing rapid change. For Boberg this meant a large number of architectural commissions, while for Larsson it meant opportunities for monumental decorative work. Sweden's rapid economic development also meant that large fortunes were amassed in private hands. Art became a central component of life for some of the wealthy. Patrons such as Ernest Thiel and Pontus Fürstenberg played a key role in furthering the careers of several artists, including Larsson.

Carl Larsson lived with his family in Stockholm in the 1890s, spending the summers in Sundborn. His affinity with both city and country is clear: in painting the rural idyll he expressed the values of the period; but his rise to fame was a product of the dynamics of the period, Sweden's technical and economic transformation, and the growth of the city.[7]

2

CARL LARSSON: HIS LIFE AND ART

Torsten Gunnarsson

Carl Larsson (1853–1919) has a unique position in Swedish art. He is a household name in Sweden, and his work has retained its popularity for a century, although he neither founded a school nor had any imitators. This was mainly due to art and life being so inextricably linked in his work that any imitation was impossible.

The chief reason for Carl Larsson's popularity must lie in the universal appeal of his depictions of everyday life. His numerous portrayals of his home and family, for instance, have increasingly become a symbol of reassurance with which a large audience can identify. The fact that his art was extensively distributed through new techniques of colour reproduction was also crucial to his success. His fame soon spread to the rest of Europe, especially Germany. The series of books illustrating scenes from everyday life, beginning with *Ett hem* (A Home, published 1899), transformed his family into public figures, and created a collective dream of family happiness and the good life.

An unfortunate aspect of this success, however, is that there have been too many poor reproductions (now sold worldwide) of his work; this has not only deprived it of its original freshness but has reduced his most popular images to mere symbols. In addition, interest has come to focus on only one part of Carl Larsson's unusually multi-faceted work. It is often overlooked that, unlike his Swedish contemporaries, he moved freely between widely differing genres. He was at once a celebrated portrait painter, a productive illustrator, a sensitive watercolourist and a skilful monumental painter.

Childhood and studies at the Academy

Carl Larsson's life had a somewhat fairy-tale quality. Despite a difficult childhood, he rose from poverty to become one of Sweden's most famous artists, a success based on recognition of his talent. He was born in 1853 in the Old Town in Stockholm. His parents were of peasant and artisan stock, but had been part of the wave of country people moving to the towns in search of work. His father was a casual labourer and was depicted by Carl Larsson as unloving and introverted, while his mother was described as trying her best to keep the family together, maintaining as bright an attitude to life as their straitened circumstances would allow. His grandmother was also an important figure, endowed with an unusual gift for telling stories. Her fairy tales were apparently the young boy's only fuel for igniting his imagination during an otherwise miserable childhood. Carl Larsson himself related how as a small boy he was often left locked in the home while his parents were out at work. At an early age he was expected to help with such household chores as carrying water, chopping wood and clearing snow, yet hunger was a constant companion. He felt intimidated and disliked both inside and outside the home.

After moving from the Old Town to an eastern district of Stockholm, Carl Larsson attended a school marked by strict discipline. His gift for drawing was noticed, however, and in the autumn of 1866 he was sent, at the age of thirteen, to the Principle School, the preparatory department of the Academy of Fine Arts. Only drawing from engravings and wooden blocks was taught in the classical academy manner. The pupils were a mixed bunch, largely consisting of the sons of craftsmen, who were complementing their vocational training without aiming at an artistic career.

Carl Larsson continued his studies in the Antique School, the first department of the Academy proper, where the emphasis was on drawing from plaster casts. Great importance was attached to learning how to create volume in drawing by means of shading, and this undoubtedly developed the students' technical skill. However, many of them felt this to be a soul-destroying exercise, since it did not encourage the development of an individual artistic style.

In the autumn of 1872 Carl Larsson finally advanced to the Life School, where drawing was from life models in Antique poses. The following year he was awarded a medal in life drawing and in 1876 he won the royal medal

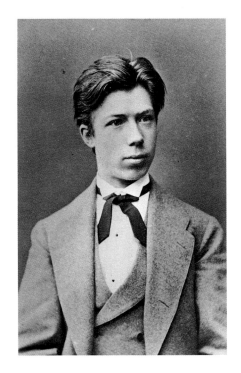

in the Academy's major annual subject competition. This was a requirement for obtaining scholarships abroad; despite repeated applications Larsson was never awarded a travelling scholarship. Instead, he supported both himself and his parents by working as a photograph retoucher and an illustrator on comic and weekly magazines. Illustration work was to remain his bread and butter for many years.

14. *Portrait of Carl Larsson, 1872.*
This portrait of Carl aged 19 was taken by A. Roesler, for whose studio he began working as a retoucher in 1872, in order to support himself as he studied at the Academy of Fine Arts. At this date he was also making illustrations for periodicals.

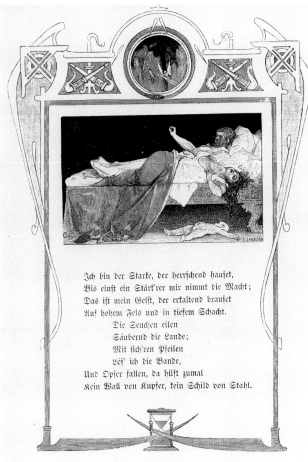

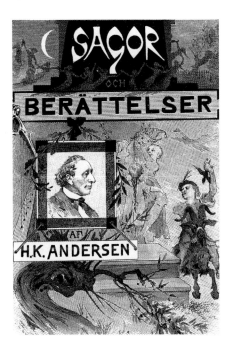

15.[3] *W.F. Meyer after Carl Larsson. Title-page to Hans Christian Andersen, Sagor och berättelser (Stories and Tales), 1877. Wood engraving. Even at this early date Larsson's work showed a marked sense of ornamental design.*

16.[6] *J. Engberg after Carl Larsson. Illustration to Johan Olof Wallin, Des Engel des Todes (The Angel of Death). Wood engraving.*
Carl Larsson designed the whole of this book, including a cover, for a Swedish edition in 1880. It was shown in a gloomy 'vanitas' still-life of 1881 entitled 'Résignation, c'est la dernière religion', painted in Paris when Larsson was at his lowest point. The handling of the illustrations, recalling such German printmakers as Max Klinger, was not to be repeated by Larsson.

Paris and Stockholm, 1877–1882

After completing his studies at the Academy, Carl Larsson travelled to Paris for the first time in the spring of 1877. He was determined to be a success in academic painting, but his very first experiment with a three-metre canvas remained unfinished due to lack of money. Instead he exhibited a portrait of his fellow artist Carl Skånberg at the Salon of 1878, but it was hung so high that no one could see it. Financial considerations then forced Larsson to return temporarily to Sweden and his illustration commissions. Even after returning to Paris in 1879, he continued within the academic tradition and refused to move in the direction of realism, despite his lack of success.

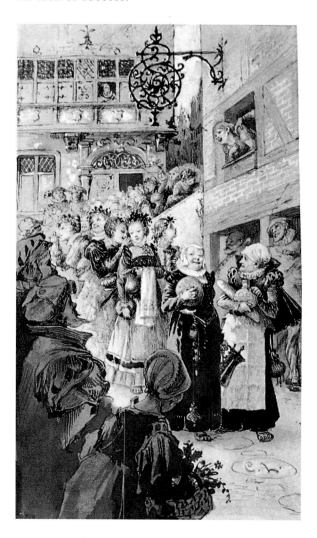

17.[80] Carl Larsson.
The Journey to the Bridal Bath, 1881-2. Pen and ink and wash.
Illustration to August Strindberg, Svenska folket i helg och söcken *(The Swedish People on Weekdays and Sundays), 1881-2.*
Larsson's illustrations for Strindberg's social history of Sweden were extremely carefully studied, right down to the smallest detail of clothing. Each illustration was drawn to a detailed programme prescribed by the author.

After a further period in Sweden, where he began illustrating his friend August Strindberg's *Svenska folket i helg och söcken* (The Swedish People on Weekdays and Sundays), Carl Larsson returned to Paris for the third time in the autumn of 1881. Firmly resolved to avenge his earlier rejections, he put all his efforts into a large painting in eighteenth-century style for the Salon, entitled *At the Court Painter's*. Its refusal by the jury in the winter of 1882 marked Larsson's final defeat in the struggle for recognition. Without a scholarship or admission to the Paris Salon all avenues seemed closed. Having cut his painting into pieces (see fig. 18), which he then distributed among his friends, he fell ill, weakened by starvation and hardship.

The *plein-air* painter in Grez-sur-Loing, 1882–1884

At this nadir, in the spring of 1882 Carl Larsson was persuaded to move to the village of Grez-sur-Loing by his fellow artist Karl Nordström. This move proved to be a crucial turning-point. It coincided broadly speaking with the transition to *plein-air* realism among young Swedish artists studying in France. According to Strindberg, who pushed literary realism to new limits, Carl Larsson represented a new type of artist, one who achieved success solely through his own work and not thanks to the Academy. In this not entirely impartial characterization of Larsson, Strindberg went on to claim that the whole situation of art was new. It could not continue to be aristocratic while the spirit of the age was democratic. Art had changed, and had now reached the masses for the first time thanks to the printing press. At the same time, it had returned with the aid of realism to its true, original source, that is nature.[1]

Grez-sur-Loing, some seventy kilometres south of Paris near the forest of Fontainebleau, was (along with Skagen in Denmark) the foremost Nordic artists' colony during the 1880s. The village, which was also frequented by English, American, Norwegian and Japanese artists, was not remarkable in itself. Its importance lay in offering a stimulating combination of a peaceful environment and unconventional comradeship. It was also the scene of experimentation for a number of Swedish painters, where the new French techniques could be tried out and further developed. The art created at Grez during the first half of the 1880s is now considered to be among the very best of nineteenth-century Nordic painting.

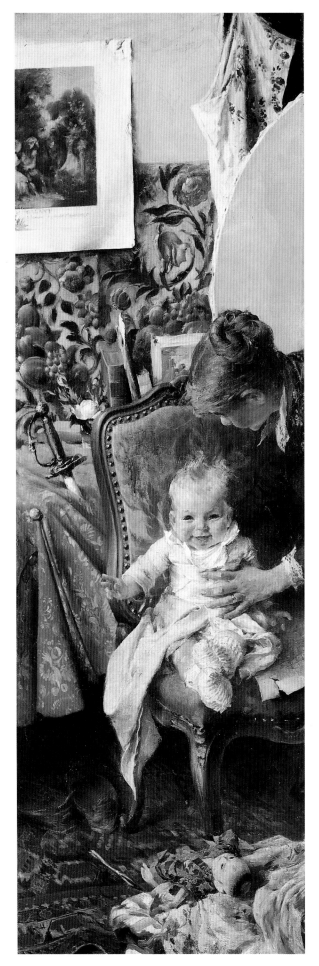

Carl Larsson's rapid transformation from academic studio painting in oils to subtle *plein-air* realism in watercolours is unique in Swedish art. The log-jam was broken and he never looked back. After only six months in Grez he had fully mastered watercolour technique, and in 1883 he received a medal at the Paris Salon for *October* and *November*, which were purchased unseen by the influential Swedish collector Pontus Fürstenberg, later to become Larsson's principal patron. That year, too, the French state purchased *The Pond* (now in the Louvre).

Carl Larsson's private life also took a new and decisive turn in Grez, thanks to his meeting with the painter Karin Bergöö. They were married in Stockholm in June 1883, but returned to Grez, where their daughter Suzanne was born the following year. The watercolours that Larsson painted in Grez, such as *Autumn* with its sensitively graded and constantly shifting hues, belong to a clearly defined period in his artistic career. His concentration on the medium of watercolour also marks the beginning of his transition to maturity, when his work was to include such widely differing genres as watercolour and monumental painting.

18. Carl Larsson. Little Suzanne, *1885. Oil on canvas. The figures have been added to a narrow strip cut from a picture called* At the Court Painter's, *painted in 1882 but destroyed by Larsson after it had been turned down for the Salon.*

19. Carl Larsson. Autumn, *1884. Watercolour. The model is Suzanne's nurse Zerline, who is wearing copies of 18th-century clothes. A hint of narrative is provided by the torn-up letter on the ground.*

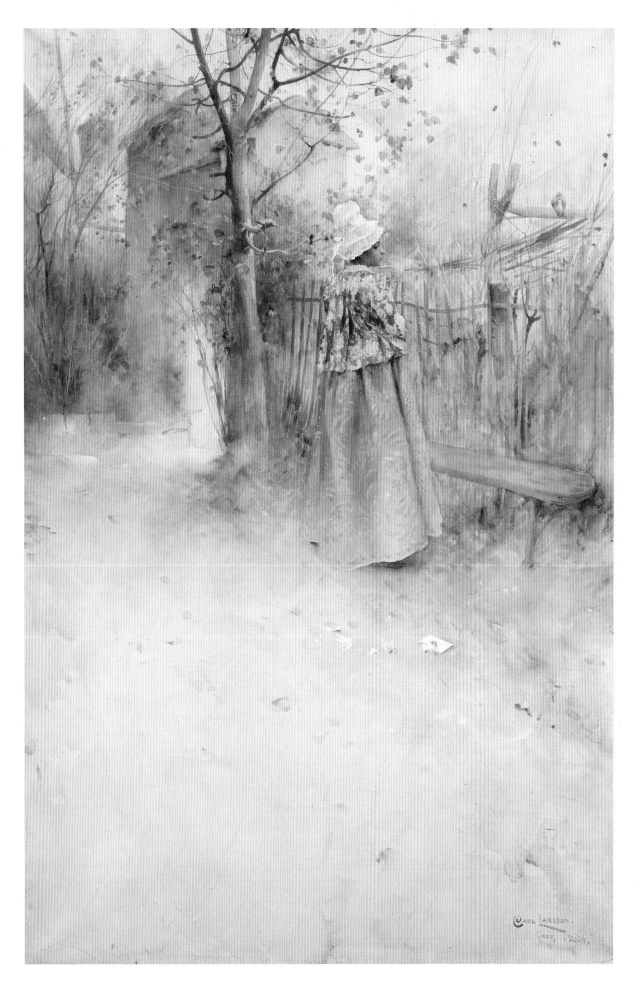

Abroad and at home, 1884–1889

In the spring of 1884 Carl Larsson first met his future patron and friend Pontus Fürstenberg in Paris. This wealthy Gothenburg merchant, who was thirty years Larsson's senior, made considerable purchases at the Salon for his private gallery and for a number of years supported Larsson loyally through commissions great and small.

That same year Carl Larsson was offered associate membership of the Academy of Fine Arts in Stockholm, an honour he declined on the grounds of the Academy's previous unwillingness to grant him a scholarship. Instead, he joined the 'Opponents', a group of young Swedish artists in Paris who professed themselves supporters of realism and opposed the Academy. The opposition movement itself began in the late autumn of 1884, and the new, French-inspired painting made its first breakthrough in Stockholm the following year with the exhibitions *From the Banks of the Seine* and *The Opponents' Exhibition*, which Larsson took an active part in organizing.

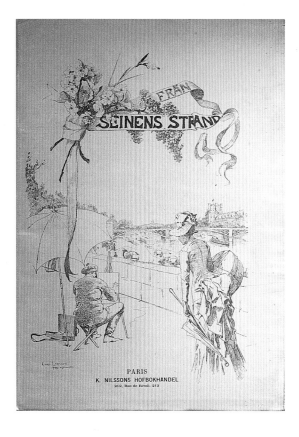

20.[9] Carl Larsson. Title-page for Från Seinens strand *(From the Banks of the Seine), 1884. Line block printed on silk. Karin is in the foreground; the painter C.W. Jaensson, called Spada, is seated at the easel. This is the first illustrated catalogue to an exhibition in Sweden.*

21. Carl Larsson. Interior of the Fürstenberg Gallery, 1885. Watercolour. Pontus Fürstenberg is in the foreground; in the background the artist Ernst Josephson paints Fürstenberg's wife Göthilda.

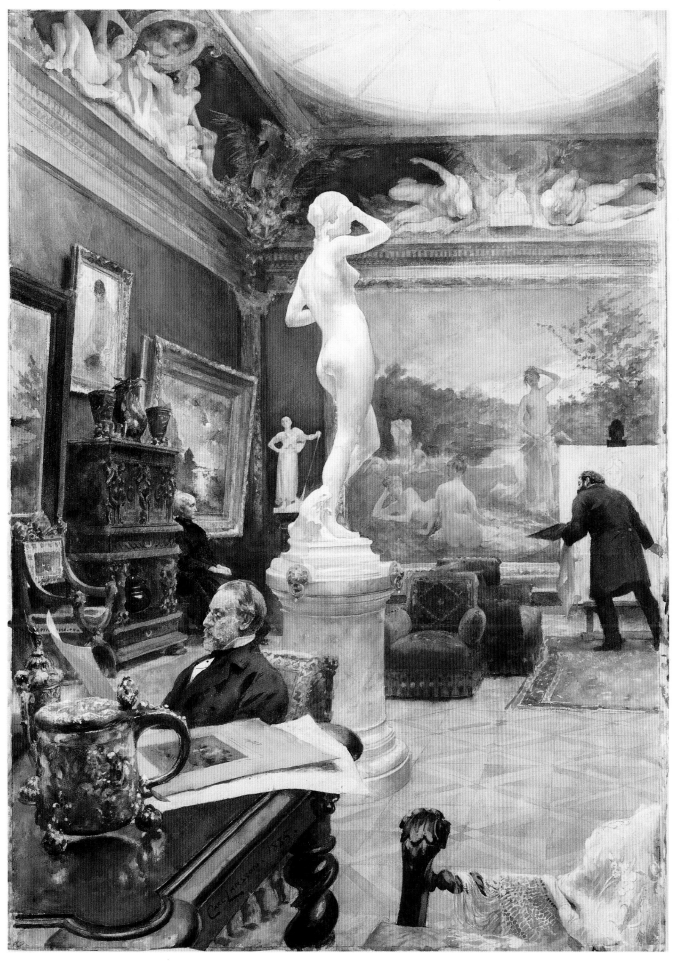

After visits to Grez and London, in the summer of 1885 Carl Larsson went with his father-in-law, Adolf Bergöö, to the village of Sundborn in Dalarna. This was the location of Lilla Hyttnäs, a small property then inhabited by his father-in-law's two sisters (see fig. 219). According to Carl Larsson, it was 'a small, humble, ugly and insignificant building, situated on a slag heap'.[2] A few years later Carl and Karin Larsson began to transform this house into their remarkable artists' home.

In the autumn of 1885 the family settled in Stockholm, but the following year Carl Larsson travelled with the painter Ernst Josephson to Paris and Italy. He now began to show an interest in monumental painting, expressing particular admiration for Tiepolo's frescoes in Venice and Michelangelo's Sistine Chapel ceiling.

A teaching post at the newly opened Valand School of Art in Gothenburg, brought him back to Sweden in the autumn of 1886. His friendship with Fürstenberg continued to develop and the following year they travelled together to Paris, where Larsson had been invited to exhibit at the Galerie Georges Petit.

In 1888 Carl Larsson made a breakthrough in the field of monumental painting. Fürstenberg commissioned him to paint a triptych for the entrance hall of his combined home and gallery in Gothenburg.[3] The theme of this first monumental commission was a symbolic representation of the Renaissance, the Rococo and modern art. The work was to be executed in Paris at Fürstenberg's expense, and Larsson now put all his efforts into carrying out the commission. He gave up his teaching post, left Suzanne and her baby brother Ulf with Karin's parents, and in April 1888 the couple set off together for Paris.

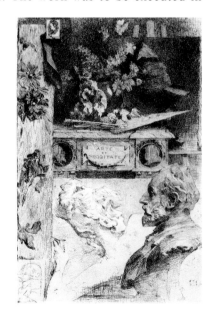

23.[14] Carl Larsson. Profiles, 1888. Etching. This complex image combines a hymn of praise to Fürstenberg (his bust by Per Hasselberg on the right and details from the triptych frame) with references to other people in Larsson's life, including Strindberg (top left), the artists Hugo Birger and Carl Skånberg (centre) and Karin on the easel behind; there is also a self-caricature at the bottom left.

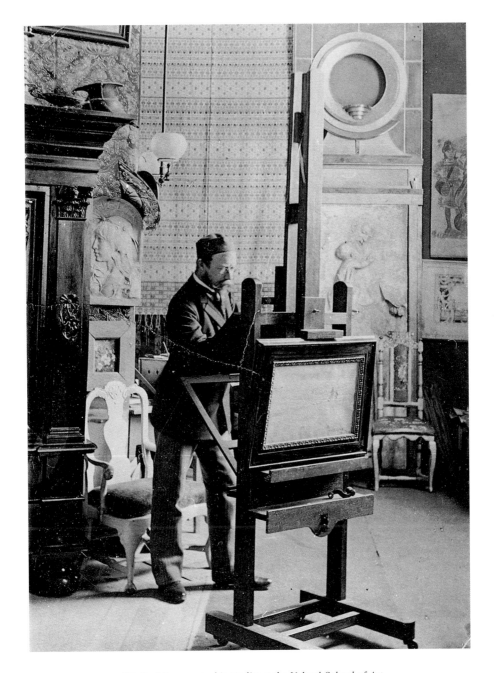

22. *Carl Larsson in his studio at the Valand School of Art,*
Gothenburg. c. 1890.
On the back wall are a textile decorated in the folk style and a
copy of part of the frame for the Fürstenberg triptych.
This picture was taken during Larsson's second phase of teaching
at Valand. Photograph by Johan Lagergren.

The work on the triptych proved to be extremely demanding, but it was completed in time for the 1889 Paris Exhibition, where it was shown in a Japanese-style frame designed by Carl Larsson. The panel *Modern Art* is an allegory of realism, and stands out as the most fully developed of the panels (fig. 24). A variation on the legend of Pygmalion, it shows a sculptor, in his pursuit of the perfect portrayal of reality, witnessing his sculpture coming to life and beginning to shape her own form.[4] In the left background Larsson himself is seen as a *plein-air* painter, watched by a Japanese colleague – a reminder of the importance of Japanese art as a source of inspiration, which Larsson also stressed in other contexts.

In the summer of 1889 Carl and Karin Larsson returned home to Sweden with their third child, Pontus, born in Paris. At first they lived with Karin's parents in Hallsberg; it was in this home that Carl Larsson first decorated a room, also designing doors, fireplaces and furniture – a symbolic prelude to the many years of work on the house at Sundborn, which Karin's father had given to the couple the previous year. In July 1889 the family moved to Sundborn, but at first spent only the summers there. The former town-dweller wrote contentedly to Fürstenberg about his newly discovered enjoyment of the fresh, beautiful landscape and his fine vegetable plot.

Carl Larsson's interest in monumental art also began to increase at that time. Despite the arduous work on the Fürstenberg triptych in Paris, he had found time to take part in the prestigious competition for the fresco decoration of the stairwell at the National Museum in Stockholm and had won second prize. No decision on its execution was made, however, and a new competition was announced in 1890, in which Larsson again took part. In the hope of improving his prospects by demonstrating his aptitude for a similar commission, he succeeded in obtaining Fürstenberg's financial support for a series of murals on the theme *Swedish Womanhood through*

24. *Carl Larsson.* Modern Art, *from the Fürstenberg triptych, 1888-9. Oil on canvas and gilt and painted wood.*

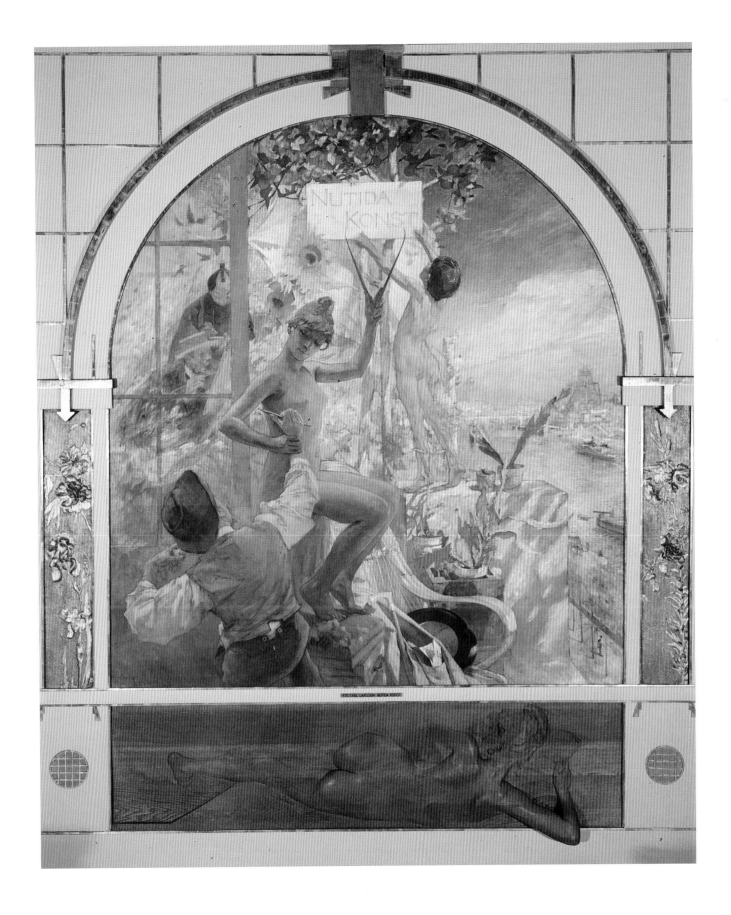

the Centuries at the New Elementary Grammar School for Girls in Gothenburg. The extensive sequence fills the entire stairwell; it was a social project, in the spirit of the age, to take art to the people, an aim that was close to Larsson's heart. The paintings were well received, and were also regarded as confirmation of his talent as a monumental painter.

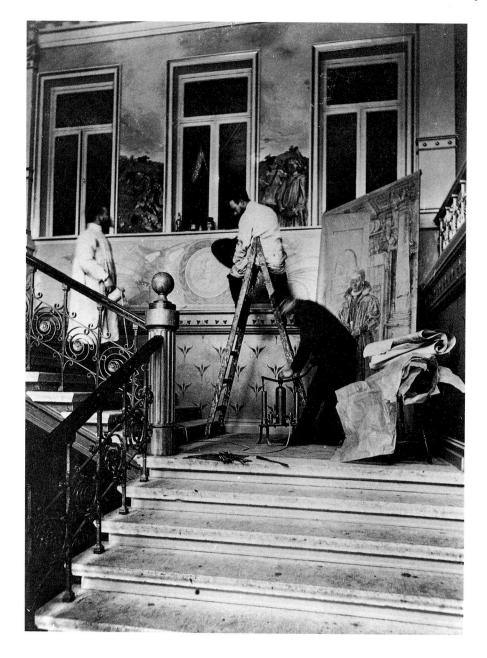

25. Carl Larsson and assistants painting the stair hall of the New Elementary Grammar School for Girls in Gothenburg, 1890. The series of murals is on the theme of 'Swedish Womanhood through the Centuries'; the stair hall takes the story from the Stone Age (on the ground floor) to the Gustavian period (at the top). Here Larsson paints a trophy incorporating the portraits of the King and Queen, but made up of symbols of industry and agriculture, including light bulbs and the bogey of a railway carriage. Above the trophy modern schoolgirls are shown collecting plants for botany. A cartoon, also to be seen in fig. 139, is on the stairs. Photograph by J. Jonasson.

The 1890s

During the first half of the new decade, Carl Larsson's painting became generally more stylized, resembling the decorative quality of line which he was developing for monumental painting. He expounded his particular view of this genre in a letter to the Director of the National Museum, Gustaf Upmark, in which he said that he regarded monumental painting as a branch of illustrative art, but practised on a higher plane. This doctrine was not put into practice, however, until the large oil painting of 1892 *De mina* (My Loved Ones; Frontispiece). Despite the realistic family subject, Carl Larsson here chose to use a stylized form with outlines and simple planes of colour. This approach, influenced by French Symbolist painting, was also

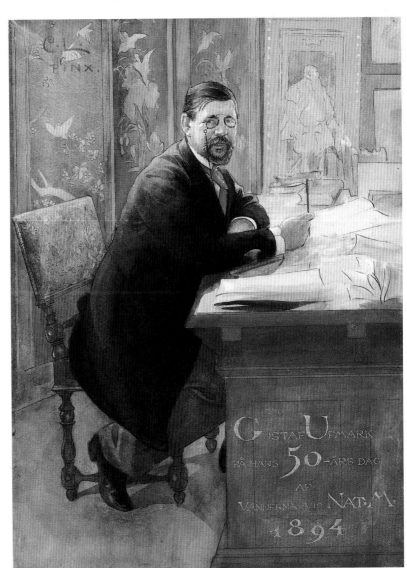

26.[17] Carl Larsson. Gustaf Upmark, *1894. Watercolour.*
Inscribed 'To Gustaf Upmark on his 50th birthday from his friends at the National Museum, 1894'.
Gustaf Upmark was Director of the National Museum during the period when Carl Larsson was working on the frescoes in the Museum's stair hall. The portrait was painted two years before this prestigious commission, and is one of Carl Larsson's best character sketches. It conveys much of the esteem felt between the two men, later also expressed in Upmark's unreserved defence of Larsson's innovative monumental style.

largely characteristic of the period. It is also relevant to note that some of Carl Larsson's contemporaries became engrossed in studying Gauguin's painting that year.[5]

Around the mid-1890s Larsson increasingly developed his quality of line, which was in many respects to become his distinctive characteristic. This mainly took the form of strengthening the outlines of the watercolours in black, as in *On Christmas-day morning* (1895; fig. 28). The watercolours in the series *Ett hem* were, however, the first consistently executed example of this new technique; begun in 1894, this series was published in book form in 1899.[6] More than any other work it has contributed to Carl Larsson's renown.

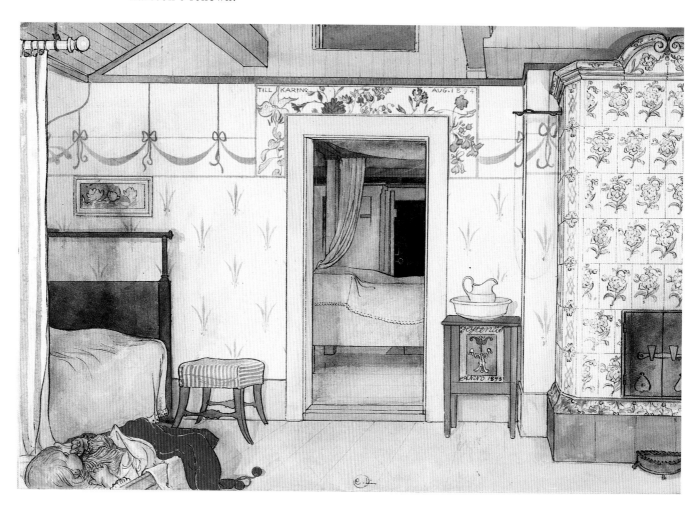

27. *Carl Larsson.* Brita's Little Nap, *1894. Watercolour. from the* Ett hem *series.*
Ett hem *(A Home; 1899) was Carl Larsson's first and most popular book on the subject of his home and family in Sundborn. Subsequently published in innumerable editions in many languages, it contained reproductions of 24 watercolours, which established the slightly stylized line as Carl Larsson's distinctive, artistic characteristic; 20 of the original watercolours were exhibited at the Art and Industry Exhibition in Stockholm (1897) under the title* A Home in Dalarna. *Carl Larsson himself regarded them as models for a practical, new way of furnishing the home, and had therefore wanted to exhibit them in the craft section. This picture shows Karin's bedroom at Lilla Hyttnäs; Carl's bed is through the door.*

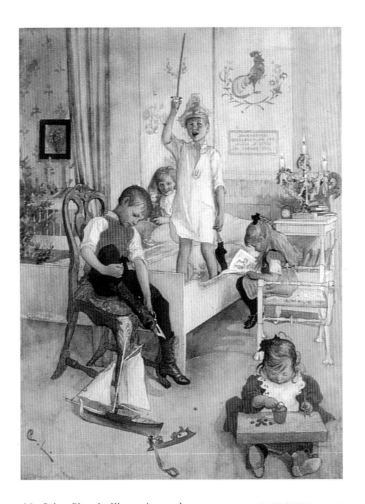

28.[23] Carl Larsson. On Christmas-day morning, *1895. Watercolour.*

29. Oskar Pletsch. Illustration to the poem 'Poverty and Pride' in Barndomsbilder (Pictures of Childhood), *1862. Wood engraving. The apparent immediacy of Carl Larsson's pictures of children and interiors was to a considerable extent the product of careful study of earlier illustrators, especially German artists of the mid-century, whose cosy idealized images were reworked by Larsson into real settings. Pletsch's book, which is still in the library at Sundborn, lay behind a number of Larsson's compositions, for example the poses in* On Christmas-day Morning *(fig. 28).*

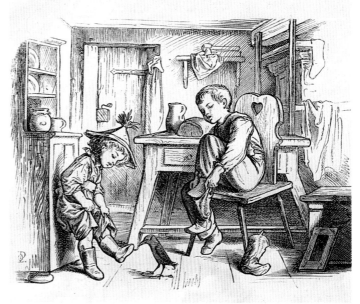

Each figure and object was outlined by an unbroken, dark line, while the surfaces were filled with watercolour in relatively uniform and light tones. This new quality of line created an unusual equality of value between the painting's various components, a feature which was to become characteristic of Carl Larsson's mature art. Objectivity was combined with the desire to make reality into ornament. This approach was also reflected in the deliberate mixture of styles in the Sundborn home, which sprang from the intrinsic value of the objects rather than from the whole. Everything appears to be of equal importance in these paintings, a fact easily tested by comparing the human figures and their settings. It was

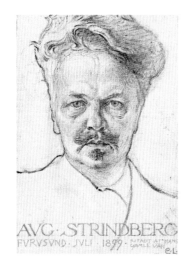

characteristic of Larsson's pictures of the home that the members of the family depicted were rarely portrayed as individuals. Instead they tended to form an integral part of the environment and were subordinate to the whole.

This was not the case in the portraits. Carl Larsson was an unerring portrayer of character, capable of capturing the personality of the subject within his highly original approach to formal stylization and often tension-filled compositions. The portraits, which ranged from self-portraits and official commissions to portraits of Sundborn craftsmen, were mainly painted around the turn of the century, and also included leading cultural figures and authors, such as August Strindberg and Selma Lagerlöf (figs 30, 31).

30. *[30] Carl Larsson.* August Strindberg, *1899. Charcoal and oil on canvas. Inscribed 'August Strindberg, Furusund, July 1899, drawn by his old friend C.L.'.*
Strindberg and Carl Larsson had known one another since their youth in the 1870s. Like almost all Strindberg's personal relationships, theirs was riven by disagreements. The decisive break occurred in 1908, due to Strindberg's personal attack in En ny blå bok *(A New Blue Book). This portrait of 1899 was executed at Strindberg's request for reproduction in a magazine; he asked Larsson to leave it in an unfinished state.*

31. *[37] Carl Larsson.* Selma Lagerlöf, *1908. Oil on canvas. Selma Lagerlöf was one of the great Swedish narrative writers of the late 19th century. Her widespread popularity, which was finally established through* Nils Holgerssons underbara resa genom Sverige *(Nils Holgersson's Wonderful Journey through Sweden; 1906-7), may be said to match that of Carl Larsson. Behind her here is a tapestry made by Anna Wettergren-Behm, the design of which is taken from Lagerlöf's book* Jerusalem.

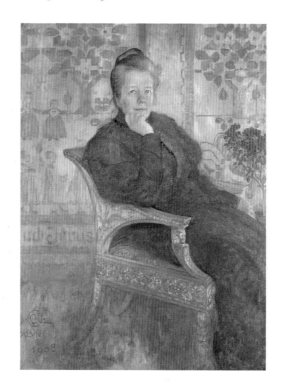

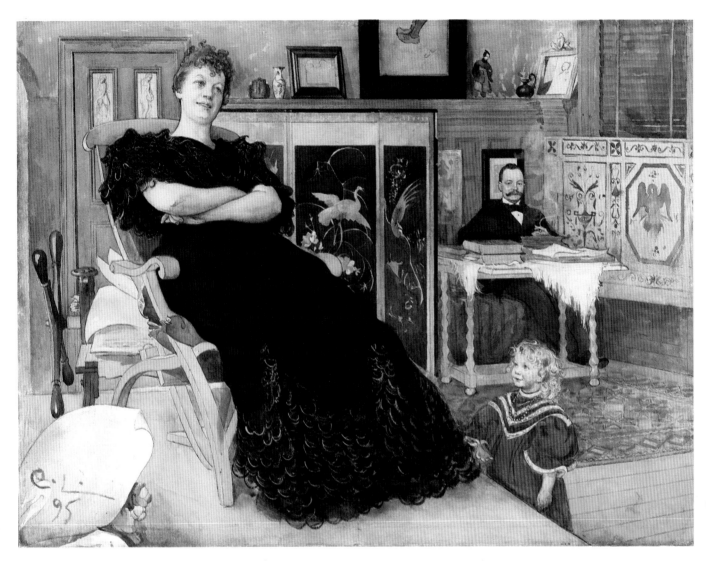

32. *[29] Carl Larsson.* The Singer Anna Pettersson-Norrie, *1895. Watercolour.*
This is one of Carl Larsson's most unconventional portraits. It documents not only the model, but also the creation of the painting itself. The scene is the studio in Carl Larsson's Stockholm flat, where the popular opera singer and later theatre director Anna Pettersson-Norrie poses boldly and impressively, accompanied by her husband and child.

33. *[32] Carl Larsson.* Convalescence, *1899. Watercolour.*
This portrait of Karin in the Stockholm flat was painted while she was recovering from pneumonia.

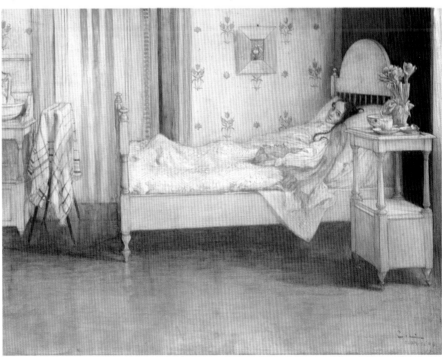

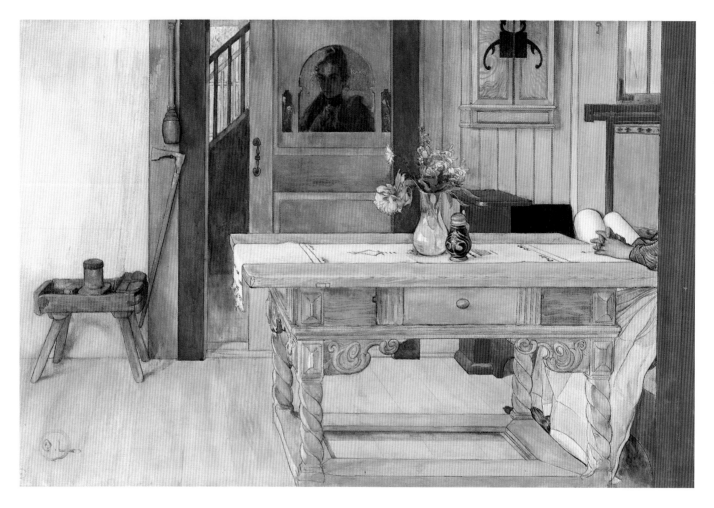

34.*[169] Carl Larsson.* Sunday Rest, *1900. Watercolour. Reproduced in* Larssons, *1902.*
Sitting in the workshop at Sundborn, Karin is recognizable only from her hands, but Carl's
portrait of her is on the door at the centre of the picture. In his book Larssons *he describes how*
the picture shows Karin left at home as the others went to church. The picture prompted
Strindberg to sketch out the plot of a dark drama.

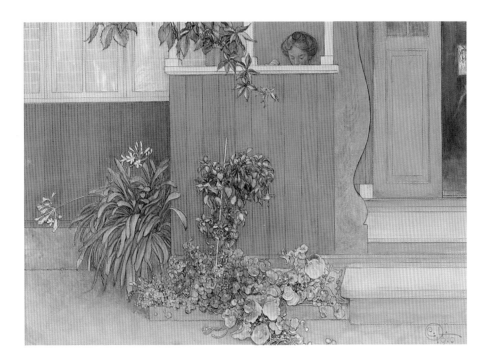

35.[104] Carl Larsson. Suzanne on the Porch, *1910. Watercolour.*

Carl Larsson's characteristic quality of line had several sources of inspiration, of which the most important were *art nouveau* or *Jugendstil* and an admiration for Japanese coloured woodcuts. The transition to an emphasis on the expressive line must also have been natural to Larsson, who had worked extensively as an illustrator ever since his early youth and for a large part of his adult life.

Along with the bold compositions of the Grez watercolours, the Japanese style first became clearly apparent in the frame of the Fürstenberg triptych, and in the inclusion of the Japanese artist in *Modern Art*. In 1895 Larsson freely declared the influence of Japanese art in his first book, *De mina* (My Loved Ones): 'as an artist Japan is my homeland!'.[7]

More than any other Swedish artist, Carl Larsson was to base his compositions on Japanese pictorial ideas to create variety and to charge the numerous portrayals of his home with an unexpected visual energy; such works are filled with tension in the spirit of Hiroshige. The large-format watercolours *Sunday Rest* (1900) and *Suzanne on the Porch* (1910) are examples of his individual mastery of this genre (figs 34, 35). The former in particular has a limited angle of view: Karin is discernible at the end of the table only by her folded hands and her freshly starched apron.

Two further sources of inspiration for Carl Larsson's quality of line may be mentioned. The first was the early Italian Renaissance, of which he had made a special study before working on the National Museum frescoes.

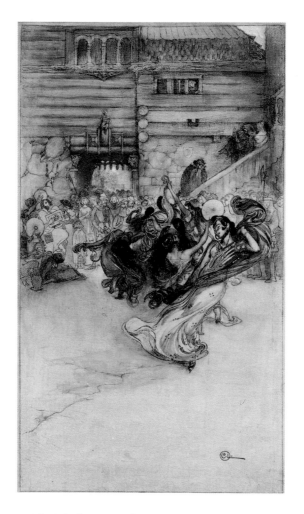

36.*[26] Carl Larsson.* The Strangers from Egypt, *1894.*
Illustration for Viktor Rydberg's Singoalla, *1894. Pen and wash drawing heightened in white.*
Viktor Rydberg's romantic medieval novel Singoalla *tells the love story of the knight*
Erland and the gypsy girl Singoalla. Larsson had received a number of extensive commissions
of this type, but this set was the last. As always, he prepared himself carefully by making
studies from nature and live models.

Impressions from the Renaissance and *art nouveau* were fused, and are re-echoed in the flowing, rhythmic line of such different works as the museum frescoes and the illustrations for Viktor Rydberg's *Singoalla* (figs 36, 37). The second, often overlooked, was Swedish folk art. Carl Larsson particularly admired the distinct lines and clear colours of painting from Dalarna and southern Swedish wall hangings (fig. 55), and he acknowledged his debt to these painters in the text of *Ett hem*. Despite the obvious differences, it is not difficult to find links between Dalarna painting and the fairy-tale atmosphere and clear colours of, for example, *Gustav Vasa's Triumphal Entry into Stockholm* (fig. 37).

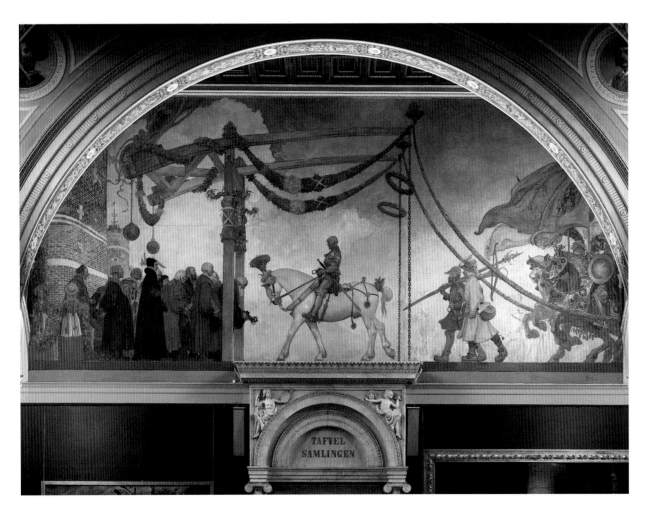

37. *Carl Larsson. Gustav Vasa's* Triumphal Entry into Stockholm, *1908.*
Oil on canvas attached to wall of the hall of the National Museum, Stockholm.
The impressive, monumental style of this work combines sources as different as the Italian Renaissance and Swedish folk painting.
Unlike the earlier museum frescoes and the later Sacrifice at the Winter Solstice, *it was an immediate success.*

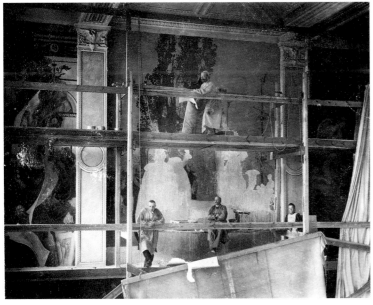

38. *Carl Larsson, Gustav Fjaestad and the Italian stuccoist Antonio Bellio at work on the National Museum frescoes in summer 1896.*

During the second half of the 1890s Carl Larsson received both small- and large-scale commissions, all of which contributed to his unique position in Swedish art. In 1896 he reached the high point of his artistic career with the National Museum frescoes. All six large sections were executed in four months with the help of Italian craftsmen; none the less, the work was extremely demanding, and at times brought the artist to the verge of despair. In his autobiography, he describes one of the most critical parts:

Once I was working on a piece for sixteen hours on end – it was on the section with Gustav III; it was autumn and it started to get dark; it looked as if I wouldn't finish it. If I didn't get it done, the whole piece would have to be torn off again. I was so tired, so desperate that I was in tears...[8]

Even in these scenes from the history of the Museum's collections and of Swedish art, Carl Larsson showed himself to be above all a draughtsman. The consistently emphasized outline at the expense of volume made the frescoes a highly original contribution to nineteenth-century decorative painting. Despite their innovative character, they were well received by the critics, but the Museum's own mural committee was divided, and several members called for alterations. Larsson refused to bend: the paintings were eventually approved, while further work on the two walls of the upper stairwell was postponed. Even this final stage was to prove full of obstacles, and was to result in the greatest setback of his career.

Meanwhile he completed several other monumental commissions, including the ceiling and lunettes in the gold foyer of the Stockholm Opera (1897) and the symbolistic *Birth of Drama* at the Royal Dramatic Theatre (1907; fig. 39). The latter is a Baroque composition reinterpreted in the *Jugendstil* manner, filled with floating figures and foreshortened perspectives, illustrating the marked development that Larsson's monumental painting had undergone since the National Museum frescoes. With its deep and intense colour treatment, it is also his most successful monumental work after the National Museum frescoes.

While the monumental paintings were important in that they reached a large public, the printed edition of *Ett hem* (1899) was of still greater significance. Although the book itself was only within the reach of a bourgeois public, one of Carl Larsson's aims was to present a model for functional and inexpensive interior decoration for the masses. In doing so, he was fulfilling a social duty, which he had described ten years previously in a letter to the writer Viktor Rydberg, asserting that the Academy of Fine Arts had failed in its duty to lead artists towards the great task 'of being priests of art, of going out and preaching the beautiful and joyful message of art to all the people'.[9] The concept of the duty of art to create mental well-being in everyday life was also put forward at this time in Ellen Key's pamphlet *Skönhet för alla* (Beauty for Everyone; 1899). These ideals had their origin in John Ruskin. The importance and spread of English influences through the magazine *The Studio* have often been emphasized in connection with the interior decoration by Carl and Karin Larsson of Lilla Hyttnäs in Sundborn (see chapter 3). It is sufficient to note here that the diffusion of ideas must have been wider than that, since the Larssons' remodelling of the house in Sundborn was begun before the first issue of the magazine was published in 1893.

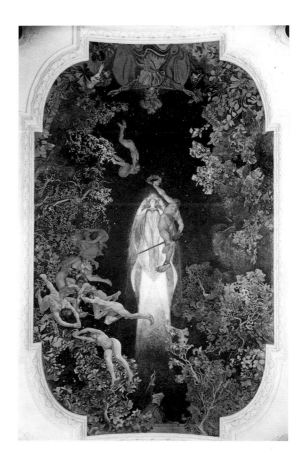

39. *Carl Larsson.* The Birth of Drama, *1907. Painted ceiling on canvas for the Royal Dramatic Theatre, Stockholm. The symbolism in Carl Larsson's monumental painting found its highest expression in this work. The large ceiling takes the form of a Baroque composition reinterpreted in the* Jugendstil *manner, filled with floating figures and foreshortened perspectives, carried out in deep and intense colours.*

The last two decades, 1900–1919

This last period of Carl Larsson's life may be described as the true Sundborn epoch, which extended from the family's settling permanently at Lilla Hyttnäs in 1901 to Carl Larsson's death in 1919. A contributory factor in the decision to leave Stockholm was Larsson's increasing nationalism, which developed in parallel with his dissociation from modern French art towards the turn of the century.

Another important factor was his affection for the Swedish soil, which was reinforced with the acquisition of the small farm Spadarvet in Sundborn in 1897. Spadarvet had a symbolic significance for Larsson: at a time when the disintegration of peasant society was gaining momentum, he himself could renew his links with the land his forefathers had cultivated. His attitude towards modern developments became increasingly conservative. He maintained that peasant culture represented the firm foundation of society, and paid homage to it in his book *Spadarvet* (1906).

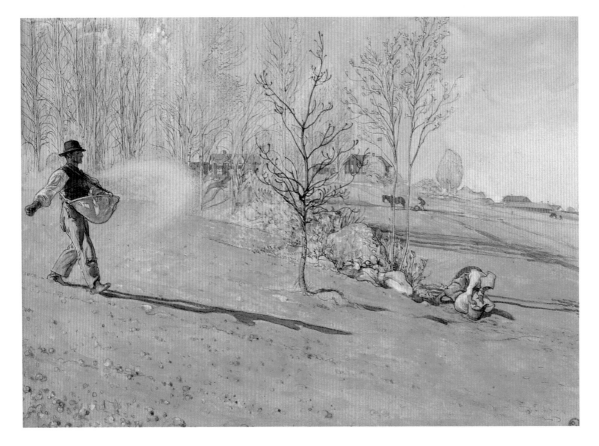

40. *Carl Larsson. Sowing, c. 1905. Watercolour. Reproduced in Spadarvet, 1906. Spadarvet was Carl Larsson's homage to Swedish peasant culture. It also marked the artist's increasingly obvious rejection of modernity, which included developments in industrial society and in art.*

The concept of 'the Sundborn epoch' can also be more broadly applied to the whole time in which Lilla Hyttnäs played a role in the Larssons' life and art. In this sense it stretches from 1888, when the couple was given the original cottage by Karin's father, until Carl Larsson's death. During this period the home directly and indirectly represented the central and most personal part of Carl Larsson's work. This is also true of Karin Larsson, who used the creation of Lilla Hyttnäs to develop her ideas in furniture design, interior decoration and textiles. There is no documentary evidence on the couple's individual contributions to the overall creation of the home, and they probably worked as a team. The timelessly austere textiles and the purely designed furniture in the large studio show, however, that Karin's contribution was both independent and significant. Carl's faith in his wife's artistic judgement, manifest in the fact that no composition was allowed to leave the studio without her approval, also points to her central role in designing the home.

From an art-historical point of view, the Sundborn motifs may be regarded as Carl Larsson's personal answer to the question which confronted all Swedish artists returning home from Paris in the late 1880s: how does one create a new and genuine Swedish art on the basis of French realism? In search of an answer, most of them set off for new, artistically undiscovered parts of the country, and claimed them as their own provinces. From the late 1880s Swedish art consequently acquired a new, national direction, enriched by its regional and symbolistic roots.

Carl Larsson went his own way in this development, and found national expression in a poetic idealization of his own home and family life. Both the creation of the home in Sundborn and its representation in art served as compensation for his own difficult childhood. Lilla Hyttnäs came to represent the dream of happiness, re-created in three-dimensional reality, by a person whose only capital was his own talent.

The key to Carl Larsson's artistry is to be found in these images, reproduced with graphic precision. 'Look, the thing is I want to be loved! It's love and not honour I've sought', he confessed in his autobiography.[10] He also described his art as directly associated with his home in Sundborn:

My art: it's just like my home: fine furniture is out of place in it, there's not even anywhere for a Haupt chest of drawers. It's modest but harmonious, quite simply. Nothing extravagant, nothing for connoisseurs. But good and solid work.[11]

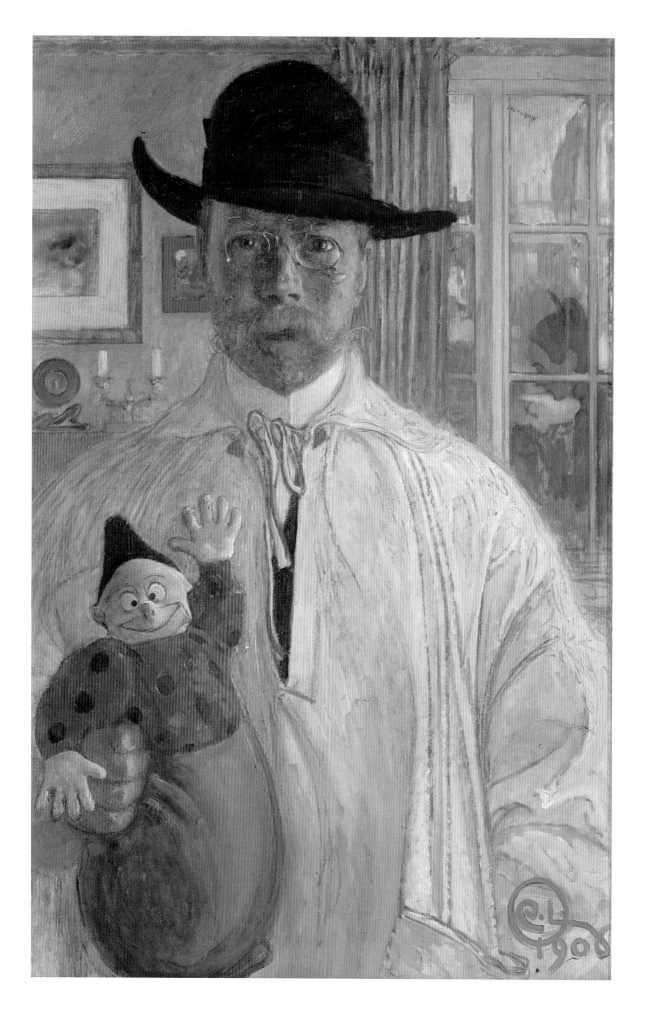

48

The stylized and ornamental character of the portrayals of the home also had a distancing effect: Larsson wanted to prevent them from being too personal, and emphasized that the images should not necessarily be identified with reality. His character also had its dark sides, even though these were not fully revealed until the posthumous publication of his autobiography (1931). This includes a description of a nightmare, which he interprets as an allegory of his life, and expresses his split personality in the words 'My constantly smiling face. My hidden horror of life'.[12]

In 1905 the Larssons suffered great grief due to the death of their eldest son, Ulf. Without affecting his artistic productivity, this event also brought out the latent pessimism in Carl's character. His last years were further darkened by an unexpected attack from Strindberg in *En ny blå bok* (A New Blue Book), published in 1908. Without mentioning his old friend's name, Strindberg described Carl Larsson as a man who had built his whole personality on lies. Even though Strindberg was wide of the mark, he must have understood intuitively how Larsson had to some extent become a victim of his own myth. Behind the constant joker and cheerful soul, there was an individual who occasionally suffered insecurity and anguish, seldom allowing such emotions to be embodied in his art; one of the rare examples is the small etching *The Writer's Ghost* (1896; fig. 42).

41. *Carl Larsson.* Self-examination, *1906.*
Oil on canvas.
Larsson, in the drawing-room at Sundborn, scrutinizes himself in the mirror in the most critical of his self-portraits. He holds the ever-cheerful clown doll, his 'alter ego', the smiling face that usually concealed the inner pessimism of his depressive character. Karin is there too, a shadow bent over her sewing in the workshop through the window. The picture was bought by the Uffizi in 1911 for its gallery of artists' self-portraits.

42. *Carl Larsson.* The Writer's Ghost, *1896.*
Etching.

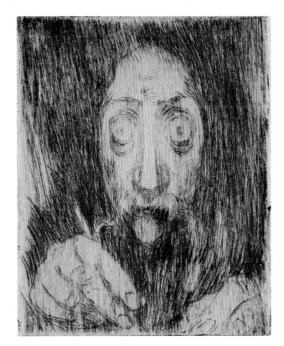

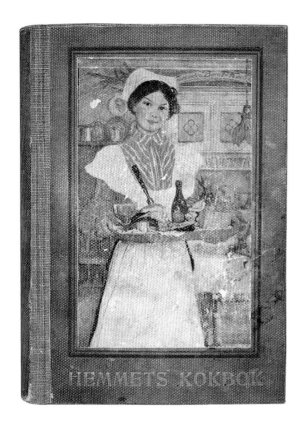

HEMMETS KOKBOK

43. Hemmets kokbok *(The Home's Cookery Book; 1912). The cover, first used in 1909, is taken from Larsson's painting* Martina with the Breakfast Tray *(1904), set in the dining-room at Sundborn. In 1907 the painting was sold to the Gallery of International Modern Art in Venice. This is the Sundborn copy of the book.*

Artistically, the first decade of the new century was very productive. It included the painting *Martina with the Breakfast Tray*, a Larsson icon, which reached hundreds of thousands of Swedish homes as the cover of *Hemmets kokbok* (The Home's Cookery Book, 1909; fig. 43). It also included several significant portraits and monumental works, such as the ceiling of the Royal Dramatic Theatre and *Gustav Vasa's Triumphal Entry into Stockholm*, as well as the book *Åt solsidan* (On the Sunny Side). Carl Larsson's popularity in Europe also became firmly established at this time. In 1910 alone his work was shown in Buenos Aires, Vienna, Munich and Rome. In Germany the book *Das Haus in der Sonne* had been published the previous year, and almost 200,000 copies were sold before the artist's death.

Carl Larsson could still not, however, relinquish the idea of the uncompleted series of paintings at the National Museum. Through his persistence and initiative, he had succeeded in acquiring all but one wall. He now wanted to fill this wall with an Old Norse *Sacrifice at the Winter Solstice*, but he met with resistance in a wider circle, which finally proved impossible to break. Both the subject and the execution aroused hostility in the dawning age of Modernism; after several years of trying discussions, the finished painting was rejected in 1916 (fig. 44). This was Carl Larsson's first artistic defeat since his youth, and his last years were embittered on two counts: he felt not only that his artistic prestige had been shattered but that the world around him was still indifferent to the national ideals which he had come to embrace with increasing fervour.

The public debate on the exhibition of *Sacrifice at the Winter Solstice* at the National Museum flared up again in connection with its sale in the 1980s, and is still not over. The painting has been on loan to the Museum since 1992, when it was borrowed for the major Carl Larsson retrospective.

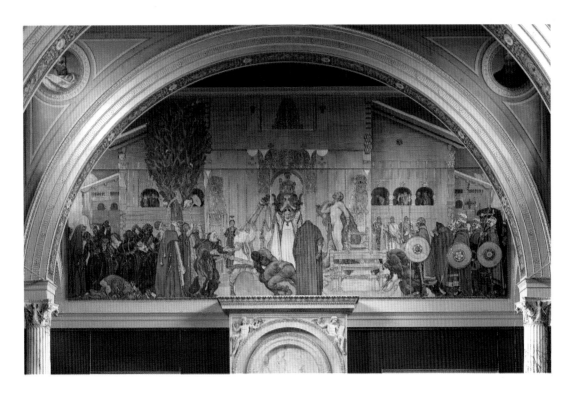

Conclusion

Carl Larsson distinguished himself early on as a gifted draughtsman. His eye for the lively and tension-filled line also remained his principal strength. Particularly in the Grez watercolours of the 1880s, he also showed himself to be a sensitive colourist. During this period, he produced several major works, which rank among the very best European watercolours of that time.

Influenced by *art nouveau* and Japanese art, Larsson went his own way in the early 1890s, avoiding the symbolistic twilight moods of Swedish National Romanticism. Instead, he developed a graphically exact line, notably in his watercolours, with his home and family as his main themes. Although the ideals of brightness, simplicity and happiness were consistent, as much in his art as in his life, they did not reflect his whole personality.

From *Ett hem* (1899) onwards, Larsson's images attained unprecedented distribution in Europe, especially in Germany, laying the foundations of his lasting popularity. During the course of the twentieth century his home in Sundborn has been transformed into a Swedish ideal whose importance has by no means diminished. The poetry of everyday life, as expressed in his best paintings, is nostalgically recaptured as a song of praise to a traditional and simple way of life, even in a world dominated by new technology. These paintings represent a dream of being secure within the home and family.

Yes, life is secure and pleasant here in Sundborn. I'm painting a corner of my yard, with one of my children and a red peony in the foreground, while Karin sits beside me peeling rhubarb.[13]

44. Carl Larsson. Sacrifice at the Winter Solstice, *1914–15.* *Oil on canvas.* *The picture is now on loan to the National Museum, Stockholm, from a private collection.*

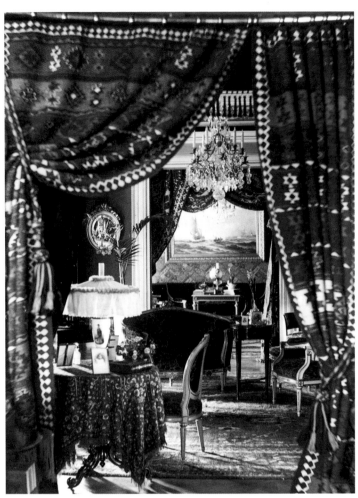

45. *View of an upper-middle-class interior on Strandvägen in Stockholm, 1891.*
Photograph by Viktor Odelberg.

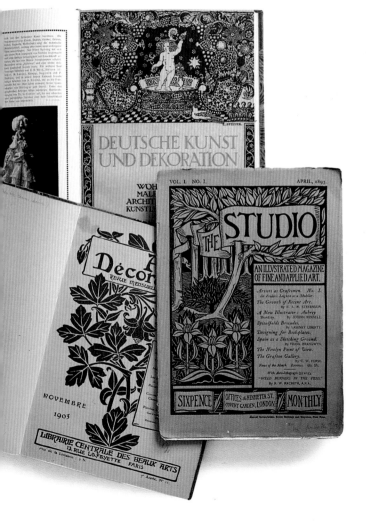

46. *Foreign art magazines from the library at Sundborn:* The Studio, Deutsche Kunst und Dekoration *and* Art et Décoration.
The Larssons also had books in German, French and English.

3

A HOME OF ITS TIME – BUT COMPLETELY DIFFERENT

Elisabet Stavenow-Hidemark

'The lamps and the lampshades! The plush, the cretonne! The master and mistress sit in misery surrounded by that gaudy rubbish, happily wearing that confident smile which proclaims that they have fully met the demands modernity makes on high society.'[1] With these words, Carl Larsson expressed his loathing for the interior design of the middle-class home in his book *Ett hem* (A Home), published in 1899. The same year the social reformer Ellen Key, that bold and aesthetic champion of a freer and more beautiful life, described Swedish taste as the most magnificently vulgar, Germanic taste.[2]

What was it that made the Larssons' home so extraordinary that it transformed contemporary ideas of interior decoration which continue to hold a century later? In Sweden the house came to embody the very concept of a national home; at the same time in Germany it came to exemplify the home as the sanctuary of the family and a temple of art. Its rustic and unpretentious qualities, combining the everyday with the colourful, remain as captivating as ever. The answer lies in the fact that Carl and Karin Larsson were not only children of their time but were active in shaping it. They were well-read and widely travelled, they subscribed to German, French and English art journals, and they kept up with current ideas both social and moral.[3] A potent combination of their art, their lifestyle and not least their home enabled them to influence their age and the future, especially through the widespread distribution of Carl Larsson's work.

German, French and Japanese influences

The late nineteenth century was marked in Sweden both by social unrest and the disintegration of peasant society. There was a feeling that a new age was dawning. The world was becoming more accessible: with improved communications and press coverage of cultural life, influences were flooding in from every direction.

In interior design German neo-Renaissance styles had dominated middle-class Swedish homes for two decades. Jacob von Falke, whose book *Die Kunst im Hause* (Art in the House; 1874) profoundly influenced interior design of the 1870s and 1880s, had spent a summer at Karl XV's summer palace, Ulriksdal, where he catalogued the King's collection of antiquities. His book had been translated into Swedish in 1876, and his design ideas were keenly taken up in Stockholm. These involved dark wallpaper, ornamented ceilings, heavy curtains and draperies, and large bouquets of dried flowers in the dark corners of rooms. On many occasions, however, they also led to a genuine feeling for history and a search for artistic inspiration in the national heritage. Knowledge of sixteenth- and seventeenth-century interior design reached a peak in the late nineteenth century. Svenska Slöjdföreningen (The Swedish Society of Crafts and Design), which was active in promoting Swedish applied arts and was an influential arbiter of taste, supported these neo-Renaissance ideals.[4]

As in the rest of Europe, collecting antiques became popular, and the antique trade flourished. The new wealth of the middle class was displayed in silk and velvet, and in collections of paintings, weapons and antiques. In middle-class homes weapons, drinking-vessels and large metal or ceramic plates (genuine or reproduction) decorated halls and studies, or were hung on the dining-room walls (fig. 47). There were precedents for this in Germany and England. History was to be brought to life, rooms were to be bathed in a mysterious chiaroscuro, and all harsh sounds were to be softened by textiles. This was the Germanic taste which Carl Larsson loathed. But even though it was still

47. The dining-room of a newly married couple in Lund, 1893. Conventionally middle-class but up to date, the furnishings are heavy and dark in the German neo-Renaissance style. Beyond the dining-room is a drawing-room resembling a grotto of textiles. The couple no doubt regarded their home as artistic.

widespread in the late 1890s, it was going out of fashion as *Jugendstil* became established in advanced aesthetic circles.

Carl Larsson was also a collector. However, he was careful to point out that his was not the traditional style of collecting, 'everything [was] of practical use'.[5] Old furniture in the Baroque style from the houses of mine shareholders, beautiful pieces of horse harness, and various peasant textiles were incorporated into the decoration of his home. The room which became known as the Old Room was filled with old furniture, paintings and north German seventeenth-century panelling. But the room was not a museum, it was a guest room.

Despite the dominance of Germany, Swedish artists chose to travel to Paris rather than to the centre of German symbolism, Dachau. A leaning towards France was also shown in the most elegant drawing-rooms, furnished in neo-Rococo and reproduction Louis XVI, with much gilded furniture. In rich bourgeois circles, French taste was now considered superior.

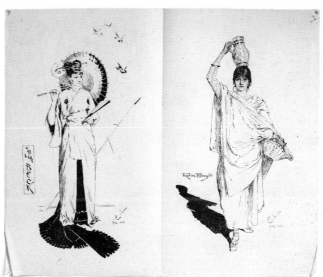

48.[73] Carl Larsson. Julia Beck and Karin Bergöö. Illustration to Palettskrap, November 1882. The two women are shown dressed for a fancy dress ball at Grez-sur-Loing, Julia Beck as a geisha, drawn in the Japanese manner, and Carl's future wife as a north African.

During the 1880s, by way of England and France, a craze for everything Japanese also developed. Artists experienced the refined Japanese approach to handicrafts, woodcuts and calligraphy. But there was also a vulgar Japanese style, regarded as artistic in certain circles. Parasols were hung in ceiling corners, and fans were put behind paintings or on window-sills. Peacock feathers, sold cheaply in Japanese warehouses, were arranged in large vases.

Carl Larsson had discovered pure Japanese art in France. There was a marked influence of Japanese art on his painting and design. In his home in Sundborn he painted Japanese-inspired flowers on the dining-room cupboard (fig. 220) and a decoration above Karin's bedroom door for her nameday in 1894. Sets of exquisite Japanese woodcuts hung in the library. The room contained a Japanese mask and a doll, but there were almost no cheap parasols, fans or peacock feathers.

In search of the essentially Swedish

Not everything, however, was foreign. On the contrary, in the late 1890s and the early twentieth century, there was a strong drive to seek national expression in art and architecture. It was like a great wave into which country after country was swept, in search of the special characteristics which lay in its history and nature. Nationalism was most strongly felt in countries where independence was suppressed or threatened, but the trend was evident even in more settled political climates such as that of Sweden.

Swedish architects studied old timber houses, and textile designers became immersed in all the variants of peasant textiles. For many designers and textile designers, Swedish flowers, stylized into ornament, were a means of expressing national identity. The sixteenth-century royal castles with their thick walls, the red-painted cottages and peasant textiles became symbols of both national and moral values.

It was during this period that artists discovered the Swedish landscape. Significantly, they did so while they were abroad. French *plein-air* painting and heavy, German symbolism transported them from Paris, Dachau and Düsseldorf back to a Sweden which they saw with new eyes. These were the thoughts of the painter Richard Bergh as he stood in a wood of stone-pines on a hill outside Florence, imagining himself in a Swedish pine forest:

A pine forest! It tore my heart. At once a longing came over me, an overwhelming longing for Sweden, that silent, white country in the North ... Then my eyes fell on the stone pines ... They suddenly seemed to me so strange ... No, spruce and pine, they are of the same timber as my own family – we are brothers! I can embrace you.[6]

In the 1890s Swedish artists were drawn to their native districts or to more remote areas, which they made their own through their painting. Anders Zorn returned to his home parish of Mora in Dalarna and settled there in 1896. Carl Larsson was given a small house in Sundborn by his father-in-law, which became the family's summer cottage from 1889 and a permanent home from 1901. Karl Nordström settled down in his native district on the

49. Anders Zorn. Midsummer Dance, *1897.*
Oil on canvas.
The sun's first rays strike the house gable as the short midsummer night turns into day.
The young people of Mora dance on the greensward – exhaustion and the opalescent light produce
a charged erotic atmosphere. This is no romantic depiction of folk life but a great artist's realistic
rendering of an annual custom. Zorn, who had his roots in Mora and actively worked to
preserve (and revive) its folk culture, described this painting as containing all his deepest feelings.

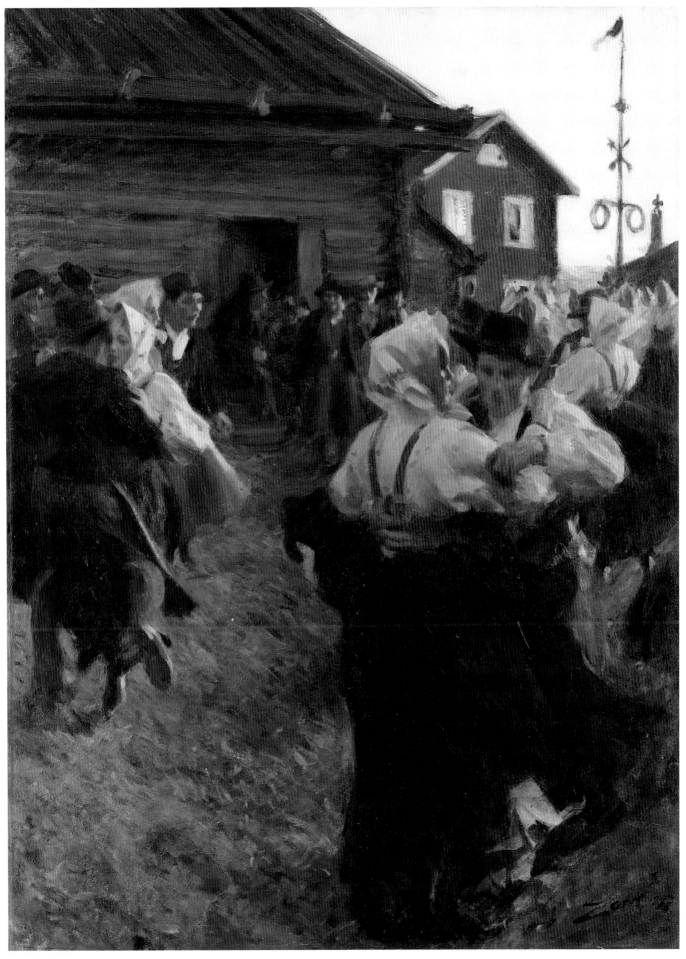

west coast, and painted Varberg fortress with heavy symbolism. Carl Wilhelmson returned to the fishing village of his childhood, among the barren rocks of Bohuslän, and painted the population at work and leisure. At the turn of the century an artists' colony was founded at Arvika in Värmland. One of the members was Gustaf Fjaestad, who was to become the country's foremost painter of snow scenes.

Young architects remained based in Stockholm, but made walking tours of the remote countryside with their rucksacks and sketchbooks. They discovered how features of the old peasant buildings could be reinterpreted into modern villa architecture. But this process was preceded by study tours to England: Carl Westman and Lars Israel Wahlman, both of whom became influential architects, went there in 1900 and saw how the heritage was preserved as well as being thoroughly absorbed into modern domestic architecture.

Folk culture and the Vikings

Seeking artistic inspiration in the history and distinctive character of one's own country was in fact nothing new, it had merely changed expression. During the 1830s a group of intellectuals began to study old folk culture.

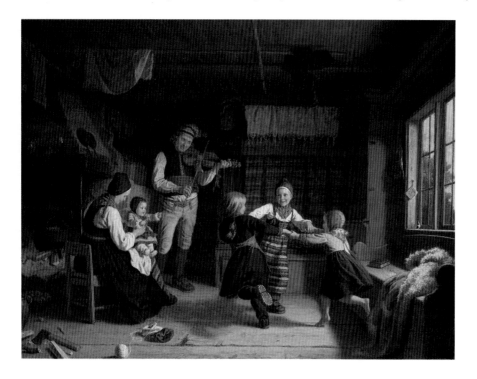

50.[68] Amalia Lindegren. Sunday Evening in a Cottage in Dalarna, 1860. Oil on canvas. Amalia Lindegren was one of the few woman painters to make her mark in nineteenth century Sweden. Her paintings of folk life were extremely popular and were widely reproduced in illustrated magazines. Although sentimental in tone, they were accurate in detail; this scene takes place recognizably in a cottage in Rättvik.

Men like Gunnar Hyltén-Cavallius, Per Säve and Nils-Gabriel Djurklou recorded folk tales, and Nils Månsson Mandelgren made inventories of artefacts. Similar activities were also taking place in Norway, Finland and elsewhere in Europe; the aim was always to discover a distinctively national material culture.

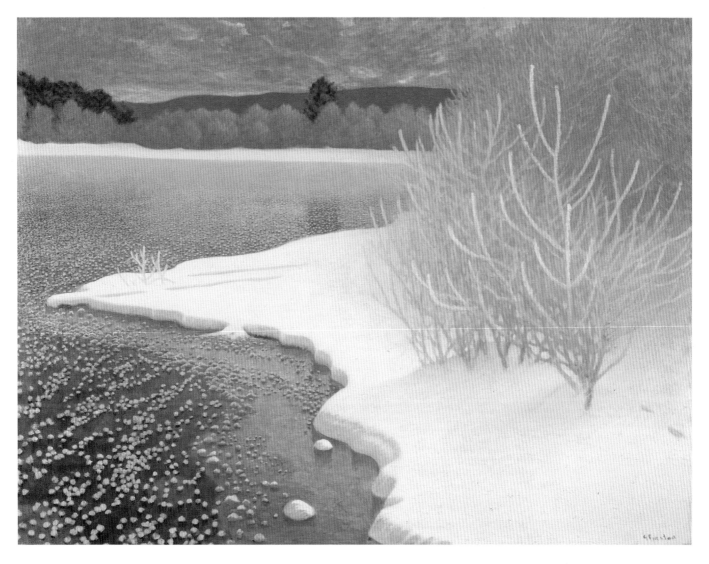

51. *Gustaf Fjaestad. Hoar-frost on Ice, 1901. Oil on canvas*
Fjaestad is the foremost painter of the Swedish winter; he was also a clever skater. In the 1890s a colony of painters formed around him when he was living near Arvika, a town in Värmland not far from the Norwegian border. It was at that period in which artists went to the Swedish countryside and painted landscapes with symbolic overtones, especially at dawn and dusk. The unusual phenomenon of hoar-frost on shining ice is caused during a cold winter by the sudden arrival of damp air followed by extremely low temperatures.

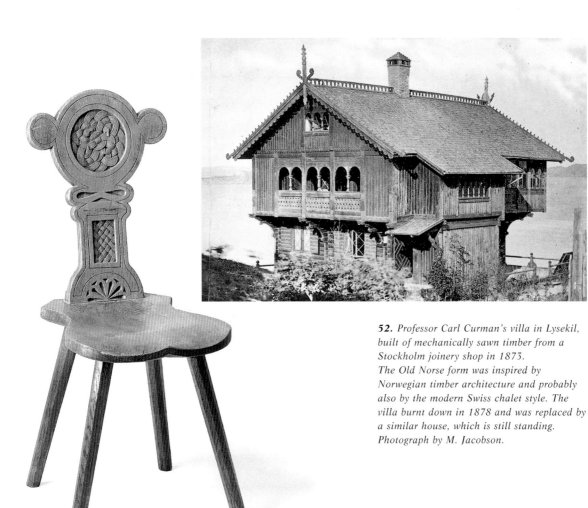

52. *Professor Carl Curman's villa in Lysekil,
built of mechanically sawn timber from a
Stockholm joinery shop in 1873.
The Old Norse form was inspired by
Norwegian timber architecture and probably
also by the modern Swiss chalet style. The
villa burnt down in 1878 and was replaced by
a similar house, which is still standing.
Photograph by M. Jacobson.*

53.*[66] Oak chair
designed by August
Malmström c. 1870
and made for
Professor Axel Key's
summer villa
Bråvalla at
Gustavsberg in the
inner archipelago
of Stockholm.*

Attempts to create a national style in timber architecture, furniture, porcelain and textiles – the 'Old Norse' or 'dragon' style – were another expression of the same movement. Interest in the Vikings had culminated in the early nineteenth century in poetry and sculpture. During the second half of the nineteenth century, the historical Old Norse home was seen as an expression of the heart of society and a symbol of a patriarchal and conservative ideal.

The Old Norse style was most fashionable in the early 1870s, largely through the efforts of two influential doctors who commissioned summer villas in the style. Professor Axel Key's villa Bråvalla was at Gustavsberg in the inner archipelago of Stockholm, and Professor Carl Curman's villa in the west coast resort of Lysekil, where he was the resort doctor (fig. 52).[7] The villa style was inspired by the wooden storehouses of Norwegian farms. Both villas were furnished with oak furniture in 'dragon' style, created by the artist August Malmström (fig. 53). The Gustavsberg porcelain factory supplied both villas with porcelain featuring a dragon design, while the Almedahl linen factory wove a dragon pattern in white damask linen, a pattern which remained in production until about 1990. Carl Larsson was clearly influenced by this. He put animal finials on the roof ridges and Old Norse hinges on the shutter to the front of the house – probably a way of accentuating the Nordic character of his new home. But that was enough. The 'dragon' or Old Norse style was short-lived in Sweden, hardly outliving the 1880s; however, it later gained a foothold in Norway, where it became a key expression of national identity, in silver, wood carving and textiles.

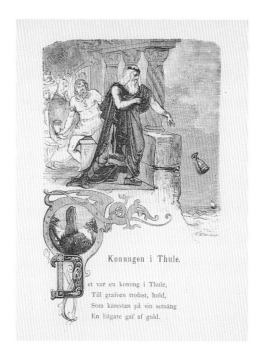

54.[67] C. Weydenhayn after Carl Larsson.
Illustration to The King in Thule
from a Swedish edition of Goethe's Ballads,
translated by Carl Snoilsky (1876).
Wood engraving.

The Nordic Museum and Skansen

This interest in folk culture was most clearly expressed by the creation of the Nordic Museum, founded in 1873, and the open-air museum Skansen, which opened in 1891.[8] These linked institutions, both in Stockholm, were founded by Artur Hazelius, an academic and linguist who was seeking to purify the Swedish language. In his youth he had taken part in Scandinavian student meetings, huge gatherings in which the historical and cultural affinity between Sweden, Norway and Denmark was expressed in enthusiastic speeches and songs and a sense of brotherhood. On journeys in the Swedish and Norwegian countryside (Sweden and Norway were united until 1905) he had seen how industrial products were gradually creeping into people's homes and driving out the old folk art. This gave him the incentive to create a museum about the life and work of the Nordic peoples as a whole. Collecting began in 1872 and inspired extraordinary

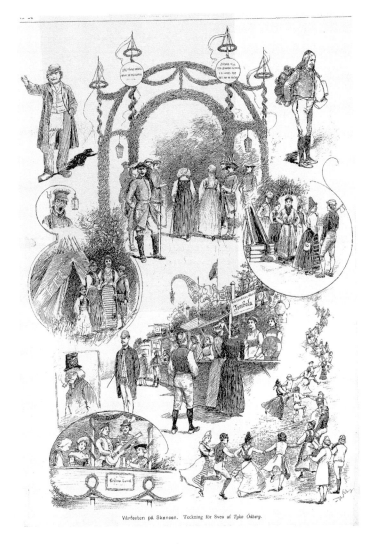

55. *Tyko Ödberg,* Spring Festival at Skansen, *from* Svea, *1894. Wood engraving.*
The open-air museum Skansen in Stockholm was famous for its spring festivals, which earned it much money. Smart people from Stockholm flocked to see the folk costumes, Lapp encampments and amusement stalls. The medallions on the triumphal arch expressed Skansen's aims for both national culture and nature: 'Swedes, learn about Sweden' and 'Hark to the sighing of the fir, at whose root your dwelling is founded'.

Vårfesten på Skansen. Teckning för Svea af Tyko Ödberg.

enthusiasm. The museum became a national movement: representatives from all over Sweden helped with collecting, while the citizens of many towns organized bazaars to raise funds. The resulting collections were displayed in local groupings, thus creating provincial identities; this had both advantages and disadvantages. Hazelius's other project, Skansen, was designed as a Sweden in miniature, with whole rural buildings brought from different parts of Sweden, set up as farms and surrounded by the appropriate vegetation, fencing and livestock. The caretakers and attendants came from the appropriate districts. Wearing folk costume and speaking in their local dialects, they described life on the farm as it used to be. Skansen, as an expression of a desire to celebrate national identity, was of interest only to the middle class and the conservative peasantry; the labour movement was indifferent for a long time to national manifestations of this type.

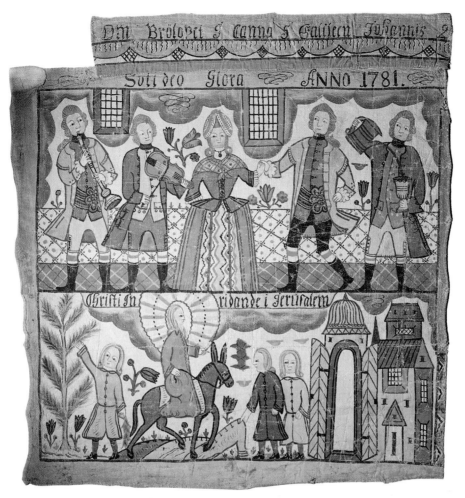

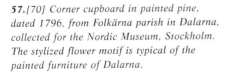

56. *[71]* The Marriage Feast at Cana *and*
Jesus entering Jerusalem. *Painted wall
hanging, dated 1781, from southern Sweden.
The fresh directness of such Southern Swedish
paintings, abounding with figures, had a
strong appeal for Carl Larsson. This example
was collected for the Nordic Museum,
Stockholm.*

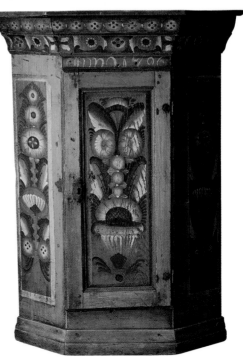

57. *[70] Corner cupboard in painted pine,
dated 1796, from Folkärna parish in Dalarna,
collected for the Nordic Museum, Stockholm.
The stylized flower motif is typical of the
painted furniture of Dalarna.*

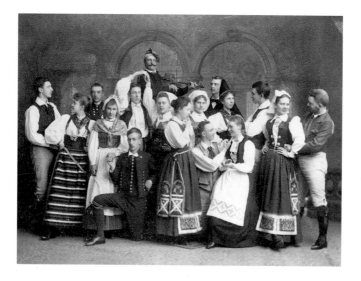

58. *The* Konstnärsring *(Artists' Ring), a folk-dancing team in Stockholm c. 1896.*
At the top of the picture is a folk musician from Skansen. The young people are wearing folk costumes combining traditional elements from various parts of Sweden with newly invented elements in the folk manner. Several of the dancers were from the families of Stockholm's cultural élite: Upmark, Curman, Gödecke and Cederström. These Folk-dancing teams were found all over the country.

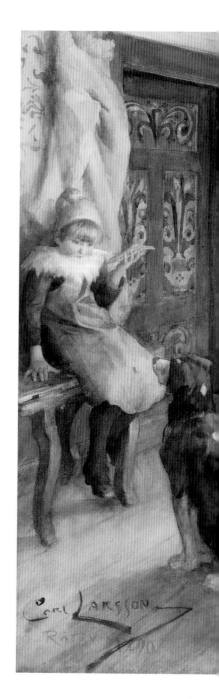

Hazelius's work contributed to the renaissance of folk costumes, but they were not worn by country people, except in Dalarna. Middle-class children and young people were, however, dressed in folk costumes on festive occasions from the 1880s up to the First World War. Skansen also contributed to a greater appreciation of vernacular architecture, but not in the case of the Larssons. Carl and Karin Larsson were keenly interested in folk culture and national values, but they were unable to appreciate the little house in Sundborn. Having referred disparagingly to its 'rural plainness', Carl Larsson felt the need to tell readers of *Ett hem*:

'Oh, goodness me!', you say, 'it's fine like that too'.
No, to be honest, not for my wife and me.[9]

And so the changes to Lilla Hyttnäs began, the first step towards making it probably the most publicized artist's home in the world.

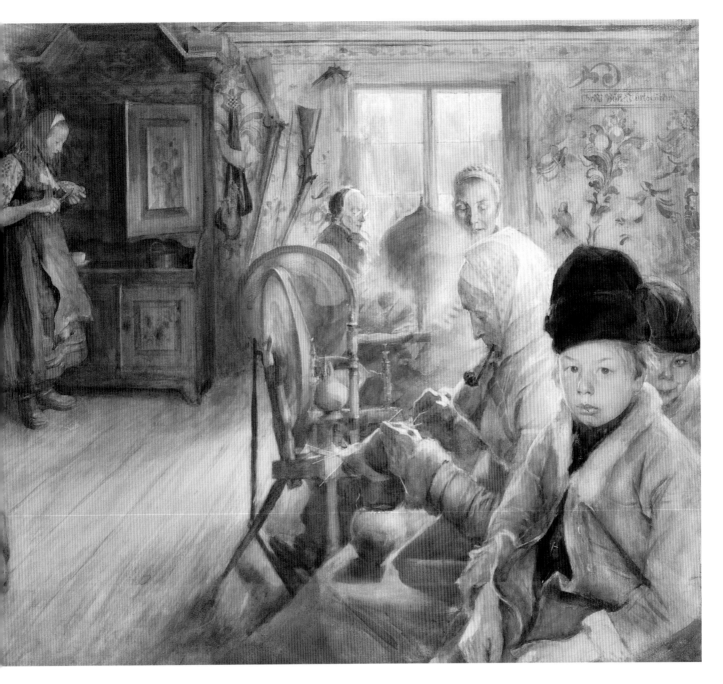

59.[69] *Carl Larsson*. The Winter Cottage, 1890. Watercolour.
The Larssons' interest in Dalarna folk culture was greatly increased by a visit in the winter of 1890 to Bingsjö near Rättvik, north of Falun, at a time in which they were just starting to work on the house at Sundborn. Karin was taught to weave, and Carl was delighted to find folk dress still worn daily, traditional crafts still practised and walls decorated with biblical texts, as in this view of a painted interior at Danielsgården. Suzanne is seated on the bench to the left.

The Gustavian legacy

The light tone of the Larssons' drawing-room at Sundborn has become part of the history of Swedish interior design. Based on the legacy of Gustav III, who reigned from 1771 to 1792, it brought into vogue a new simplicity, rural yet elegant.

The Gustav III style is a Swedish variant of that of Louis XVI. In the 1880s the French style had left its mark on the elegant drawing-rooms of Sweden; in the 1890s people began to be conscious of the Swedish legacy

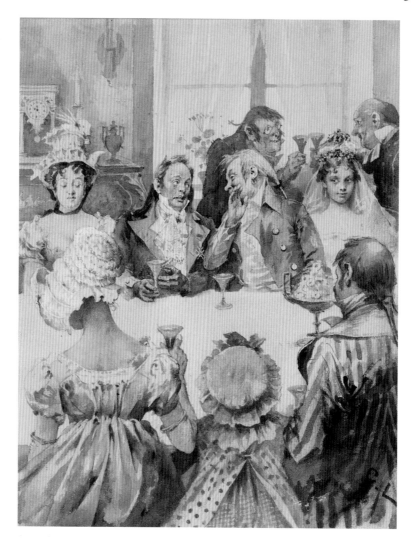

60.[83] Carl Larsson. The Skipper and the Shipowner, 1883-4. Illustration for Anna Maria Lenngren, Samlade skaldeförsök (Collected Attempts at Poetry, 1884). Pen and ink and wash.
Behind the Larssons' use of late 18th-century styles at Sundborn lay Carl's long acquaintance with and fondness for the period in his painting and illustration work. For the highly detailed Lenngren illustrations, which were made in France, Larsson studied extensively in libraries and museums. In the 1890s he gave some 18th-century clothes from his own collection to the Nordic Museum.

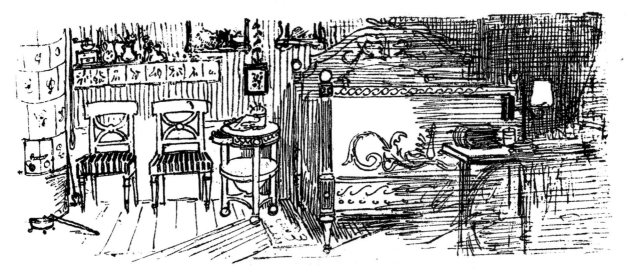

61. [82] Carl Larsson. Illustration for the poem 'Gammalstämning'
(The Good Old Days) in the magazine Svea, 1890.
Larsson's poem (reprinted as 'Mormor' (Grandmother) in De mina, *1895, but without this picture) was*
a hymn to the good old days and to his mother's mother, the widow of a decorative painter in
royal service. He describes her room as filled with things in the Empire and Biedermeier styles,
but whether it really was like this is not known. The chairs shown here with their striped covers and
the table are remarkably similar to those originally at Sundborn.

of the eighteenth century. When Svenska Slöjdföreningen mounted a major exhibition of the Gustavian style in 1891, it was a sign that the style was coming back into fashion, while the exhibition itself encouraged an even greater interest. Significantly, it was at precisely this time that Carl Larsson redecorated the drawing-room in Sundborn in a late eighteenth-century style and divided the walls with green mouldings.

It is perhaps only through our modern eyes that we want to see a more intimate tone creeping in, and detect a new appreciation of the simple pearl grey chairs, the floors scrubbed white, and the plain tiled stoves decorated in green or blue. A striking example is the small apartment decorated in blue, which John Böttiger, Steward to the Royal Household and the Royal Collections, furnished at Gripsholm Castle in 1893 (fig. 62). The castle was being restored, and its sixteenth-century interiors renovated, but the building was also associated with the period when Gustav III stayed there with his court in the 1780s. The apartment was accordingly declared to have been occupied by the chief lady-in-waiting to the King's sister, Princess Sofia Albertina. Red and white checked linen from the castle's storerooms was made up into bed curtains, a simple, small, green tiled stove was installed, a dressing-table was hung with light, white curtains, and simple chairs with a round, openwork back were placed on the wide floorboards. The result, in its strictly artistic authenticity, is still loved as the most genuine eighteenth-century interior a Swede can imagine. The low rooms, with their naive interior design, have often been compared with the Larssons' contemporary interiors, which were also characterized by rusticity, simplicity and a light colour range.

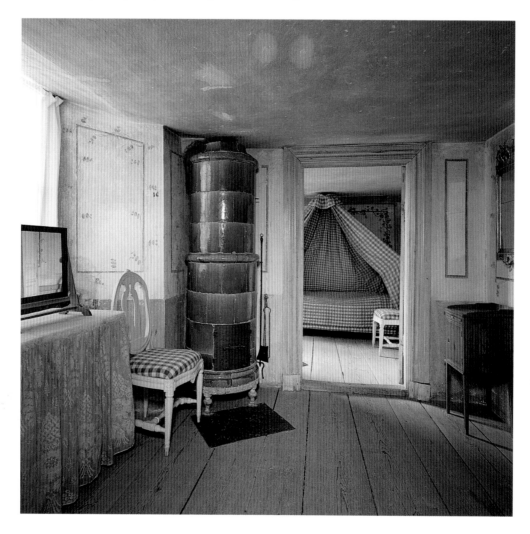

62. *These rooms at Gripsholm Castle, although apparently authentic examples of furnishing from the 18th century, were in fact furnished in this way in 1893, a sign that the simple Gustavian interior was again popular.*

A treasury of peasant textiles

Sweden has a unique treasury of surviving peasant textiles. In the second half of the nineteenth century this formed the basis of a new textile tradition, mainly through the activities of two associations. Föreningen för Handarbetets Vänner (The Association of Friends of Textile Art) had been founded in 1874, to promote Swedish textiles in an 'artistic and patriotic spirit'.[10] At first the Association's designers drew designs with dragon-style interlacings, but they soon began to incorporate designs based on peasant weaving techniques; countrywomen with first-hand knowledge of the old techniques were brought in to pass them on. The Association made a substantial contribution in artistic terms. The stylized flora of *Jugendstil* never found a more beautiful expression. Having taken part in the World Exhibition in Paris in 1900, the Association was offered a chance to exhibit and sell through the leading firm L'Art Nouveau S. Bing.

The peasant legacy was also passed on by Föreningen för Svensk Hemslöjd (The Swedish Handicrafts Association), founded in 1899 by Lilli Zickerman, with the painter Prince Eugen as chairman. An inventory was made of old textile handicraft in rural areas, on the basis of which new products were created, providing work for the rural population as well as goods which could be sold to a discriminating Stockholm public.

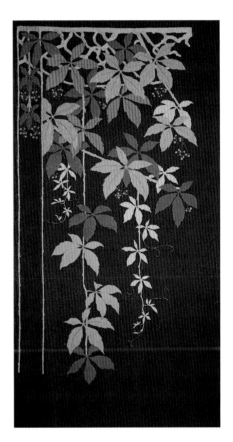

64. Embroidered door curtain with a Virginia creeper motif, designed by Gunnar Gunnarson Wennerberg in 1899 and made by Föreningen Handarbetets Vänner *(The Association of Friends of Textile Art). Founded in 1874, the Association was famous in the 1890s for its modern textiles and embroidery for which skilled designers created stylized plant motifs for interior decoration.*

63.[72] Carriage seat cushion from the province of Skåne in southern Sweden, late 18th or early 19th century, now in the library at Sundborn. It is made in the rectilinear tapestry technique known as 'rölakan'.

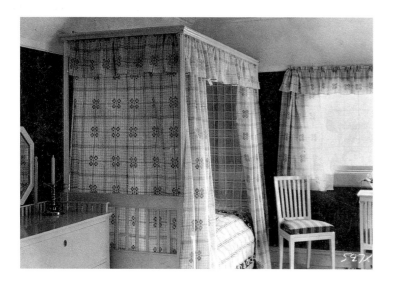

65. *Interior as shown by Föreningen för Svensk Hemslöjd (The Swedish Handicrafts Association) at its exhibition of 1904. The furniture and textiles together created a light environment similar to that of late 18th-century interiors*

The Association's textiles, furniture, basketwork and wrought ironwork were characterized by an exemplary high quality and by traditional techniques and designs. The light interiors, which the Association promoted, were related to those of the eighteenth century. It upheld, in principle, the same interior design ideals as Carl and Karin Larsson put forward with the paintings of their drawing-room and as those which Ellen Key described in *Skönhet för alla* (Beauty for Everyone). A light, Swedish style of interior decoration was thus created, with light-painted furniture, rep-woven runners, thin white curtains, and checked and striped textiles, a style that remains very much alive. But while these two associations were clearly national in their textile creation, Karin Larsson was completely free of such tendencies in her textile art. She did not copy peasant textiles, and used whatever materials she came across, with no concern as to whether they were hand-woven or vegetable dyed. In this respect, she was totally original.

What was England's role?

English ideas about the reform of art and design were certainly to be found in Sweden, but their effect was very subtle. The Pre-Raphaelites had been introduced to the Swedish public, both as artists and writers, by the art historian Carl Gustaf Estlander in 1867[11] and later in a series of articles by the English critic and linguist Edmund Gosse. His 'Letter from London' began in the spring of 1877 in *Ny illustrerad tidning* (New Illustrated Magazine), a cultural weekly with a large readership. The first serious presentation of the ideas of John Ruskin was apparently in an article by Gustaf Steffen written in 1888.[12] Steffen was a scientist and particularly interested in social issues; since 1887 he had been working as a foreign correspondent in London, where he was on social terms with William Morris's daughter May and her husband. Steffen described Ruskin as the great moralist on aesthetic and social questions. (The first Swedish translation of a work by Ruskin was not published until 1897.[13]) He also wrote about William Morris, giving a detailed description of how Morris's home in Hammersmith was decorated and furnished and an account of his workshops, fabrics and wallpapers as well as his socialism.[14]

When the first issue of *The Studio* was published in April 1893, a number of Swedish artists and architects became subscribers, including Carl Larsson, who showed an early interest in the English aesthetic movement. At Sundborn there is still a copy of *Smått folk* (Little People), a translation of Kate Greenaway's *Under the Window* (1878) published by Bonnier in 1882. Any child who read it might be affected by its summary of English aesthetic and educational ideas, its depictions of quaintly dressed children in the safety of the garden landscape, its evocations of beauty and good. Carl Larsson's illustrations for *Samlade skaldeförsök* (Collected Attempts at Poetry; 1884), an anthology of pieces by the late eighteenth-century Swedish poet Anna Maria Lenngren, are clearly influenced by Greenaway. Contact with England was maintained through Karin Larsson's sister Stina, who was married to Frank Bather, a geologist at the Natural History Museum in London. In her letters to Karin, Stina described how she was furnishing her Kensington home in the style of the English aesthetes, with green and rose as the dominant colours.[15]

A more general interest in the English aesthetic and Arts and Crafts movements was awakened in Sweden through Germany as Swedes came to read well-informed and well-illustrated articles about these issues in German art journals. Furthermore, Swedish craftsmen had been visiting England since 1890; their views on William Morris, Jeffrey & Co. wallpapers and William de Morgan's ceramics were published in *Svenska Slöjdföreningens Meddelanden* (The Swedish Society of Crafts and Design Review). For a few years in the 1890s there was even a small shop, Sub Rosa, which sold exquisite, modern English decorative arts in Stockholm.[16]

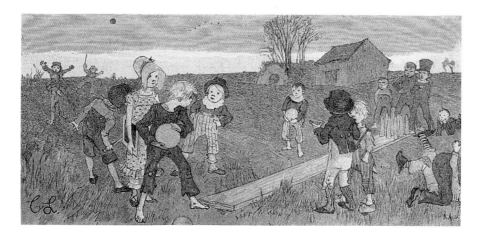

66.*[85] Carl Larsson.* The Boys. *Wood engraving. Illustration for Anna Maria Lenngren,* Samlade skaldeförsök *(Collected Attempts at Poetry, 1884). The influence of Kate Greenaway is clearly apparent.*

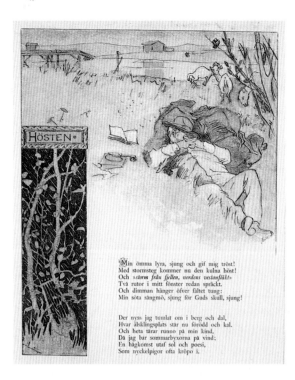

67. *[76] Carl Larsson. Illustration and decoration for the poem 'Hösten' (The Autumn) in Elias Sehlstedt,* Sånger och visor i urval *(Selected Songs and Ballads, 1892-3). Carl Larsson's knowledge of English design is also shown in his illustrations and page decorations for Sehlstedt, begun in 1890, which are close to the Japanese-influenced designs by Walter Crane and Randolph Caldecott.*

68. *Hanna Pauli.* Friends, 1900-7. *Oil on canvas. Several members of Sweden's intellectual élite belonged to the group* Juntan, *shown here at a meeting in Hanna and Georg Pauli's flat in Stockholm. She reads aloud, perhaps from the manuscript of one of her next pamphlets or from something by a modern foreign author. The listeners include Larsson's publisher Karl Otto Bonnier and one of his great supporters, Carl Laurin.*

Ellen Key, a bold pioneer

Ellen Key's pamphlet *Skönhet för alla* (Beauty for Everyone), one of a series by the radical students' association Verdandi, was first published in 1899 (and in many later editions) (fig. 69). Verdandi's programme included public information on social, political, health and aesthetic issues. Ellen Key was strongly influenced by English writers such as Herbert Spencer, Ruskin and Morris, and was certainly aware of the numerous English and American publications about Art in the Home that appeared from the 1870s to the 1890s. Through Svenska Slöjdföreningen, she probably also knew of the existence of an association in France by the name of *L'Art pour Tous*.

Ellen Key's main thesis was that beauty is not a luxury, and that it ennobles and enriches man. 'People work better, feel better, and are more amiable and happier if they experience beautiful shapes and colours in the objects with which they surround themselves at home, however humble it may be.' Here she was primarily addressing members of the working and lower middle classes, concerned that everyone should learn how to 'avoid ugly things and be surrounded by beautiful objects through simple, inexpensive means'.[17] According to Key, too many homes from the 1870s to the 1890s were made ugly through senselessly decorated, dark wallpapers and heavy curtains which shut out the light. Her ideal of beauty was a light-filled rectory or manor-house drawing-room, with pearl grey furniture, plain deal floors and thin white curtains which let the sun shine on the plants on the window-sills. An appreciation of beauty was widened by good art and good books. She praised Föreningen för Skolans Prydande med Konstverk (The Association for School Decoration with Art), which supplied good reproductions in new printing techniques. She was pleased with the activities of public libraries and also advocated that every home should have a shelf of good books.

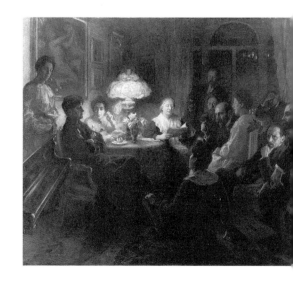

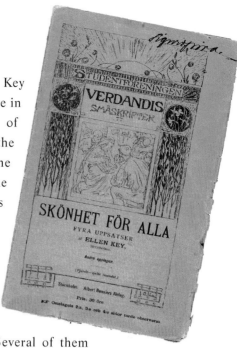

At the Art and Industry Exhibition in Stockholm in 1897, Key had seen Carl Larsson's series of watercolours from his home in Sundborn. In *Skönhet för alla* she described the effects of colour in the rooms, the simplicity of the arrangement and the artistic whole. In later editions, after staying with the Larssons and seeing their home, she extended the text. She held their home up as an aesthetic ideal and their lifestyle as a model. Carl Larsson's picture book *Ett hem*, also published in 1899, provided illustrative material, which reinforced her aesthetic programme.

As an ardent feminist, Ellen Key wrote controversial books about women's issues, children's upbringing, the ennobling effect of art and social reform. Her books were translated into many languages, especially into German. Several of them were translated into English by the American Mamah Bouton Borthwick, who lived with the architect Frank Lloyd Wright for many years.[18] However, *Skönhet för alla* seems to have been published only in Swedish.

69. *Ellen Key's set of essays* Skönhet för alla *(Beauty for Everyone) appeared in 1899 as a pamphlet in a series published by Verdandi, a radical students' association in Uppsala. This is the second of three editions to appear in 1899, with the standard cover designed by Carl Larsson for the series in 1888.*

Carl and Karin Larsson and their age

The Larsson home was to a great extent a product of its time. The Larssons collected antiques, but treated them as they thought fit. They had furnished the dining-room and drawing-room consistently, but moved the furniture all over the house. The drawing-room, with its inherited furniture, was in the late Gustavian style and was very light. The dining-room was fairly dark, with high panelling and a shelf for ornaments. In this respect, they followed a middle-class pattern. But the colour of the furniture and the walls was personal and innovative. As Swedish textile art began to flourish, with improved techniques and imbued with national self-esteem, Karin executed her timeless embroideries; in this area she was totally original, if not always good technically. Interestingly, she liked to use bright aniline dyes, which the leading textile artists hated.

The concept of the home as the heart of society expressed itself more strongly at Sundborn than anywhere else. The Larsson home was in keeping with its time. The most varied currents of the period met here, yet everything was carried out in a different and personal way. The home became a living and changing work of art.

4

DOMESTICITY AND DESIGN REFORM: THE EUROPEAN CONTEXT

Gillian Naylor

The road from the village of Shirley, near Addington, where my mother and father are buried, to the house they lived in when I was four years old, lay, at that time, through quite a secluded district of field and wood, traversed here and there by winding lanes and by one or two smooth mail coach roads, besides which, at intervals of a mile or two, stood some gentleman's house, with its lawns, gardens, offices and attached fields, indicating a country life of long continuance and quiet respectability. Except such a one here and there, one saw no dwellings above the size of cottages or small farmsteads; these, wood-built usually, and thatched, their porches embroidered with honeysuckle, and their gardens with daisies, their doors mostly ajar, or with one half shut to keep in the children, and a bricked or tiled footway from it to the wicket gate, – all neatly kept, and vivid with a sense of the quiet energies of their contented tenant, – made the lane-turnings cheerful, and gleamed in half-hidden clusters beneath the slopes of the woodlands ... there were not signs of distress, of effort, or of change; many of enjoyment, and not a few of wealth beyond the daily needs of life.[1]

The recollected landscapes of Ruskin's childhood evoke a natural order, a rural Arcadia of 'quiet respectability' where the man-made harmonizes with nature, and the rich and not so rich share the pleasures of the simple life. Such idyllic evocations of the past have a long pre-history;[2] they are defined by contrasts – past and present, town and country, rich and poor – and since they are reactions to change, industrialization intensified their potency. Industrializing societies throughout Europe and America constructed variants of the ideal, and related them, like Ruskin, to policies for social, moral and aesthetic reform.

In England Ruskin had articulated values that stimulated action: guilds and societies were formed to promote workmanship, protect the past and created good citizens for the future. And, according to the Ruskinian ideal, the virtues of this good citizenship were to be demonstrated in a domestic context: the order of the home became a metaphor for the order of society, and its ambience – its family hierarchies, its furniture and furnishings, its structure and its setting – demonstrations of social and cultural regeneration.

Observations about the nature of the home and the values it represented to the British idealists can be revealing: 'Why cannot we have ... simple and beautiful dwellings fit for cultivated, well-mannered men and women and not for ignorant, purse-proud digesting machines?'[3] This was William Morris in 1883. And Ruskin's more familiar definition: 'This is the true nature of home – it is the place of Peace; the shelter, not only from all injury, but from all terror, doubt and division. In so far as it is not this, it is not home ... And wherever a true wife comes, this home is always around her.'[4]

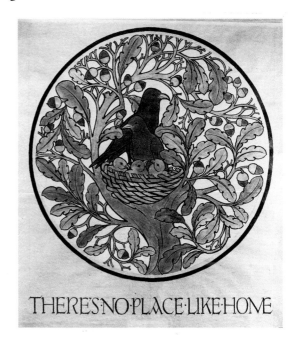

The references here are complex and they are worth some analysis since they locate the anxieties as well as the aspirations of this generation of design reformers. Both descriptions imply threat and disintegration. The 'simple and beautiful dwellings' William Morris so often described are defined against the degradation of poverty, but they also defy vulgarity, and vulgarity is associated with the bourgeoisie, those 'digesting machines' – producers as well as consumers of the new wealth and all that wealth can devour. Morris's ideal home is peopled by 'cultivated, well-mannered men and women': like the cottagers and landowners of Ruskin's childhood, their homes relate to a golden age, where the

70. Charles Francis Annesley Voysey.
Design for a poster for the Central Liquor Control Board,
c. 1915-18. Pen and ink and watercolour.

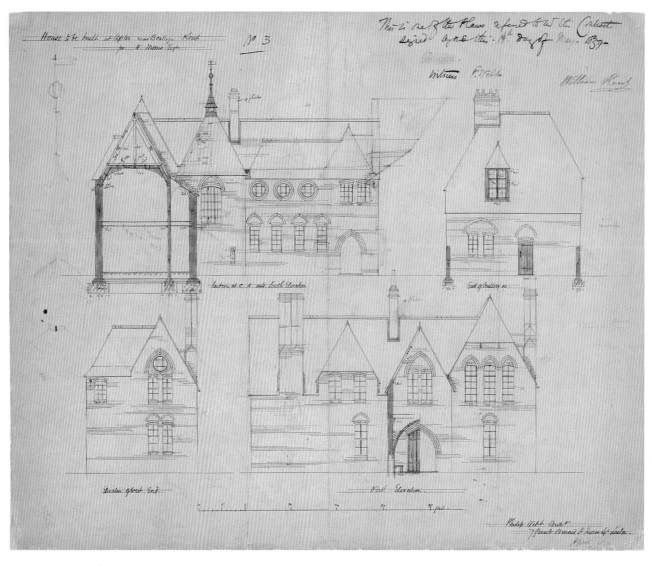

71. *Philip Webb. Design for the north and south elevations and details of Red House, Upton, Kent. 1859.*
Pen and ink and wash.
Built for William Morris, the house was filled with furniture by Webb and decorated by Dante Gabriel Rossetti and Edward Burne-Jones

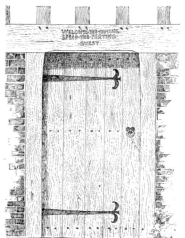

72. *M.H. Baillie Scott. Design for a Front Door. Illustration from* The Studio, *April 1895.*

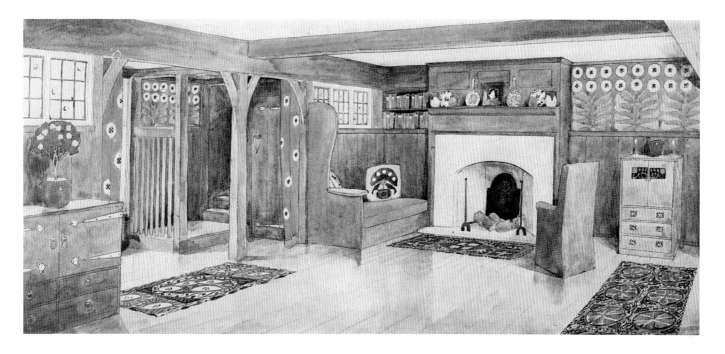

73. M.H. Baillie Scott. The dining-room, Falkenwood. From Houses and Gardens, *1906.*

order of the household was sanctified by a benign social and political economy – a Utopia Morris believed to be retrievable given 'a properly ordered state of Society'.[5]

For Ruskin the true home is also a private sphere, and a defence against the 'hostile society of the outer world'; it is the man's duty to defend and maintain it, while the woman's role is to 'secure its order, comfort and loveliness'.[6] The home, therefore, and the family unit were seen as microcosms for a wider harmony – the health, as well as the wealth of a nation.

Such civilized and civilizing aspirations were, of course, persuasive, and in some measure achievable, at least in England, since they obviously appealed to those with the means to invest in ideals. Architects such as Voysey, Baillie Scott and Lutyens were commissioned to build their affluent clients dream houses: houses that acknowledged local traditions of building and workmanship, and that celebrated country life (fig 73). Similar values inspired urban and suburban housing: the town houses of Norman Shaw, for example, especially the Queen Anne houses in Bedford Park[7] which were built for a middle-class market, represented a potent symbol of 'modern' living (fig 74). More modest equivalents were re-created in English Garden Suburbs and work-related communities such as Bournville and Port Sunlight; their furniture and furnishings complemented the ideal, and they were admired, as well as analysed by Continental and American observers of this English renaissance in design and architecture.[8]

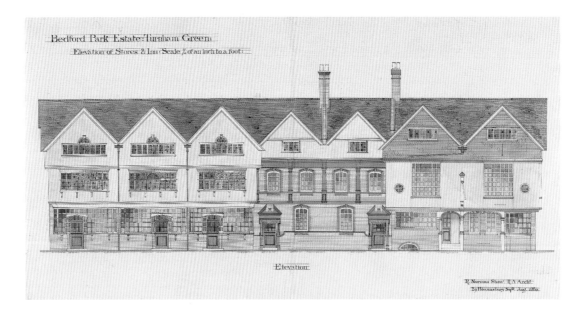

One of the most important of these appraisals was that of Hermann Muthesius, a civil servant with the Prussian Board of Trade, who was attached to the German Embassy in London from 1896 to 1903. His brief, to report on developments in English architecture and design, resulted in several books, including *Das englische Haus* (1903–4) and *Stilarchitektur und Baukunst* (1902).[9] As the title of the latter indicates, Muthesius was debating and defining the qualities he associated with the art of building – qualities, he maintained, which transcended academic and socially divisive preoccupations with style. The English approach to the building arts, he wrote, was:

> nothing other than a rejection of architectural formalism in favour of a simple and natural, reasonable way of building. One brought nothing new to such a movement; everything had existed for centuries in the vernacular architecture of the small town and rural landscape ... Here, amid the architectural extravagance that the architects promoted, one found all that one desired and for which one thirsted: adaptation to needs and local conditions, unpretentiousness and honesty of feeling; utmost cosiness and comfort in the layout of rooms, colour, an uncommonly attractive and painterly (but also reasonable) design, and an economy of building construction. The new English building-art that developed on this basis had now produced valuable results. But it has done more: it has spread the interest and understanding for domestic architecture to the entire people. It has created the only sure foundation for a new artistic culture: the artistic house.[10]

74. Richard Norman Shaw. Design for the Hostelry and Stores, Bedford Park, 1880. Pen and ink and wash.

Muthesius's reactions are worth recording, not only because of his subsequent influence on European policies for design reform,[11] but because they indicate shared concerns. By confronting the problem of the house, the English (or so it seemed) had confronted the social dislocation implicit in industrialization. At the same time their concern for national or regional traditions of building and work processes had preserved the distinction associated with craftsmanship, and this had contributed to the production of what he described as a 'genuine' or 'natural' art. Again, by concentrating on art in workmanship, the English had also challenged the hegemony of the fine artist, the easel painter, and had restored art to everyday life.

This concentration on the social and redemptive role of art privileged the designer and the architect, and it also privileged the object. It was more important to design a cup or a chair than to devote one's life to what Walter Crane described as 'the more expensive kinds of portable picture painting';[12] and since the home was the focus of this 'new artistic culture', every householder was a potential artist, and every home a potential work of art.

This was, of course, a middle-class vision: it reflected the prestige and élitism associated with 'high art', and at the same time it romanticized the role of the working class. By aiming to transform factory hands into creative and contented artisans, and by concentrating on vernacular ideals

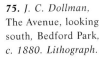

75. *J. C. Dollman,* The Avenue, looking south, Bedford Park, *c. 1880. Lithograph.*

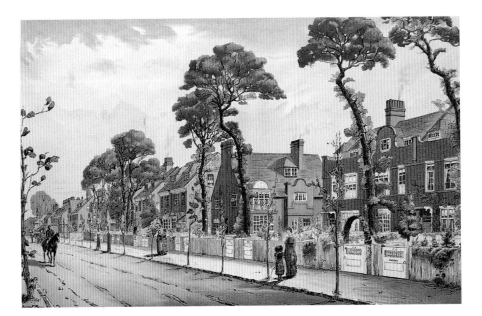

of workmanship, this generation of design reformers also challenged the policies of their predecessors rejecting any form of training programme based on attempts to control or rationalize the design process. Students at the Berlin *Kunstgewerbeschule*, for example, had been guided by the *Vorbilder für Fabrikanten und Handwerke*r, a prestigious pattern book of design exemplars for manufacturers and craftsmen selected by Karl Friedrich Schinkel and Peter Beuth, and distributed from the 1820s to the 1860s;[13] the South Kensington Schools of Design system, co-ordinated by Henry Cole after the Great Exhibition of 1851, had produced Owen Jones's influential *Grammar of Ornament* (1856), which categorized and documented the ornamental systems of a range of countries and cultures in order to demonstrate 'certain general laws' in the 'language of form'.

Such programmes were rejected by the Arts and Crafts generation because they denied the role of individuality and creativity; they were devised to impose rather than generate order, and they isolated the object from the context of making and use. But while the alternative – the ideal of small enterprises supporting communal endeavour – was considered both radical and humanistic, it was founded in economic expediency, especially in countries such as Sweden and Germany, where forms of 'guild' enterprise had survived into the nineteenth century.

In Germany the surviving guilds were involved with trade rather than craftsmanship; they included shop-keepers, butchers, bakers and carpenters, and they resisted industrialization on economic rather than ideological grounds. But while their laments for the loss of the past recall the idealism of Ruskin and Morris, these small tradesmen became a powerful reactionary force, and their resistance to change was seen as a bulwark against social disorder. As Shulamit Volkov has pointed out, it was also 'the mental response of men who found themselves overwhelmed by material hardship and social pressure ... suffering from an unfulfilled need to belong, and a deep-seated feeling of homelessness'.[14] The restoration of the ideal and the reality of the home, therefore, became a political as well as a social necessity.

Policies to improve standards of workers' housing had been instigated in Germany in the 1840s,[15] and the association of *Wohnungsreform* (the reform of the dwelling) with *Lebensreform* (the reform of life) acknowledged the English celebration of home. In Germany, however, the home came to be associated with the homeland, *Heimat*, that powerful and politically compromised symbol of national unity and continuity. *Heimat* was (and is) a value-laden concept, and is therefore difficult to translate; it signified home, locality and country, as well as a sense of belonging, and the inheritance of a shared past. Unlike Morris's gentle Utopia, however, *Heimat* was *somewhere*; its roots were in the German soil and the German homestead, and in the bitter struggles for the survival of the German race.

Wohnungsreform, therefore, was identified with national unity and national identity, and it was an obvious response to the pressures that led to unification in 1871. As in England, it was associated with social and economic stability, and it was also the focus of attempts to establish a German culture of art and design. The English had demonstrated the virtues, as well as the value, of the domestic arts, and according to Muthesius, they had also proved that these arts could and should be the 'natural' products of a collective endeavour. The *Werkstätte* (or workshops) which were set up in Munich and Dresden in 1898[16] represent one response to the English achievement: the founder members of the Munich enterprise included Peter Behrens and Richard Riemerschmid, both converts to the ideal of a social art. Another founder member, however, was Paul Schultze Naumburg, author of *Art and Race* who was president of the *Deutscher Bund für Heimatschutz* (established in 1904) and who was to organize the dissolution of the Bauhaus in Dessau in 1930.[17]

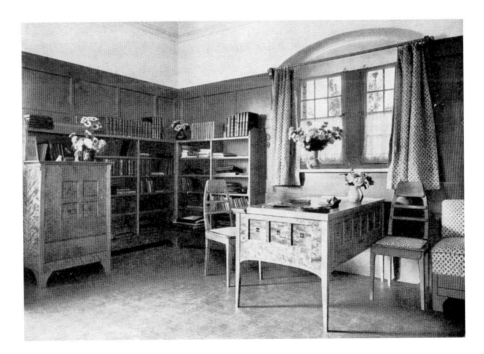

76. *A study with furniture designed by Richard Riemerschmid, made in birch veneer. From Hermann Muthesius,* Landhaus und Garten, *1907.*

The political ambiguities of these campaigns to protect the homeland and promote a national and social policy for German art and design are now obvious, and their implications confound interpretations of domesticity. The style associated with *Heimat*, preoccupied as it was with national identity and folk traditions in design and architecture, was obviously not confined to Germany; its association with racial supremacy, however, denied the Arts and Crafts concern for a shared symbolic order of workmanship. Karl Schmidt, for example, founder of the Dresden *Werkstätte*, claimed to be expressing 'the inner feelings of our nation' when he called for 'our Germany [to] remain in possession of the German race'. 'The understanding for this', he continued, 'can ... only be awakened, preserved and empowered if the works of our forebears find more appreciation, if everything foreign is held distant from the crystallization process and simply, or rather predominantly, the national element is emphasised.'[18]

Karl Schmidt had been trained as a carpenter and had visited England, and the success of his Dresden enterprise led to the development of a Garden City commune in nearby Hellerau. As well as the workshops, there was a training school, and a theatre (dedicated to music and dance); there were schools for the children, shops and communal facilities, and the enterprise was dedicated, according to Schmidt, to 'an aristocracy of workers that transcended traditional class distinctions'.[19] The *Typenmobel* (or type furniture) they produced was intended to meet the needs of this new aristocracy. It combined hand techniques with the use of machinery and was made from standardized components. The use of different finishes and woods produced unity in variety, so that every room in the house could demonstrate consistency of style.

By relating the craft ideal to serial production, these similar German organizations promoted concepts of art in industry. Although most of the work produced was beyond the means of the working classes, it offered the middle classes – the *Mittelstand* – the opportunity to furnish their homes with practical, well-made, unostentatious designs that demonstrated the German ideal of *Sachlichkeit* – simplicity, sobriety and a sense of order. When the Germans began to publicize and exhibit these models of *Wohnkultur*, they were seen as a challenge both to Arts and Crafts achievements and to the French hegemony in the decorative arts. For example, when designs from the Munich Werkstätte were included in a

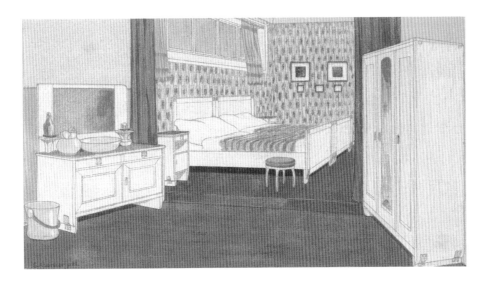

77. *Gertrud Kleinhempel. Design for a Bedroom, c. 1902.*
Made for the Dresdener Werkstätten *of Hellerau.*

Salon d'Automne exhibition in Paris in 1910, one French critic wrote: '[they have reformed] the aesthetics of the home to make the modern house a combined work of art, a practical construction of simple and dignified beauty'.[20]

At the turn of the century, therefore, Germany was not only demonstrating its industrial power, it was also proving that its domestic consumer products could compete on an international level. The strength of the *Heimat* was reflected in the commercial supremacy of the nation, reinforcing the economic potency of the domestic ideal. By establishing a national identity for a domestic art that was achievable, practical and exportable, the Germans presented a new model for European design reform. For although English Arts and Crafts achievements were still acknowledged at the turn of the century, they certainly did not celebrate democracy in design. 'The curse which weighs upon their products is one of economic impossibility', wrote Hermann Muthesius in *Das englische Haus*.[21]

Muthesius's interpretation of design reform was reflected in the policies of the *Deutscher Werkbund*, which was set up in Munich in 1907 in order to promote 'the best in art, industry and trade'. The inclusion of industry and trade in this triumvirate challenged the English design reformers' concentration on social redemption through art and craftsmanship, and it also acknowledged economic reality. The craft ideal, nevertheless, survived in attempts to signal a secession from imperialist dominance in countries such as Hungary, Poland, Norway, Finland and Ireland, where 'craft' was more closely associated with a surviving vernacular, and with regional peasant art and culture. Research into vernacular design and building, peasant dress, folk songs and folklore, for example, which took place throughout Europe in the nineteenth century, was intensified in these 'peripheral' countries. Here the need to identify and celebrate a national past was associated with political independence; the language of the vernacular was a language of resistance, and although Ruskinian idealism contributed to these movements, campaigns for 'design reform' focussed on cultural autonomy rather than on problems associated with industrialization.[22]

Various arts and crafts and 'home industry' organizations were formed to promote these campaigns, including the Friends of Finnish Handicrafts (1879), the Norwegian Society for Home Industry (1891) and the Society of Polish Applied Art (1901). These were essentially middle-class initiatives, and they were associated with historical and archaeological research, the formation of national collections of folk art and design, and the promotion of training programmes to support and sustain traditional methods of building and making. The focus of this concern was the home or the homestead, and its ideal was generally located in remote peasant communities – in Karelia (Finland), Transylvania (Hungary) and the Tatras (Poland).

In Zakopane, for example, the Polish architect and designer Stanislaw Witkiewitz based the design, decoration and furnishings of his impressive wooden villas on the Tatran mountain cottage;[23] in Hungary, the artists of the Godollo community produced stained glass, tapestries, furniture and embroideries to celebrate the Hungarian past, while architects such as Károly Kós explored Transylvania for models for both urban and rural living (fig. 78).[24] Architects and designers, therefore, manipulated the language of local vernacular style to signal a shared inheritance; and since these achievements were widely publicized in books and magazines, as well as in exhibitions, they contributed to an international ideal of domesticity. In Finland, for example, Hvitträsk, the house designed by and for the architectural partnership of Gesellius, Lingdren and Saarinen to demonstrate their interpretation of the 'Finnishness' of Finnish design, was celebrated by a European élite that included Alma Mahler and Maxim Gorky.

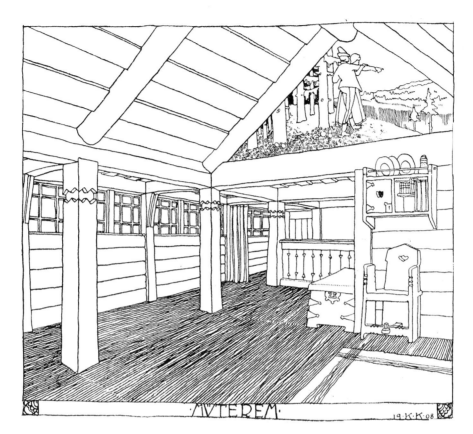

78. *Károly Kós. Design for Studio I, from* Magyar Iparmüvészet *(Hungarian Applied Art), 1908.*

These attempts to transform the peasant home into a *Gesamtskunstwerk* (unified work of art) celebrated a sophisticated ideal of the simple life, and as in England and Germany, it appealed to those with the means both to create and sustain it. At the same time, however, designers and architects in these 'peripheral' cultures were able to draw on surviving peasant traditions and skills in order to proclaim the nationality, as well as the democratic intent of their design, and these policies, as we have seen, were determined as much by economic necessity as by social and aesthetic idealism.

One of the earliest of these European 'skill-based' design reform organizations was Svenska Slöjdföreningen (The Swedish Society of Crafts and Design), which was set up in 1845, a year before Sweden abolished its craft guilds and introduced free trade. The Society's founding motto was 'Swedish handicraft is the father of Swedish independence', and its aim, in the early years, was economic survival. Sweden was then struggling to establish an industrial base in the face of competition, recession and agricultural decline, which had resulted in both urban and rural poverty, as well as the loss of prestige the country had enjoyed in the eighteenth century. In its early years, therefore, the Society had initiated training schemes, sponsored exhibitions, and published pamphlets on such diverse topics as basket weaving, glue manufacture, welding and machine techniques, and these activities, as well as its promotion of an 'art industry' to compete in European markets, represented a practical and pragmatic response to economic needs.

When 'design reform' was prioritized in the 1880s and 1890s, the model, of course, was England, and English Arts and Crafts developments. In Sweden, however, Morris's ideal of democracy in design seemed in some measure achievable, partly because the Swedish domestic industries tended to concentrate on small-scale production, and partly because of Svenska Slöjdföreningen's stress on education, for the consumer as well as the producer. Ellen Key's *Skönhet for alla* (Beauty for Everyone; 1899), for example, with its demand for practical as well as beautiful household goods, identified the priorities for Swedish design: the production of simple, affordable furniture and furnishing appropriate to the modest needs of the average household – priorities that were emphasized in the exhibitions organized by Svenska Slöjdföreningen.[25] Like

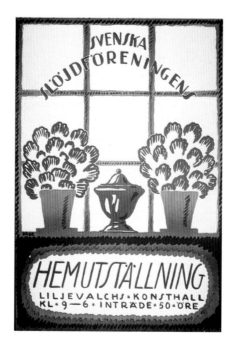

79. *Poster for the homes exhibition of* Svenska Slöjdföreningen *(The Swedish Society of Crafts and Design), 1917.*

similar societies in Finland and Poland, Svenska Slöjdföreningen also supported vernacular traditions and craftsmanship, and the focus of these endeavours, of course, was the home.

So that when Carl Larsson began to paint his loved ones and his home, celebrating the setting, as well as the rituals of his family life, he was, perhaps without realizing it, representing a European, as well as a Swedish ideal of domesticity. For these scenes of everyday life in Lilla Hyttnäs proved that Arcadia, the earthly paradise, was achievable, and that the home, as well as life within it, could become a work of art. Carl Larsson himself was the archetypal artist; he was a 'child of the gutter',[26] but he could draw, and his skills enabled him to escape from urban poverty and train as an artist. He won medals, had rejected academic conventions and he lived the Bohemian life, in France as well as Sweden; then he met and married Karin Bergöö, the 'ideal role model for all the women in the country'.[27] Karin, the 'angel in the house', was the Ruskinian 'true wife': the home that Larsson painted 'always around her' – alive with children, flowers, sunlight and colour – 'a charming home, quaint, gay and happy; so thoroughly Carl Larsson throughout, bright colours, deftly applied, and wise maxims adorning walls and doors'.[28] And, especially for the Germans, this home and its creation represented the ideal of the *Heimat*: Larsson, whose family had suffered from urban poverty, homelessness and the loss of an agrarian past, was determined that his children's childhood would not be like his. He and his wife took over this simple country cottage and transformed it into their ideal of home. It was not, to quote Larsson, 'a lifeless object', it was 'alive and like all living things it must obey the law of life and must change from moment to moment'.[29]

The changes they made there celebrated the fusion of art and craft; the household objects, the furniture and the furnishings (and the clothes they wore) represented William Morris's (and Hermann Muthesius's) ideals for domestic art – they acknowledged tradition, and a revival of handicraft that was founded in the family and supported by local skills. All those involved were artists: to quote Friedrich Naumann, who was active in the German design reform movements: 'The architect, the carpenter, the upholsterer, the painter, the decorator, taken together, give life to a new figure of the artist, in whom re-appear all of these specialisations'.[30]

Above all, however, life in Lilla Hyttnäs represented what Ferdinand Avenarius described as 'the central importance of joy in life': 'We must take into account', he wrote, 'the enormous importance of the ordinary joy, that basic nutrient of the human spirit. We sadly lack a social hygiene of the mind. Keeping in mind the central importance of joy, artists should represent the phenomena of life as joyfully as possible.'[31]

5

LOOKING
AT LILLA HYTTNÄS

Michael Snodin

Welcome to Sundborn

The village of Sundborn, some 238 kilometres north-west of Stockholm in the province of Dalarna, is much the same today as it was when the Larssons lived there. It has of course grown, but it still contains the scatter of old farms which Carl recorded on his first visit in 1885 (fig. 80). Passing by the small hydro-electric power station, built in 1904, you finally reach the Larssons' property, Lilla Hyttnäs or 'little furnace point', its name commemorating the industrial activity which once dominated the area.[1] Still in the hands of the family, the plot of land is not large, and is today all but filled with a scatter of wooden outbuildings clustered around the main house (fig. 81).

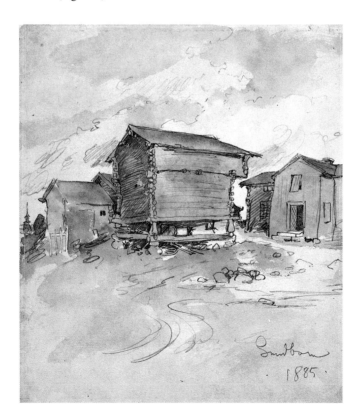

80.[90] *Carl Larsson*. A View of Bondesgården, Sundborn, *1885. Watercolour.*

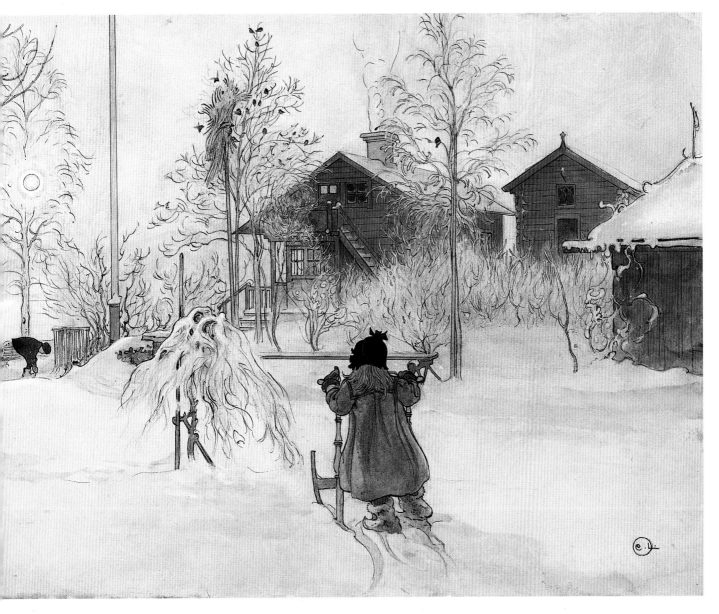

81.[99] Carl Larsson. The Front Yard and the Wash-house, *1897.*
Watercolour, from the Ett hem *series.*
The area in front of the cottage at Lilla Hyttnäs in the winter. The large building is a laundry
and sleeping-quarters built in 1896. Behind it is an old härbre *or storehouse also adapted for*
sleeping. Before 1901 the Larssons spent only summer and Christmas at Sundborn.

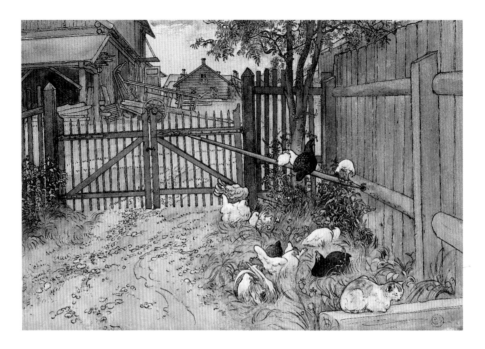

82. Carl Larsson. The Gate, *probably 1897.*
Watercolour, from the Ett hem *series.*
This drawing shows the first gate to Lilla Hyttnäs, looking towards the village.
In 1904, with the addition of land due to the building of the electricity power station,
the site of the gate was moved and its design changed.

Once through the gate, you forget the village behind you. For those who have seen Carl Larsson's illustrations, coming to Lilla Hyttnäs can be like a waking dream or like meeting a famous face for the first time – extremely familiar yet oddly unreal. Those less well acquainted with Larsson's seductive images can perhaps more easily take it all in. We are facing a large and glittering sheet of water, part of the Sundborn river. It is bordered by low tree-covered hills, while directly in front is reflected a wooded island and the sky (fig. 83). The main house is L-shaped, with the end of one arm close to the water to the south. It is surrounded by lawns, flowerbeds and the delicate freshness of silver birches (fig. 84). Contrasted with these natural forms are the straight lines of a boat dock delineated by crisp white fencing and an arched bridge. The very image of peace and retreat from the world, it is easy to understand why the town-boy Carl Larsson felt he had come home when he came to own this spot in 1888.

83. *[101] Carl Larsson.*
Viking Raid in Dalarna,
1900. Watercolour.
The Larsson children, drawn
from the bank at Lilla
Hyttnäs. In the background is
the island of Bullerholmen,
which also belonged to the
Larssons and was the scene of
crayfish and bathing parties.
This image of summer
childhood was made into
one of the most popular of the
colour lithographs after
Larsson's watercolours.

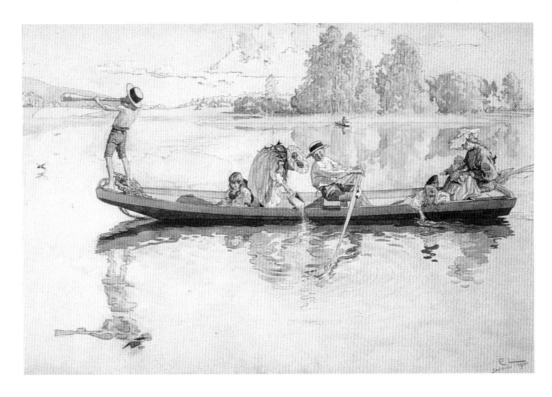

84. *Lilla Hyttnäs from*
the river.

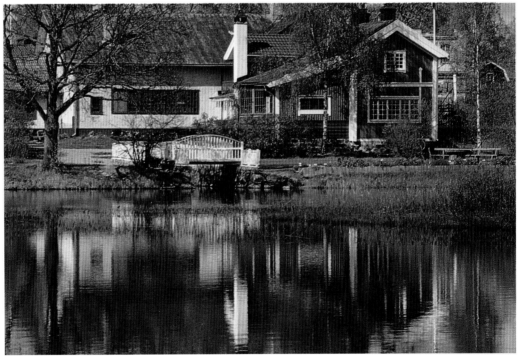

85. *[98] Carl Larsson.* Crayfishing, *1897.*
Watercolour, from the Ett hem *series.*
The opening of the crayfishing season in early
August is one of Sweden's great annual
events. When this painting was made,
showing the Larssons' party on the island of
Bullerholmen, the custom was relatively new,
initiated by laws to prevent overfishing.
In 1899 this image, accompanied by a verse
to Swedish nature and to friendship, was
made into a tapestry; it has since become an
emblem of the whole custom.

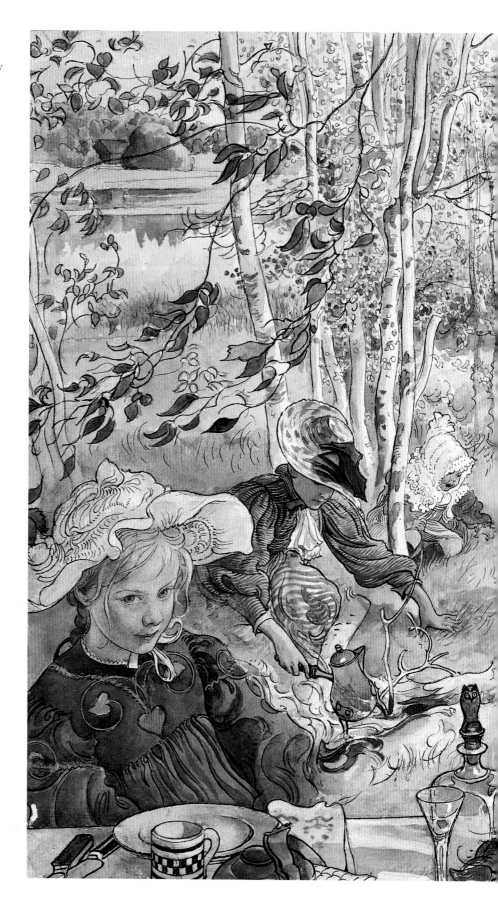

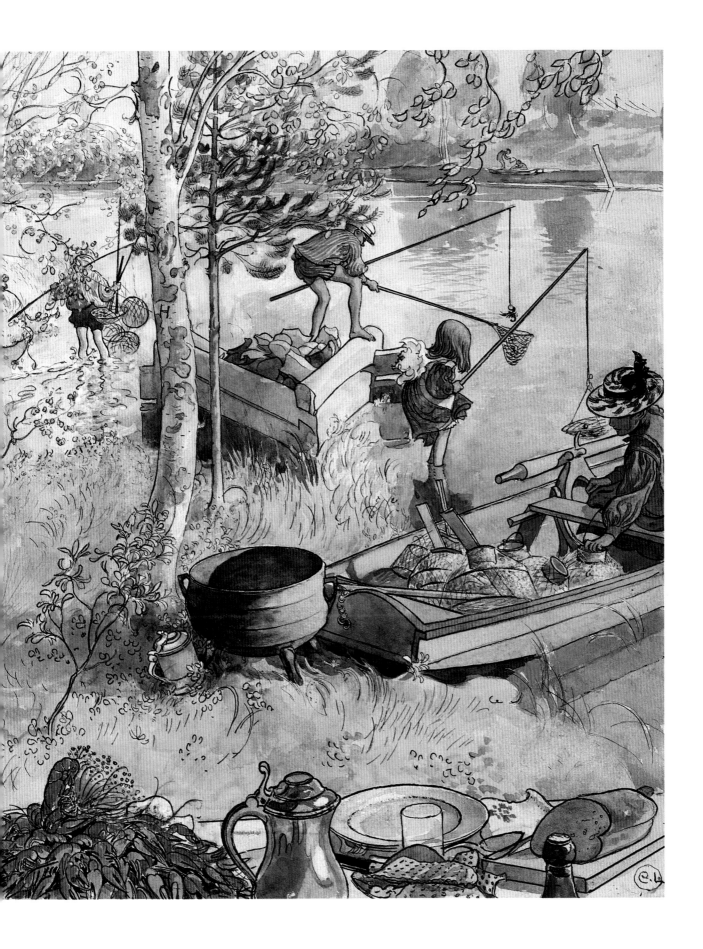

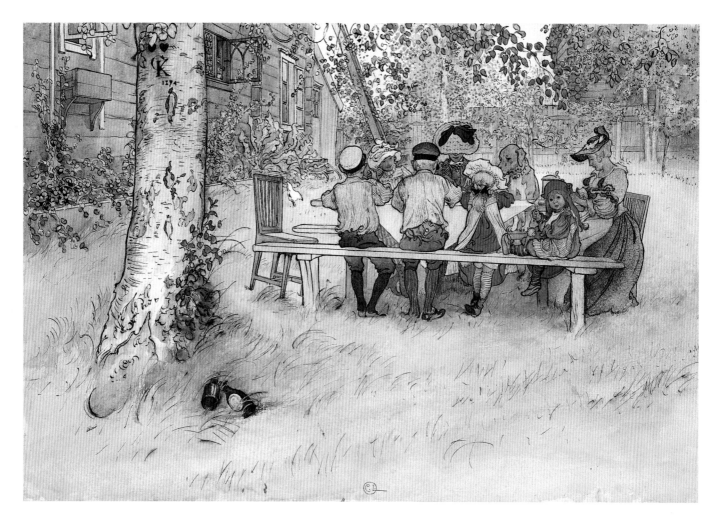

86. *[97] Carl Larsson*. Breakfast under the Big
Birch, *1896. Watercolour, from the* Ett hem *series.*
This picture of the Larssons (and their dog Kapo)
and one of Carl's models at breakfast has come to
symbolize Swedish summer, helping to form a habit
of outdoor eating. On the left is the east front of
the old cottage, still showing its log construction,
later to be almost entirely covered up. At the far
end is the converted woodshed in which some of the
children slept.

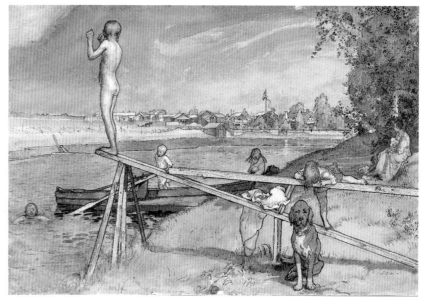

87. *Carl Larsson.* A Good Place for Bathing, *1896.*
Watercolour, from the Ett hem *series.*
The view of Sundborn from Bullerholmen, with
Lilla Hyttnäs on the right, with its railings along
the shore and the laundry under construction.

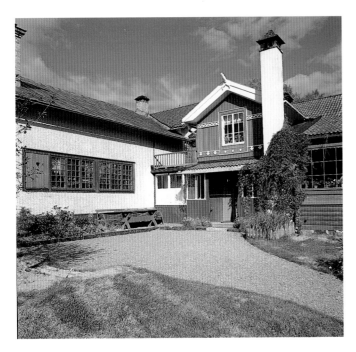

One look at the main house, however, tells us that we are here in the presence of much more than the usual Swedish country cottage. A wide variety of colours, building materials and roof lines suggest a piecemeal development. Seen from the water, the wing running north-south is made of wood painted in a cheerful combination of reds, yellows and greens; it has a tiled roof and an array of wooden ornaments, with the entrance porch on its west side. The other part of the house, very much taller, plainer and metal-roofed, is rendered in white-washed plaster; at its end is a

88. The house from the south-west.

smaller tiled extension (figs 88, 89). The wooden part, we surmise, must be an old cottage, the other a modern studio. We are only partly right, for on acquiring Lilla Hyttnäs the Larssons almost immediately began turning the simple wooden house they found on the site into something which clearly announced both inside and out that it was not only a family home and the house of an artist but also an artistic house.

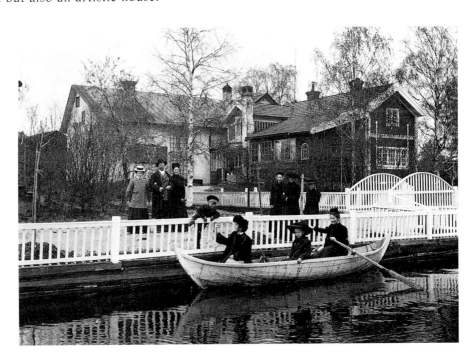

89. Lilla Hyttnäs, 1904-5.
Carl stands with two unknown ladies, Karin with Lisbeth and Brita; Esbjörn is on the fence and Kersti in the boat. This view shows most of the works associated with the Larssons' permanent move in 1901 and the increase of land which followed on from the setting up of the electricity power station, including the new studio and the bridge and boat dock.

The Larssons arrive

Lilla Hyttnäs had come into Karin's family in 1875, when it had been purchased by her father for his widowed mother and his two sisters, Ulla and Maria.[2] When Ulla died in 1888, Maria left, allowing Karin's father to give it to the Larssons, on condition that they put a sum equal to its value into the children's savings accounts. When the Larssons arrived they found little to appeal to them beyond the site itself and the possibilities inherent in the house. It was perched on what Carl called a slag heap, and was accompanied by a couple of lilac bushes, some birch trees and a potato patch. Like all the other houses in the district, it was coloured red with iron-oxide paint and built of exposed logs laid horizontally. This building method had allowed it to undergo, with little difficulty, a number of expansions since the early nineteenth century, growing from a low two-roomed cottage to one with three rooms on the ground and first floors, with at the front a two-storey projection containing the entrance hall and stairs, and at the end a lean-to storeroom.[3] The result was perhaps rather ungainly, being rather too tall for its width, and not very picturesque (fig. 90).

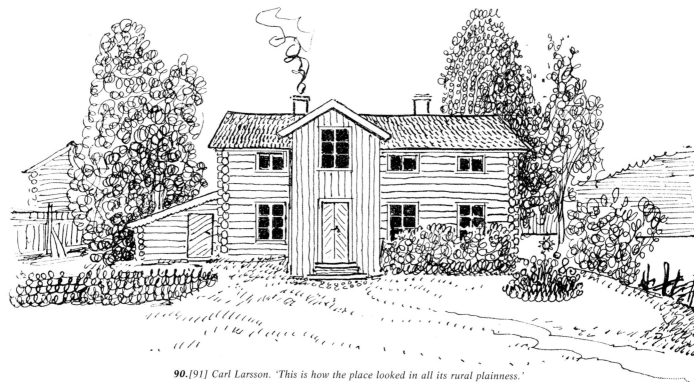

90.[91] *Carl Larsson. 'This is how the place looked in all its rural plainness.'*
Illustration in Ett hem, *1899, of the west side of the cottage as the Larssons found it. Carl has omitted another vertical log wall on the right; otherwise the drawing is accurate, showing the old log house and its later planked extension at the front for the hall and staircase. The very first cottage probably consisted of two rooms only, represented by the lower two windows on the left.*

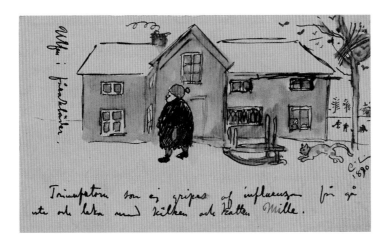

91.[92] Carl Larsson. Ulf in Front of the Cottage, *1890. Pen and ink and watercolour.*
Drawn very early in 1890, this sketch shows the first external change to the old cottage, the long Gothic dining-room window. The text reads: 'Ulf in sheep's clothing; the conqueror who no longer has influenza is allowed to go out and play with the sledge and Mille the cat.'

It was certainly too inartistic for the Larssons, while the garden (the lilacs and birches apart) was judged to be very unsatisfactory. They were obliged to bring in topsoil, starting with a load to feed a group of lilies by the porch. These marked the beginning of a notable garden, informally planted (not without a struggle) with both Swedish and more exotic flowers, which also helped to supply the Larssons' passion for plants indoors. In their first summer, 1889, nothing happened to the outside of the house, but by the winter of 1890 the first change had appeared, a long Gothic window for the new dining-room, apparently inaugurated in January (fig. 91).[4] In July the same year Carl wrote to his patron Pontus Fürstenberg, adding a sketch of the west façade, ironically titled 'The Artist's place, Sundborn's only curiosity' (fig. 92). 'You cannot imagine how extremely nice and cosy we are beginning to make Hyttnäs', he wrote, 'But there is still much to do and we will have to carry it forward a little each year'. The outside, however, was well on the way to being completely transformed into the state shown in drawings and photographs of the mid-1890s (figs 94–96).[5]

92.[93] Carl Larsson. Sketch of the cottage, in a letter to Pontus Fürstenberg dated July 1890. Pen and ink.
This drawing shows the house with most of the alterations of summer 1890; some unexecuted and unresolved features show that the letter was written before the work was complete. The annotated parts include 'wife's portrait' on the chimney-stack and Carl's initials on the windvane.

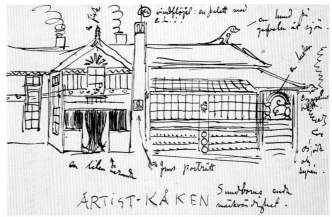

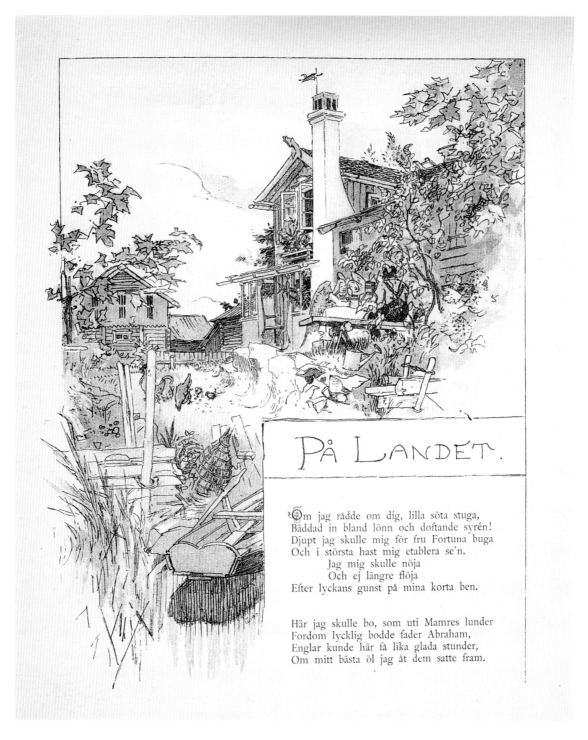

PÅ LANDET.

Om jag rådde om dig, lilla söta stuga,
Bäddad in bland lönn och doftande syrén!
Djupt jag skulle mig för fru Fortuna buga
Och i största hast mig etablera se'n.
    Jag mig skulle nöja
    Och ej längre flöja
Efter lyckans gunst på mina korta ben.

Här jag skulle bo, som uti Mamres lunder
Fordom lycklig bodde fader Abraham,
Englar kunde här få lika glada stunder,
Om mitt bästa öl jag åt dem satte fram.

93. *Carl Larsson. Illustration to 'In the Country', from Elias Sehlstedt,*
Sånger och visor i urval *(Selected Songs and Ballads, 1892-3).*
In illustrating Sehlstedt's poem, about a little cottage in the country,
Larsson shows his own house as seen from the water, probably drawn in 1890 or 1891.
The angels at the table also feature in the poem.

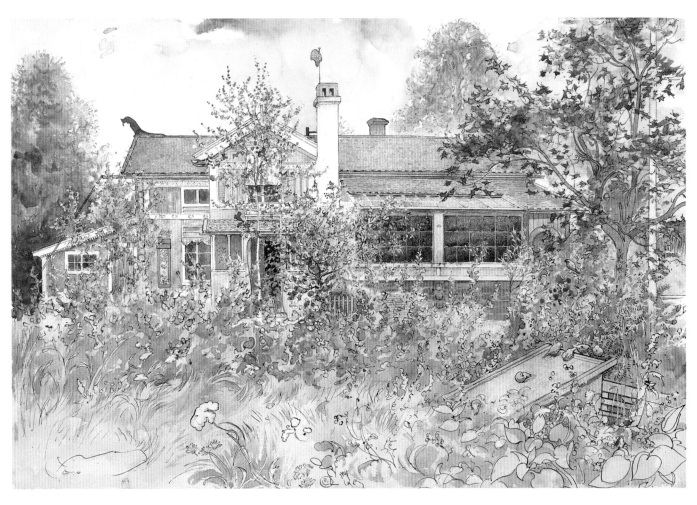

94. *[95] Carl Larsson.* The Cottage, *1894-5.*
Watercolour, from the Ett hem *series.*
In this view of the west façade Larsson has simplified the colouring of
the new woodwork, but shows clearly the bright red oil paint on the studio front,
contrasted with the less strong iron-ore paint of the old cottage.

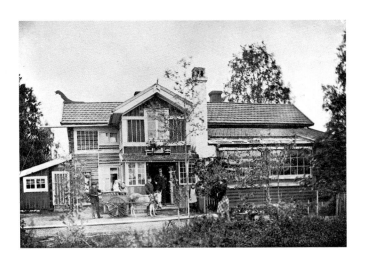

95. *The house from the west, c. 1891.*

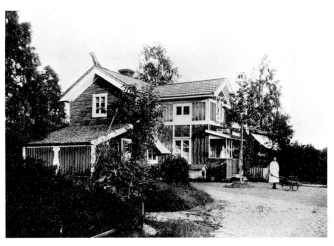

96. *The house from the north-west, c. 1897.*

Adding to the cottage

A studio and its chimney filled up the space between the extension and the main house wall, a porch had been added, and the upper walls had probably already been covered with a framework of decorative wooden elements painted white and green, disguising and unifying the combination of logs and planking. At one gable end (in the sketch shown facing the river) is a carved figure of a dog, while over the porch is a leaping fish. Carl's self-portrait appears among the carved wooden gargoyles supporting the eaves of the studio (fig. 97) and Karin's portrait (now lost) was placed on the front of the chimney. In June 1891 they were joined by the children's portraits, painted in line on the chimney in the porch (fig. 98). Above the whole composition is the wind-vane, palette-shaped and signed CL: it was an artistic house indeed.

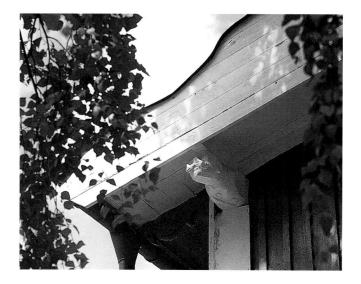

97. *A carved wooden gargoyle, depicting Carl in collar and pince-nez looking out over the river.*

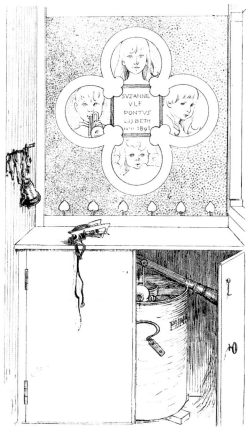

98. *Carl Larsson. The Larsson children painted in June 1891 on the plastered chimney wall in the porch; below is the fire pump. Illustration from* Ett hem, *1899.*

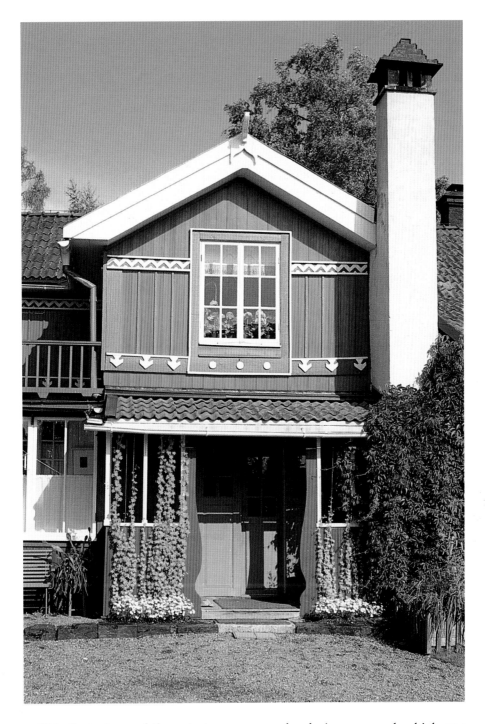

99. *The porch and part of the west front.*

This first phase of the exterior announced a design approach which was to be repeated throughout the house (fig. 99). The existing building was adapted to create a synthesis of the old and new, introducing a complex mix of historicizing and exotic elements. The result was something completely fresh yet rooted in tradition. This adaptive design technique, which Carl, in another context, described as having things 'cooked up in the Carl Larsson manner', was to some extent determined by economy and the need to use local craftsmen and labourers. The simple yet striking geometrical shapes of the additions, however, were also part of his general approach to design and ornament, as is clearly shown in his book decorations (fig. 16), the frames for the Fürstenberg triptych (fig. 24), and the early and modern parts of the mural decorations of the New Elementary Grammar School for Girls in Gothenburg. These demonstrate not only his profound grasp of and creative approach to ornament but also a very similar design method based on geometry and proportion. Behind the simple rough wood shapes on the exterior lies a sophisticated blend of elements both Swedish and foreign.

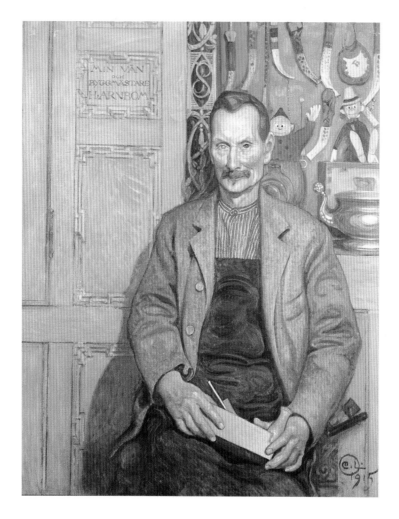

100.[35] *Carl Larsson.* The Carpenter Hans Arnbom, *1915.*
Oil on canvas.
Hans Arnbom, the village handyman, was the most important of a number of local craftsmen who helped the Larssons to realize their ideal at Lilla Hyttnäs. He is shown seated before the panelling in the new studio and Larsson's 'Lapp Museum'; Larsson himself is represented by an 'alter ego' doll. The panelling is inscribed 'my friend and my builder H. Arnbom'. From a set of portraits of local people, painted by Larsson for the parish.

Swedish influences

The dominating Swedish influence, visible in the gable decorations, the zigzag bands and the log-fronted lower walls of the studio, is that of the Viking or Old Norse style, described in chapter 3. To these was added a copy of a gilt-wood medievalizing relief, originally made to accompany a painting of 1893 (figs 101, 102). The most noticeable Old Norse feature

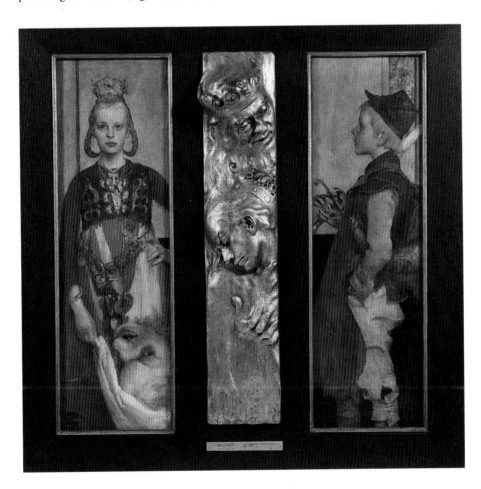

101.[18] Carl Larsson. The Princess and the Shepherd Boy:
A Swedish Fairy Story, *1893. Oil on canvas and gilt wood.*
A gilt copy of the central relief was placed on the front of Lilla Hyttnäs.
Similar reliefs on the Fürstenberg triptych were modelled by
Larsson in clay, cast in plaster and then carved in wood by another hand.
The painted figures were adapted in 1896 for the watercolour St George
and the Princess *(see fig. 246).*

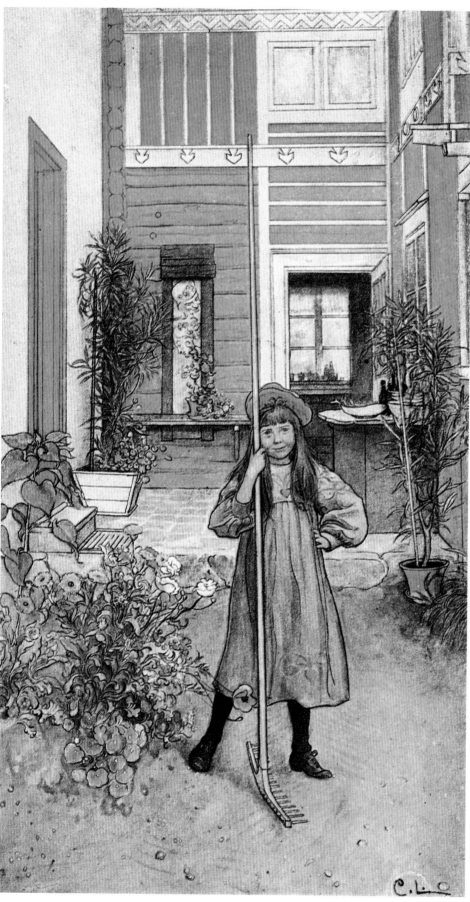

102. *Carl Larsson.* Raking.
Illustration in Larssons, *1902, after a watercolour painted in 1900.*
Raking the gravel at the front of the house on Saturdays was a regular and irksome duty. Here Brita stands in front of the north end of the west front of the old cottage, with its gilt relief; above it is the blocked-in window of the small winter studio. The rough logs contrast with the smooth white wall of the big studio, built in 1899; a kitchen door was formed from the old cottage window at the same time.

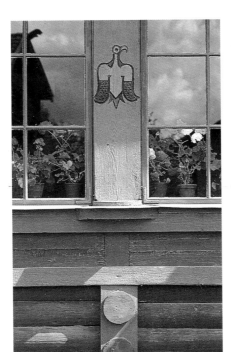

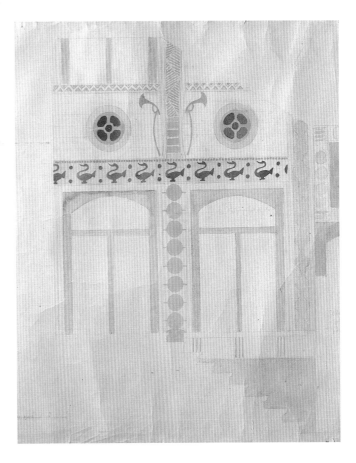

103. *Detail of the studio wall, intended to evoke an Old Norse past.*

104. *Carl Larsson. Design for the wall decorations representing the Bronze Age, painted by Carl Larsson in 1890 in the hall of the New Elementary Grammar School for Girls, Gothenburg. Watercolour.*
The rising discs beneath the frieze of ducks represent log-ends. The drawing was given to the Nordic Museum by Carl Larsson in 1897.

was the front wall of the studio, with its gargoyles, false logs with a bird decoration above, and a shuttered window like one in a stave church. The obvious falsity of the log front, with its unconvincing wooden discs representing the log ends of a non-existent interior cross-wall (fig. 103), does not seem to have worried the Larssons. To them it was clearly so much pattern, just like the strikingly similar trompe-l'oeil Viking and Bronze Age logs and ornament which were being painted on the walls of the Gothenburg school at the same date (fig. 104).[6] By 1890 Old Norse was far from revolutionary; it had in fact become one of a number of styles to be found among the villas of Stockholm's suburbs, in which applied wood strip also played a major role (fig. 9). But in making their villa in the remoteness of

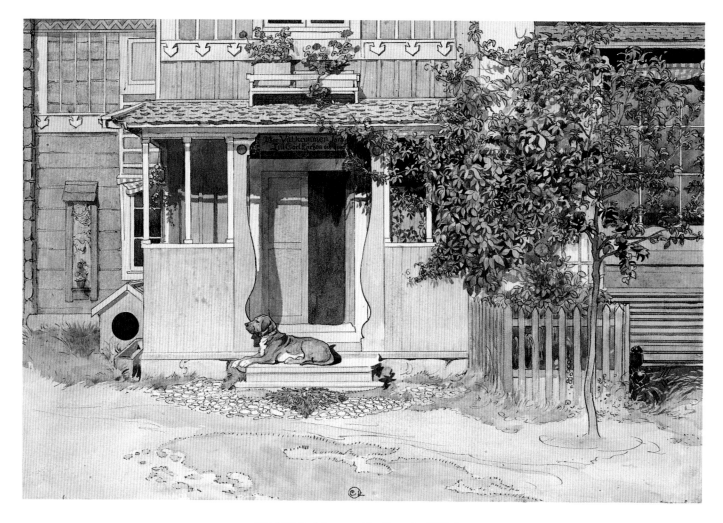

105.[96] Carl Larsson. The Veranda, 1896-7.
Watercolour, from the Ett hem *series.*
Kapo on guard; the old cottage changed dramatically with the addition
of the new studio in 1899.

Dalarna, the Larssons added an Old Norse coat to a plain and comparatively modern vernacular house in order to make a link between surviving folk culture and the ancient Nordic heroic past.[7] Even then they gave it further resonances by adding a Rococo porch derived from local eighteenth-century examples (fig. 105) and a flat Baroque baluster to the end of the house. The final folk element on the exterior is the use of colour, although the Larssons treated it in a rather unusual manner, adding elements in white and two shades of green to the red ground of the traditional cottage. While these combinations resemble the colours on folk furniture, they are not usually to be found on architectural exteriors.

Foreign influences

The foreign influences include ideas both Japanese and English. The network of applied wooden strips strongly recalls such Japanese-inspired designs as the cover for the series *Verdandis småskrifter* (Verdandi's Pamphlets) and the frames for the Fürstenberg triptych, both conceived in 1888 (figs 24, 69). The former incorporates the discs under the upper hall window, and the latter the curious downward-pointing arrows. It is significant that Carl's first exhibited view of the house and family, *De mina* (My Loved Ones), was painted to fit into the Fürstenberg frame (Frontispiece),[8] while a later cover design for the *Småskrifter* (fig. 106) combines arrows and strips in a manner even closer to the Sundborn house.[9] The position of the chimney-stack, placed on the outer wall to serve the studio fireplace, cannot be paralleled in Swedish vernacular architecture. With its cosy outline and picturesquely dominant position, it can probably be attributed to English influence, as seen in houses in the so-called Old-English, Queen Anne and Arts and Crafts styles. The top, however, is derived from a local Dalarna type.[10]

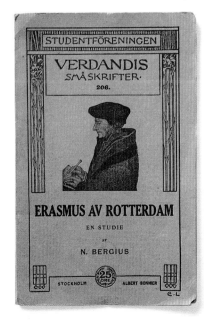

106. Example of a pamphlet from the series Verdandis småskrifter*, with a cover design by Carl Larsson first used in 1906.*

The other façades

The disposition of the ornament, and such paintings as *De mina* (Frontispiece), make it clear that the principal view of the original house was always intended to be that from the north-west. The south front facing the river lacked the elaborate decoration of the west front but did include one remarkable feature, a long multi-casement window of many small panes to the drawing-room, which was under construction from 1891 onwards (fig. 107). The Larssons were no doubt aware of long windows of this form in English vernacular buildings and their Queen Anne derivatives of the 1870s and 80s (figs 74, 75). On the other hand, such long horizontal windows were also to be found in Swedish vernacular architecture, as on the glazed-in galleries of the celebrated sixteenth-century house at Ornäs near Sundborn, a full-size replica of which was shown in the Paris Exhibition of 1867.[11] A Swedish derivation is also suggested by the use of long horizontal windows in the earlier dining-room, where they were significantly given Gothic leading. It is entirely characteristic of the house that the design of the drawing-room window is primarily determined by the demands of the room it lights, in particular the way in which the middle casement is a little larger than the others, subtly pulling the whole interior together.

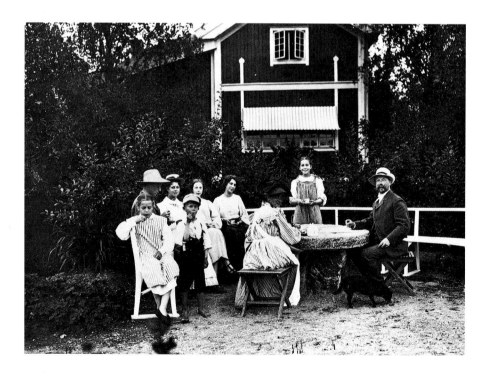

107. *The Larsson family around the millstone table before the south front, 1906-7. The planking had been added to the logs of the south front in 1904, altering the arrangement of the white woodwork. The onion-topped uprights began as abstract 'posts' at the ends of a fictive balustrade. From right to left are: Carl, Brita, the model Leontine, Karin, Lisbeth, Esbjörn, Olga Palm (a friend), Pontus and Kersti.*

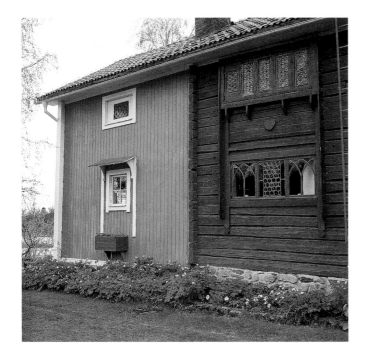

The east façade of the house now fronts the rushing water channel of the power station, but even before the channel was built this side always had an undesirable view, facing the adjoining property of Stora (big) Hyttnäs. It is perhaps for this reason that the original windows on this side were made smaller (or if enlarged were given stained glass); only the kitchen window (for the servants) was left large and unobscured, reminding us that with its back door (after 1901) this was a servants' area. Here the original logs were left exposed long after they had disappeared under planking on the other fronts, but today only one section remains on view, appropriately emphasized by an elaborate and subtly designed framework around the medievalizing windows of the dining-room and Carl's bedroom (fig. 108). This section now separates façades treated very differently, giving the almost postmodern impression of several different houses joined together (fig. 109), although whether this was intentional or simply evidence of a development process stopped in its

108. *The southern end of the east front. On the right are the logs of the original house and the windows to Carl's bedroom and the dining-room. The boarded section on the left has windows to the drawing-room and Karin's bedroom.*

109. *The east side of the house. The half-timbering of the wing built in 1901 was extended to cover the walls of the north end of the old cottage.*

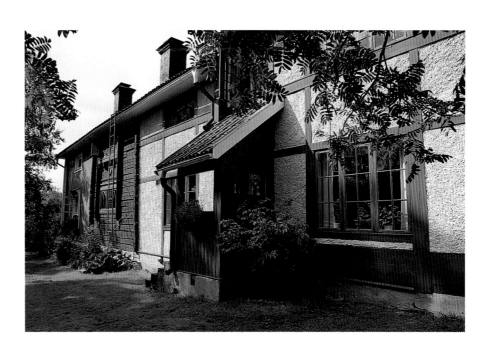

tracks is uncertain. The kitchen end of the old cottage is clad in rough-cast and half-timbering which is a continuation of the outside treatment of the final building phase of the house, which was put up in 1901 and filled the angle between the new studio and the old house. The red half-timbering and cream-painted render are derived not from local practice but probably from building techniques seen in the far south of Sweden and neighbouring Denmark.

The new studio

At the end of 1899 the Larssons inaugurated the new studio, built at right angles to the old house. Completely filling the rough-cast, metal-roofed structure was one of the biggest studios in Scandinavia, custom-built for the preparation of large-scale mural paintings and for use all the year round.[12] Indeed it marked the beginning of the transition of the Sundborn house from a summer cottage to a permanent dwelling, finally completed in 1901. Its whitewashed exterior was in marked contrast to the old house, and the building as a whole is frankly modern and utilitarian. Rough cast, which in Dalarna was to be found chiefly on churches, was used in more humble older contexts elsewhere in Sweden. Its use by the Larssons was not only practical but marked a change of aesthetic from the deliberately idiosyncratic and experimental approach of 1890 to a more mature and understated style befitting Carl Larsson's growing public profile.

The south side of the studio originally had only a small window; its enlargement to a long strip between 1905 and 1909 was, according to Larsson, the inspiration for his book title *Åt solsidan* (On the Sunny Side), published in 1910. Beside the large windows on the north side was the studio door, adapted from a spare piece from the antique panelling used inside (figs 110, 111). As a separate entrance to the studio from the drive and service area it allowed a proper separation of the living and working areas very different from the more intimate mode of the earlier years. In 1912 a further structure was added to the end of the studio to accommodate an old painted room from Lilla Aspeboda in Dalarna.

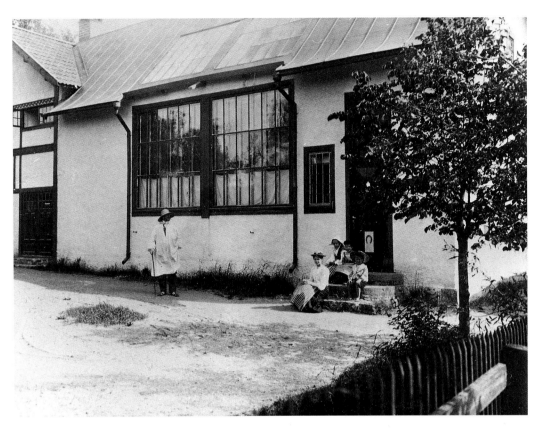

110. *The north side of the studio, 1906.*

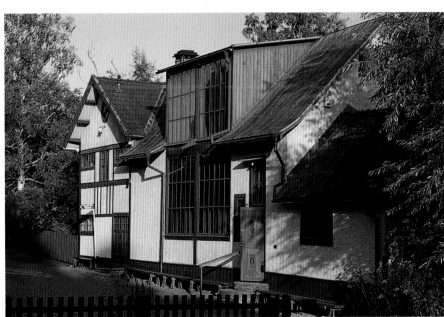

111. *The north side today, showing (from left to right) the 1901 wing, the new studio (1899) and its attached building for the Lilla Aspeboda room, added in 1912. The upper studio window was made vertical in 1910 to light new bedrooms in the roof.*

The Larssons at home

Above the front door is the first and most important of the many mottoes painted throughout the house, loosely translatable as 'Welcome, dear friend, to the house of Carl Larsson and his spouse' (fig. 112). The children are there too, depicted on the other wall of the porch, directly in front of a broad seat calculated to catch the late afternoon sun (fig. 98). The lettering and portrait frame are Gothic, but the familiar tone of the inscription (based on those on Dalarna farmhouses[13]) and frankness of the portraits (each identified by name and deliberately contrasted with the Gothic quatrefoil) must have seemed remarkably daring on a bourgeois house in a society still dominated by a rigid class structure. Even in England, where similar inscriptions over front doors and in other parts of the house were used by Arts and Crafts architects, they generally had a more impersonal tone (fig. 72). They are of course there to set the scene for what is to come: whoever you may be, you are invited to cast off formality and join in with the family; it is not simply that you have entered the house of an artist, which you might expect to be a little Bohemian, but you have entered a family home in which (the servants excepted – the Larssons were not extreme radicals) there are no divisions between the formal and informal as found in normal bourgeois homes of the time.

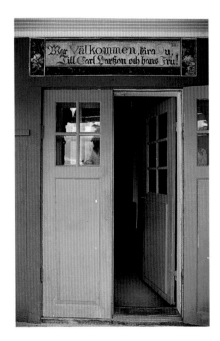

112. A text above the front door welcomes visitors.

Certainly some rooms, such as the drawing-room, were apparently more formally arranged, but this was not an expression of hierarchy (the children were allowed everywhere) but part of a style game, a sort of make-believe in which each room conjured up a different mood but all were equally important. The same lack of hierarchy lay behind the combination of furniture of different date and status in the same room, as well as the alteration of the furniture through paint and textiles. It is principally this undifferentiated quality and family centredness, combined with a sharp sense of style, which has allowed the Larssons' rooms, extremely radical in their time, to continue to seem so modern.

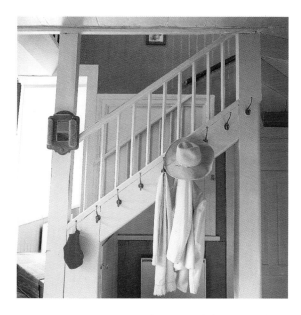

113. In a brilliant practical touch, the coat-hooks of the Larsson family are attached to the rising side of the staircase.

The room decorations the Larssons inherited at Lilla Hyttnäs were in marked contrast to the rough exterior of the house, for they had fairly recently been wallpapered and painted by Karin's aunts in the mainstream bourgeois taste of the time.[14] All this the Larssons either swept away or covered up. The hall you enter is an unpretentious space half-filled with the staircase, the set of rising coat-hooks on its side another reminder of the Larsson family (fig. 113). On the right is the room built on as the first real studio, later turned into a workshop;[15] directly in front is the dining-room, the first room to be made by the Larssons, probably inaugurated on Carl's nameday in January 1890, but not completed until 1891. The deliberately contrasted treatments of the adjacent dining- and drawing-rooms, the one rich and cosy, the other brighter and sunnier, were typical of the time, as was the Larssons' use of a broadly medieval and Renaissance style for the former and an eighteenth-century style for the latter, but there the similarity with bourgeois norms stops.

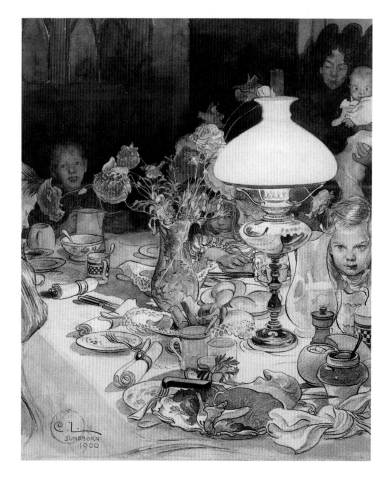

114. Carl Larsson. Around the Lamp at Evening, 1900. Watercolour.

The dining-room

This dining-room, small and low-ceilinged as it is, was the only room which Carl thought important enough to show all four walls in his book *Ett hem* (A Home; figs 115-16, 118-19). The striking green and red colour scheme (green boarding, and red shelves, windows and furniture), which just predates the similar painting of the façade, has often been described as being inspired by the English Arts and Crafts movement and the 'dragon's blood' red of William Morris.

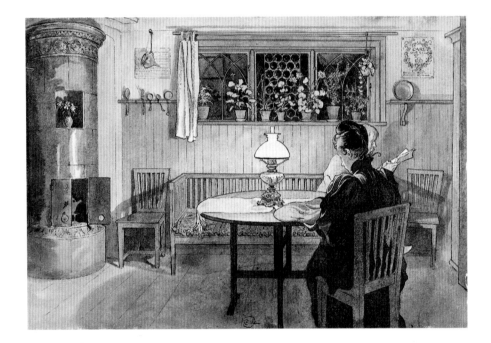

115.[107] Carl Larsson. When the Children have Gone to Bed *(the dining-room, east wall), 1894-7. Watercolour, from the* Ett hem *series. Carl reads aloud while Karin mends the children's clothes. On the wall on the right is the nameday congratulation made by Karin early in 1890. The curtain with its practical loops on a rod and embroidered pattern is an early example of Karin's simple window coverings.*

116.[108] Carl Larsson. Between Christmas and New Year *(the dining-room, south wall), 1896. Watercolour, from the* Ett hem *series. The servant Helena holds the baby Kersti. The closed door to the drawing-room, painted in 1891, is decorated with Renaissance ornament and a photograph of a late medieval Flemish painting. On the right is the cupboard painted with Japanese motifs in the same year. At this period the Larssons' winter visits were restricted to Christmas.*

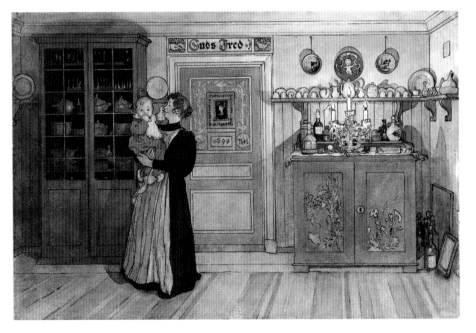

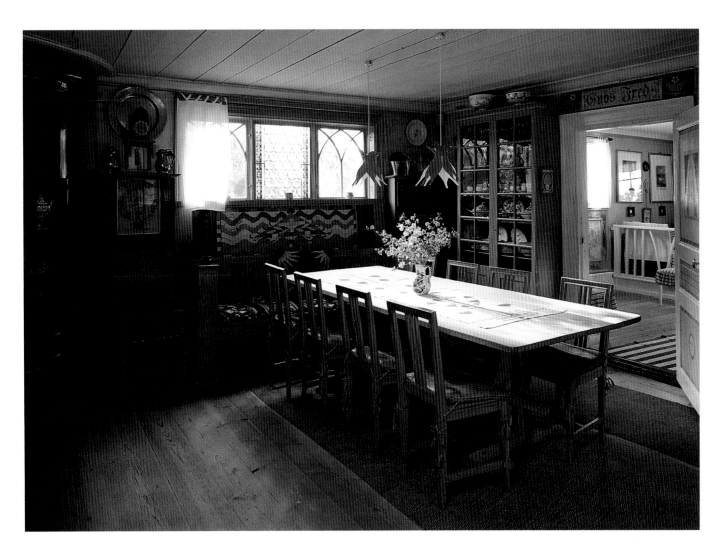

117. *The dining-room, seen from the door to the hall. On the right is the drawing-room. The wall boarding is 155 cm high; above it the wall is finished in a traditional manner with a layer of clay bound with linseed husks.*

118. *Carl Larsson. Old Anna (the dining-room, north wall), 1896. Watercolour, from the* Ett hem *series.*
In the kitchen through the open door the cook Anna butters a piece of bread for one of the girls. The branches of birch and fir in the wall decoration perhaps symbolize summer and winter. The pattern on the rugs is not shown.

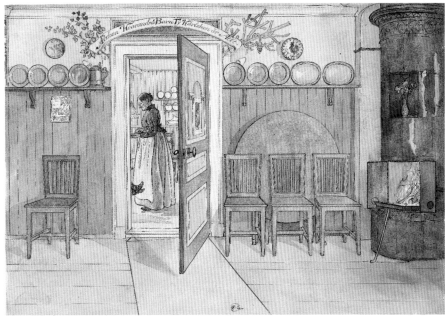

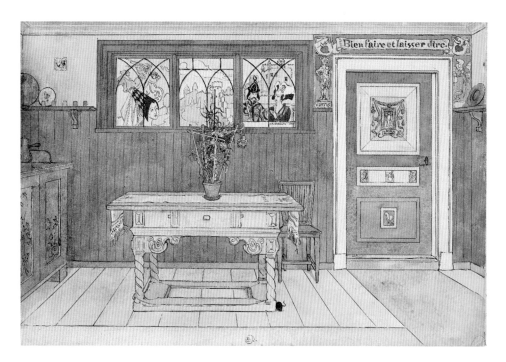

119. *Carl Larsson.*
The Dining-Room *(west wall),*
1894-7. Watercolour, from the
Ett hem *series.*
At this early date the medieval
walled town scene in the
painted window included a late
medieval couple (perhaps
intended to depict Carl and
Karin), with the man in
Mongol costume. The Flemish
style of the whole window is
underlined by the 'signature':
'stuerbouts pinxt'. By 1900 this
had been replaced by the motto
'Arte et Probitate'.

It is, however, more likely that the Larssons, like the English Arts and Crafts designers, were using red and green in the belief that they were medieval colours, and that they knew of the very similar, if rather darker, colour schemes in houses in the Old Norse style.[16] The truly revolutionary step was to turn the panelling and shelf combination of the usual Renaissance-style dining-room into an apron of simple utilitarian boarding of a type usually found in public and institutional interiors and in the service areas of country homes. Planks of this tongue-and-groove type with a beaded edge were used for wall cladding throughout Lilla Hyttnäs thereafter. The plainness of the boarding allowed the space to be more than the Gothic-style room suggested by the windows, wall painting and door decorations, so that it could easily absorb a number of objects in other styles, including a modern tiled stove, a Larsson-designed glazed china-cupboard adapted taken from Gustavian models, a japoniste cupboard (painted for Karin in 1891, see fig. 220), a seventeenth-century table and a set of Gustavian-style (probably locally made) chairs and sofa which came with the house and which, like all the furniture, were painted red to match the room.

The dining-room contains more painted inscriptions and decorations than any other room in the house. They are executed on the doors and walls above the panelling, each in a style closely related to its subject. While appropriately decorated inscriptions were a usual part of both Old Norse and neo-Renaissance dining-rooms, the visual wit of those at Sundborn suggests that the Larssons' intention was at least partly to make gentle fun of the heavy historicizing dining-rooms of the bourgeoisie. Thus above the door to the kitchen the biblical 'Love one another little children, for love is all'[17] in modern lettering on a scroll is painted so that it almost completely obscures 'Liberté Egalité Fraternité' in roman lettering on a neo-classical tablet. Over the door to the drawing-room is 'God's Peace' in Gothic lettering with decoration imitating folk art, while over the door to the hall is 'bien faire et laisser dire' with emblematical coats of arms and medieval figures, matching those painted on the window. The doors, too, are painted but this time in a Renaissance style, the one to the drawing-room (dated 1891) also carrying a photograph of a Flemish fifteenth-century painting. Several ideas from the dining-room are to be found in Carl's wall decorations of 1890 in the staircase hall of the school in Gothenburg. These include the transformation of the existing doors by paint, the use of Renaissance decoration and applied photographs[18] and even the red and green, which are the predominant base wall colours at the school.

In its first stage the dining-room, with its boarded ceiling and walls and scrubbed wood floor, had a certain awkward bareness both in design and arrangements, the furniture being perforce movable in a room with three doors. After 1900 the room began to change character, the denser furnishings distracting the eye from the panelling and gradually losing its Gothic feel in favour of a modern monumental style developed from Gustavian and Biedermeier models. In that year a table of traditional trestle type derived from medieval models was given a new top and brought in from the workshop (fig. 121),[19] to which room the Baroque table now went. In 1901 the old chairs were replaced by a set with simpler backs made by Hans Arnbom, the local carpenter (fig. 120). By 1904 a cupboard derived from a Swedish Biedermeier type had been built in under the painted

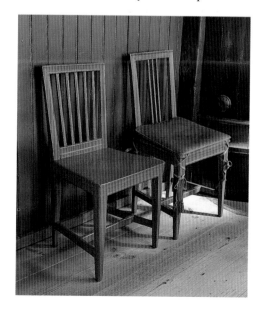

120.[114] Two chairs in the dining-room, the one from the first furnishing, the other (with a leather seat by the local saddler), made by Hans Arnbom in 1901.

121.[109]. *Carl Larsson*. For a Little Card
Party, *1901. Oil on canvas. Reproduced in
Larssons, 1902.*
*It is winter and sleeting outside. Karin is
making arrangements for a game of 'vira', to
be played in the drawing-room next door by
Carl and some men of the neighbourhood.
The large table probably arrived in the
dining-room in 1900, the chairs a year later.
The lamplight shows the room at its best.*

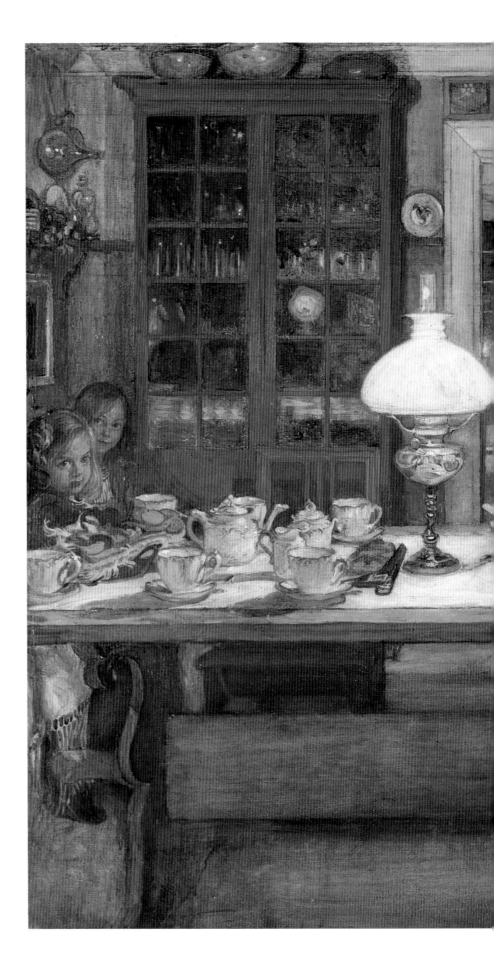

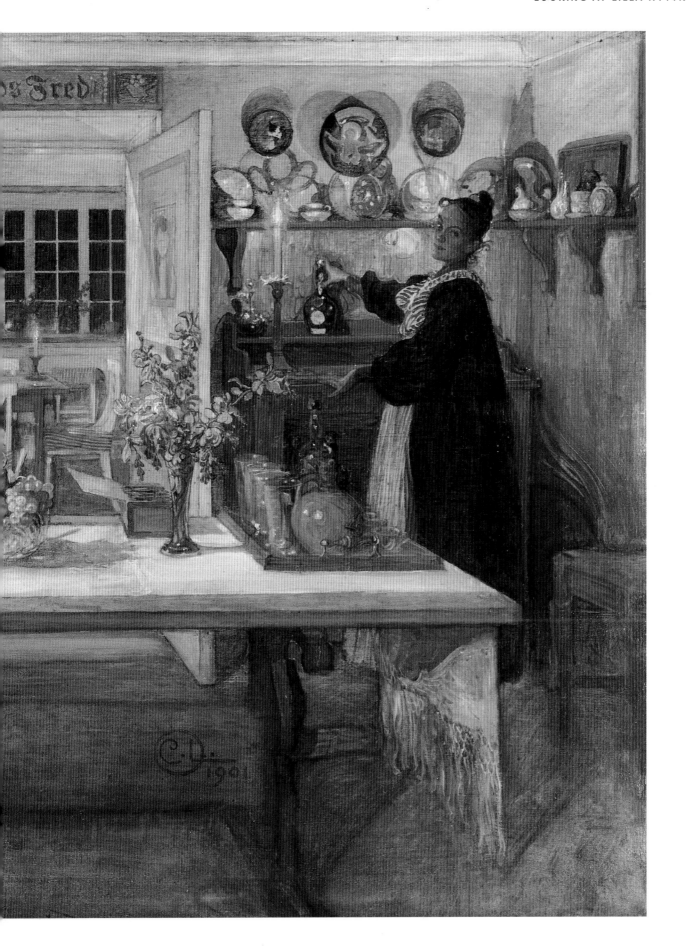

window,[20] which was itself modernized with portraits of Carl and Karin in contemporary clothes rather than the fancy-dress make-believe of before (figs 122, 124). A portrait of their son Esbjörn was added to the door. At the same time the *japoniste* cupboard was moved to the studio, its role taken over by the so-called 'sin-cupboard' for spirits and cigars, built into the space of the now-blocked door to the kitchen, with its own practical fold-

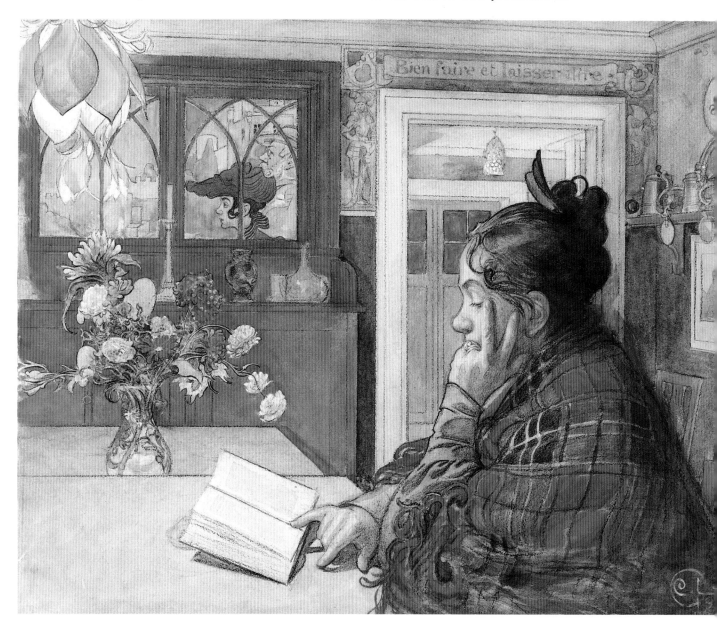

122.[110]. Carl Larsson. Karin is Reading, 1904. Watercolour.
In 1904 the dining-room had almost reached its final stage. The local power station gave electric light under paper cactus-flower shades and a new cupboard had been put in under the window. Karin's living profile is echoed by that of her portrait in the window.

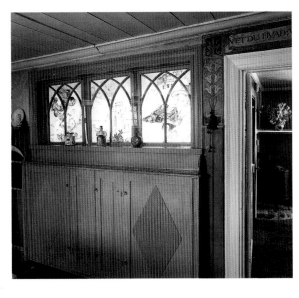

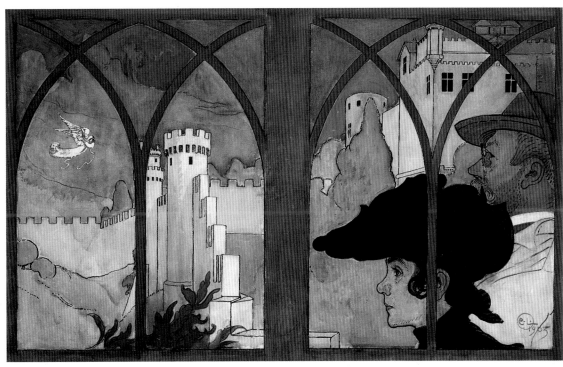

123. *The west wall of the dining-room. The cupboard is built into the thickness of the log wall.*

124.*[111]. Carl Larsson. Version of the painting on the dining-room window, 1905. Watercolour.*
By 1904 the fantasy medieval couple in the original dining-room window had been replaced by a modern twin portrait, in fact the only serious portrait of Carl and Karin together. The golden angel was never painted on the window.

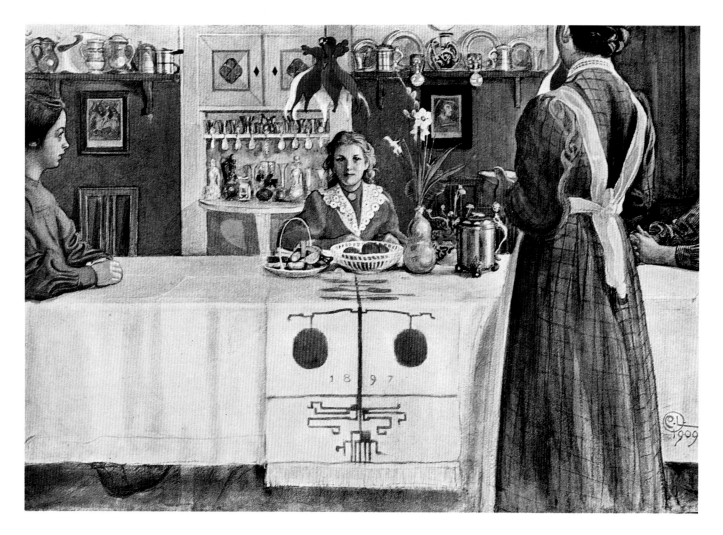

125. *Carl Larsson.* The Friend from Town, *1909. Reproduction in*
Åt solsidan, *1910, from a watercolour dated 1909.*
Hilda W. has skied from Falun and cannot stop eating, while Brita and
Kersti stare. Behind is the 'sin-cupboard' for spirits and cigars,
which by 1903 had replaced the old kitchen door. On the table is
Karin's family tree tablecloth.

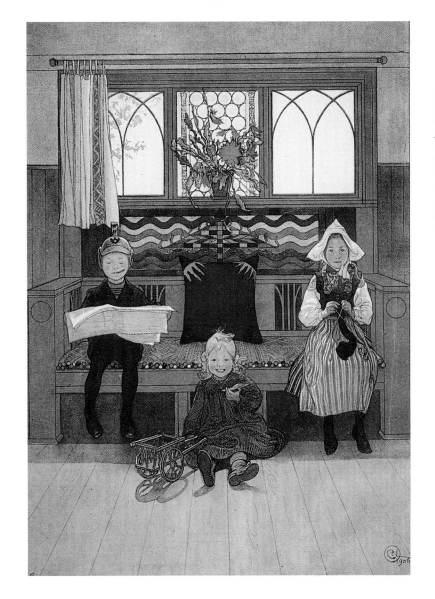

126.[112]. Carl Larsson.
Father, Mother and Child,
illustration in Jultomten, *1910,*
from a watercolour dated 1906.
The new arrangement of the
dining-room sofa, with Karin's
'Sunflower' cushion and 'Four
Elements' tapestry, is clearly
shown. The window curtain
and sofa cushion survive from
the previous scheme.

down table.[21] Electric lights appeared, with renewable red paper shades in the shape of red cactus flowers.[22] Above all, by 1903 the low Gustavian sofa had been encased in new wood, 'cooked up in the Carl Larsson manner',[23] creating a monumental rectilinear seat of honour (for Carl and his guest) at the end of the table. Topped by Karin's abstract tapestry of the 'Four Elements' it pulled the whole room together (fig. 126). Through all these changes the dining-room retained its dense display of silver, pewter and ceramics, a feature characteristic of bourgeois historicizing drawing-rooms. The Larssons' display, however, was more than the usual antiquarian collection, for it contained vernacular items from their foreign travels as well as a dinner service painted by themselves loosely inspired by eighteenth-century models.

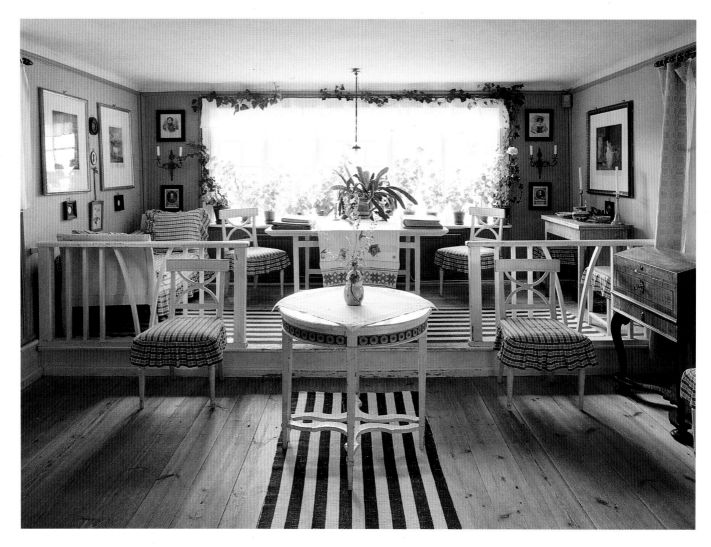

127. The drawing-room, looking south from the entrance door.

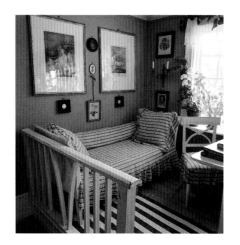

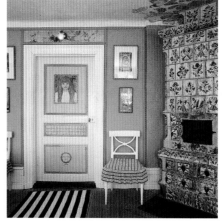

128. By the southern window of the drawing-room.

129. The northern end of the drawing-room. The door leads into the dining-room. The flowers on the ceiling, painted in the manner of vernacular decoration, echo the painting on the stove.

The drawing-room

The red and green dining-room, with its foreign mementoes and rich dark atmosphere, leads into the drawing-room, which since its publication in *Ett hem* in 1899 has been regarded as one of the most quintessentially Swedish of all rooms.[24] The overwhelming first impression is of light, flooding in from the long south-facing window onto the pink, green and white décor, the glitter of the water outside reflected on the ceiling (fig. 127). The second impression is of restfulness, chiefly produced by the horizontal emphasis of the main window, which not only makes the room seem wider than it really is, but also higher, being set right up against the ceiling. The southern end of the room is filled with a platform railed in white, to which a stripy rep woven rug leads across the scrubbed-board floor. The walls are clad in pinkish textile, formed into a series of panels by mouldings painted a fresh green. They are hung with French and Swedish eighteenth- and early nineteenth-century prints in suitable gold or black frames, some on ribbons (fig. 128). In one corner is a buff-coloured tiled stove, its floral decorations extended by the Larssons to the ceiling (and at one time to the walls too) (fig. 129). The windows, though now with light textile pelmets, were once curtainless, the long one filled with flowers in pots and framed in trailing ivy. While the Larssons radically changed two of the pre-existing windows, they left that to the west intact. It gives not on to the exterior but to the studio workshop, in which it is provided with a pair of shutters for privacy. The view through it from the workshop gives the dining-room a curiously showcase-like appearance entirely in keeping with its historicizing atmosphere.

The furniture is all late eighteenth or early nineteenth century and chiefly painted white, the chairs and sofa with blue and white stripy loose covers. Most of this furniture came with the house (figs 130, 219) and was clearly the source

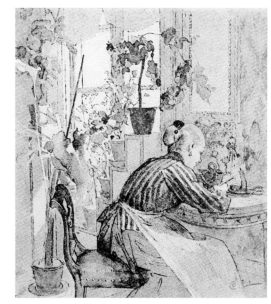

130.[120]. *Carl Larsson. Illustration to 'From a Housekeeper in the Country' in Elias Sehlstedt,* Sånger och visor i urval *(Selected Songs and Ballads, 1892-3). Half-tone after a wash drawing.*
The illustration shows the drawing-room as it was before the Larssons altered it; already present, however (and perhaps moved from another room for the picture), is the geometric plant-stand designed by Karin. The Sehlstedt illustrations were begun in 1890, a likely date for this drawing. In the summer of 1890 the studio was built on the other side of the western window shown here.

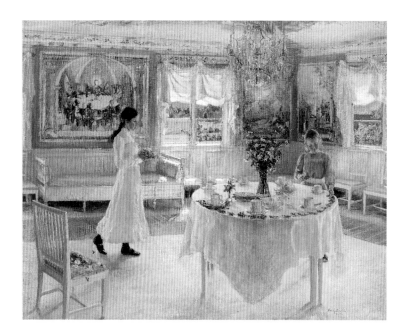

131.[87] Fanny Brate. Nameday,
1902. Oil on canvas.
This painting shows the drawing-
room at the small Brate manor house
at Bråfors in the Bergslagen district,
a well-preserved example of the type
of late Gustavian interior which
inspired the Larssons' drawing-room
treatment at Lilla Hyttnäs. In manor
houses, however, such rooms were
often on the first floor.

of the initial idea to decorate the room in a late eighteenth-century manner, albeit around a window in a different style. The particular style chosen was not the silk-and-gilt of the revived Louis XVI but that of the modest type of Gustavian room found in minor manor houses and country vicarages for which the drawing-room furniture would originally have been made (fig. 131), a style celebrated by Larsson in his poem 'Mormor', first published in 1890 and based on memories of his grandmother: 'furniture of an old cut, and like all empire, in white' (see fig. 61). The drawing-room's specific Swedishness is proclaimed in the *Ett hem* series by a Rococo chair (now no longer at Sundborn) prominently upholstered with the Swedish crowns. The next key event in the design process was the gift to Carl Larsson in 1891 of a late eighteenth-century Swedish decorator's pattern book.[25] Not only was it the source of the wall scheme and its colouring (fig. 132), but also of the painted wall decorations under the east window (fig. 133) and over the door, the latter being a typical example of the Larsson adaptive method, in which Carl turns a book and flower garland into a classical temple inscribed 'Karin', in front of a mountain (fig. 134).

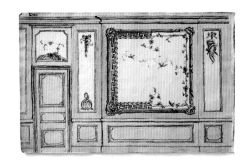

132.[121]. Anonymous artist. Page from a pattern
book of room decorations, c. 1780. Watercolour.
This particular sheet from a pattern book
given to Carl in 1891 inspired the drawing-room wall
treatments and the painting over the door.

133. *Carl Larsson. The Lazing Corner, probably 1894. Watercolour, from the* Ett hem *series.*
This picture is the core of the Ett hem *series; it is loved by Swedes and regarded as representing the essence of the Swedish style. Under the window is a river scene copied from the 18th-century pattern book. In* Ett hem *Larsson describes the drawing-room as 'the temple of laziness'. The picture's composition is directly inspired by an illustration in Oskar Pletsch's* Barndomsbilder *(Pictures of Childhood; 1862).*

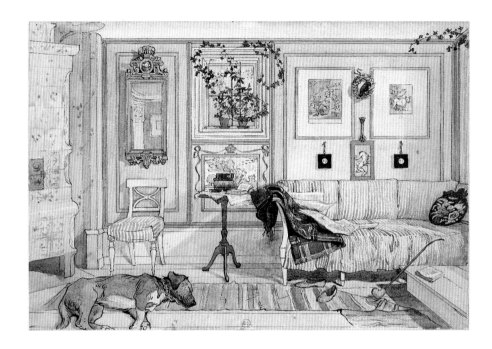

134. *Carl Larsson.* In the Punishment Corner, *1894. Watercolour, from the* Ett hem *series.*
Larsson wrote in Ett hem *that this drawing, showing Pontus banished to the drawing-room for impudence at table, was the start of the whole series, although this may not have been the case. The splendid tiled stove, made in Falun in 1754, was brought by Carl from elsewhere. The decoration on the door to the dining-room, which has now been painted over, includes a verse in English adapted from Kate Greenaway: 'There was a little woman/lived with CL/And if she is not gone/She lives there still – very well.'*

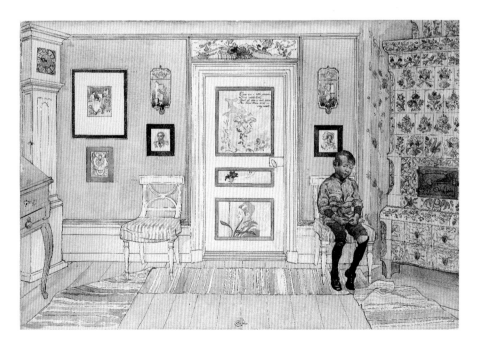

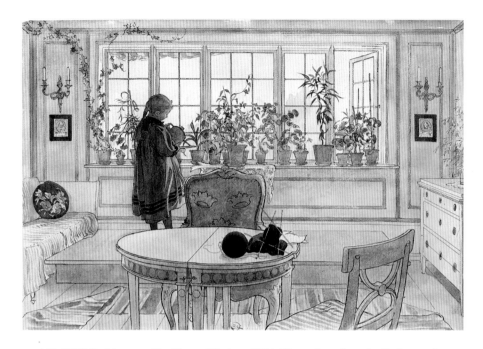

135.[122] Carl Larsson, The Flower Window, *1894. Watercolour, from the* Ett hem *series.*
Suzanne waters flowers at the long southern window of the drawing-room,
standing on the movable platform. The window is entirely free of curtains but enriched by ivy.

When first decorated, the door from the dining-room continued the hymn to Karin, being painted with an asymmetrical composition of a portrait of Karin standing before a lily, while in the top panel was a Rococo vase taken from the pattern book. It was accompanied, rather significantly, by a verse to Karin in English, adapted from one in Kate Greenaway's *Mother Goose* (1881), which had itself been illustrated in her own late eighteenth-century style.[26] At the start the other end of the room was also very different from its present appearance, being provided with a simple movable platform, which blocked the complete use of the sofa but allowed other furniture to be raised to the long southern window (fig. 135). It was probably inspired by similar platforms used for the same purpose in Biedermeier town interiors of the 1840s.[27]

The present arrangement of the room, with a platform and railings put in between 1901 and 1903, was the most dramatic of a number of changes which also included repainting the door in 1900 with a forward-facing portrait of Brita and a decorative grid and reducing the number of green mouldings. These changes can be seen as part of the modernization campaign which also overtook the dining-room at the same period, and which introduced a simplification and a greater sense of structure. Above all, the stage-like railing focuses the eye to the southern end, emphasizing with its restful horizontal line the long window. It is related to the gallery railing in the big studio, installed in 1902, which was decorated with a flower and two leaves (fig. 172), the latter appearing in abstract form in the curved elements in the drawing-room rail.[28] The flower motif was derived

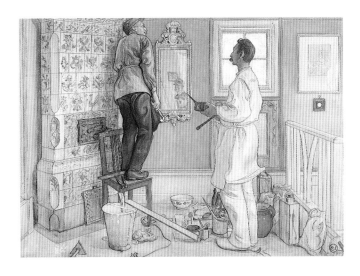

from a design by Karin for the cover of a magazine (fig. 194), but the notion of the white railings, which also appeared on the landing (significantly in an English form) and most lavishly outside at the water's edge, can most probably be traced back to the key importance of white railings in such English Queen Anne schemes as the development at Bedford Park of the 1870s and 1880s (fig. 75) and in English Arts and Crafts interiors.[29]

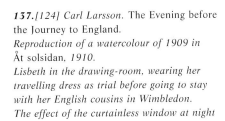

136. *Carl Larsson.* The Carpenter and the Painter, *1909. Watercolour.*
Used on the title-page of Åt solsidan *(1910).*
This picture shows the carpenter Hans Arnbom and the Larssons' house painter Carl Oscar Persson at work in the drawing-room. Larsson himself is in the mirror.

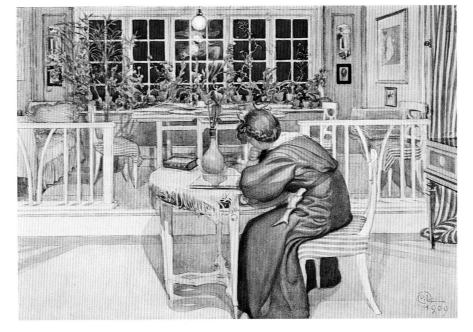

137.[124] *Carl Larsson.* The Evening before the Journey to England.
Reproduction of a watercolour of 1909 in Åt solsidan, *1910.*
Lisbeth in the drawing-room, wearing her travelling dress as trial before going to stay with her English cousins in Wimbledon. The effect of the curtainless window at night is well shown.

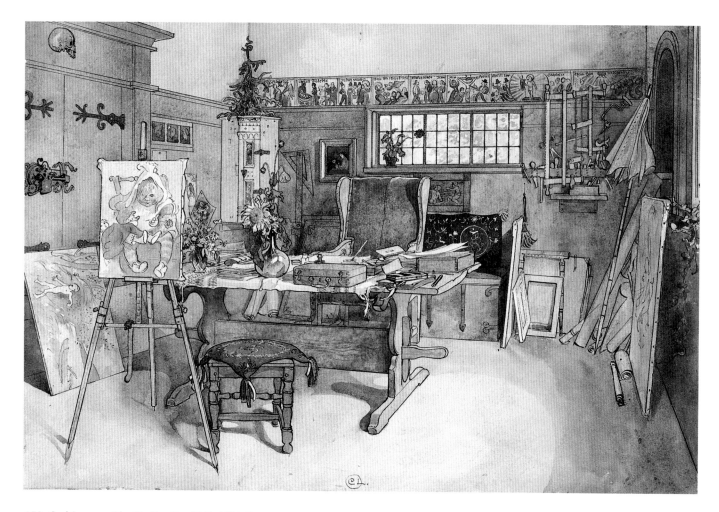

138. *Carl Larsson.* The Studio, One Half, *1894-7.*
Watercolour, from the Ett hem *series.*
The working half of the studio in its earliest form. The
long folk painting above the window showing the life of
Christ came from Halland in southern Sweden; Carl wrote
that it was far more interesting than the equally naive
and appealing paintings by Giotto. The doors on the left,
seemingly part of a large cupboard, are in fact shutters to
the drawing-room window.

139.[125] *Carl Larsson.* The Studio, the
Other Half, *1894-5. Watercolour, from the*
Ett hem *series.*
The drawing shows old Anna, the Larssons'
cook, modelling for one of the frescoes in the
New Elementary Grammar School for Girls at
Gothenburg. This project began in the
summer of 1890, just after the studio had
been built but this is a later reminiscence. To
aid the illusion Larsson has altered the dated
embroidery on the sofa end from 1892 to
1890. A child looks through from the window
in Carl's bedroom on the first floor.

The first studio

The third main room on the ground floor, the first studio, was added to the house in the summer of 1890, that is before the drawing-room was fitted out. Like many artists' studios of the period, it was filled with a suggestive collection of antiquities, old furniture and picturesque bric-à-brac and had an area for informal relaxation. In this case, however, the furniture and objects departed from the European norm (and those in Carl Larsson's town studios; see fig. 22) by concentrating entirely on Swedish things in the Baroque and vernacular styles, thus adding a third strand to the European sixteenth- and Swedish eighteenth-century themes of the dining- and drawing-rooms. This is made clear in the *Ett hem* watercolours (figs 138–9), which accentuate the objects by completely suppressing the ochre-

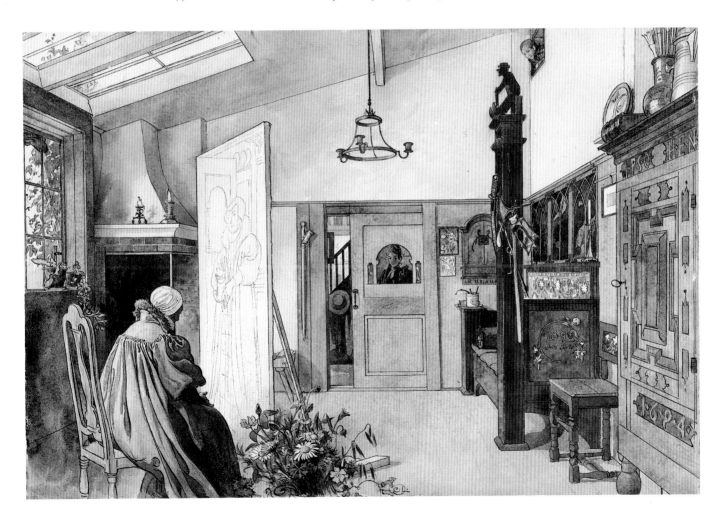

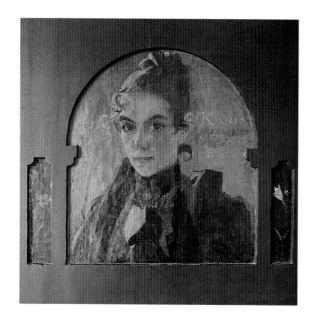

140. *Karin's portrait, painted by Carl in 1890 on the sliding door to the workshop (formerly the studio)*

yellow boarded walls surmounted by a large painted inscription, although they do show Karin's portrait painted in oil on a surface cut into the sliding door in the form of an Old Norse or Renaissance window (fig. 140). The old Swedish theme is reinforced by the long leaded window to the south and by the cupboard-like arrangement for the shutters to the drawing-room window, which are given a touch of humour by the hand-shaped hinges, the old and exaggeratedly large lock and the profile skull above. The most remarkable vernacular feature is the brick and plaster cottage fireplace at the north end, one of the earliest occurrences of this type in a bourgeois interior.

Also very probably related to the Old Swedish theme was the substantial fixed red-painted sofa facing the fireplace, made to fit under the Gothic dining-room window (fig. 142). The first Larsson-designed furniture in the house, it prefigures in its simple geometrical forms other additions to the interiors, notably in Carl's bedroom. As a fixed corner seat it certainly owes something to the elaborate built-in 'cosy-corners' which were characteristic features of English 'artistic' and Arts and Crafts interiors (and studios) from the 1870s to the 1890s. Its solidity, however, probably owes something to the monumental forms of Biedermeier sofas. Its most curious feature, the three-metre high post at one end, had both a practical and aesthetic purpose, for it served as cupboard for paints and helped to demarcate the tall open space of the studio. Of these, in *Ett hem*, Carl characteristically recognized only the functional;[30] its main purpose,

141. *Carl Larsson. Vignette from* Ett hem, *1899, showing his self-portrait in the studio.*

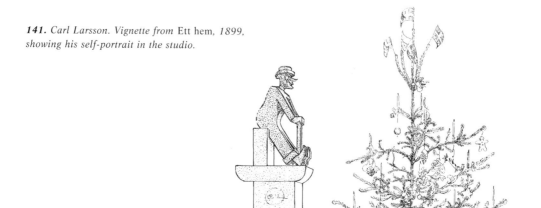

however, was to act as a symbol, which, as so often in Carl Larsson's work, was woven about with irony. The post acts as a plinth, raising high a carved wood caricature self-portrait of Carl as man about town, carved by a local carpenter.[31] Excluding the painted glass portraits in the dining-room, Karin appeared three times in the house in flattering portraits (of which one survives), Carl appears only twice, both times in caricature.

It was also in this form that he chose to depict himself at the start of *Ett hem*, showing in a vignette the studio self-portrait, which, self-deprecating yet dominating, soared over the guests in the early house's most public room (fig. 141). But the post and portrait in all probability also had an extra layer of meaning, closely related to the Old Norse character of the studio's exterior. Very similar posts surmounted by sculpture stood before the patriarchal high seat in the Old Norse hall, as depicted by antiquaries in the 1870s.[32] Such halls, general purpose living-rooms, were widely admired as an expression of ideal happiness and order, and it is not unlikely that Carl was seeking to recall them at Sundborn.

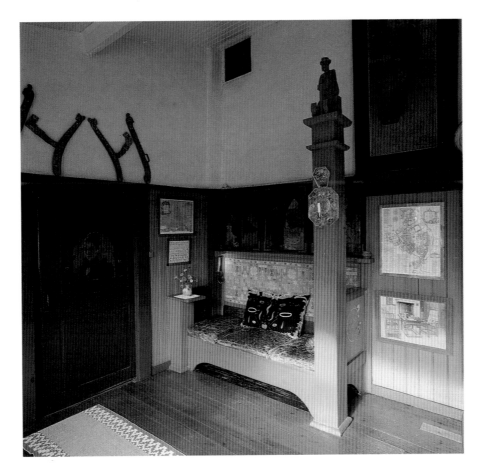

142. The sofa in the workshop (formerly the studio), with its portrait of Carl on a post three metres high.

Towards the end of the 1890s the character of the room began to change, especially after Carl had been provided with a new studio in 1899. The ceiling skylight, always impractical in a country with heavy snowfalls, had been covered in by 1896, and the rest of the ceiling was later lowered

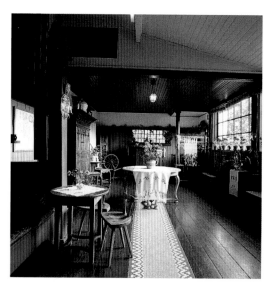

143. The workshop (formerly the studio), looking south.

to accommodate sleeping-quarters under the roof. This allowed a raised platform to be built beside the high-placed Old Norse window, which before had had little purpose, flanked by a single column supporting a baldachin (fig. 143). Now considerably less hall-like, the room functioned not only as a general living-room but became a craft workshop on the model of the vernacular craft room or *slöjd stuga*, in which the family could weave, spin and do woodwork (figs 144–6). On the platform by the window stood the sewing-machine, while for the children a miniature but working iron stove was installed beside the fireplace. The furniture, as in most rooms at Lilla Hyttnäs, changed about, but always present were the Baroque cupboards and later chairs, painted in the Larsson manner in bright blue.

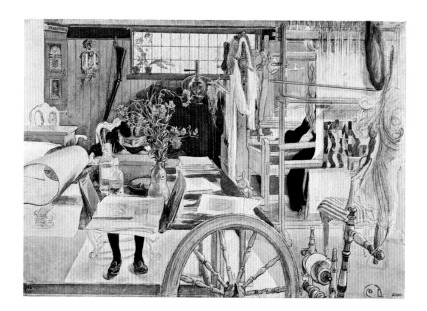

144.[128] Carl Larsson.
The Workshop. *Reproduction in Åt solsidan, 1910, of a watercolour 1908.*
The workshop, although mainly a room for Karin's textile work, was used for all sorts of activities. Here Brita writes a postcard to Pontus on Carl's etching table. Karin is just visible on the right. A copy of the 'Four Seasons' tapestry is on the loom.

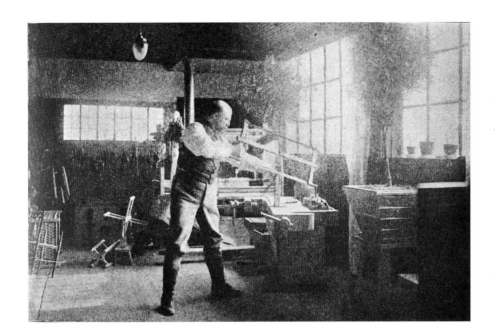

145. Carl in the workshop, 1903. Photograph from Hvar 8 dag, 31 May 1903. Note the trees in tubs, brought in for the winter.

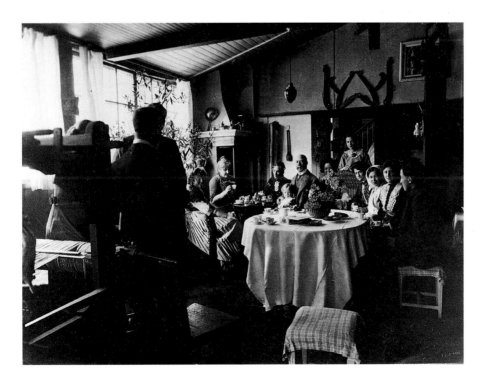

146. The workshop was also used for entertaining visitors, here the Norwegian writer Aagot Gjems-Selmer in 1913.

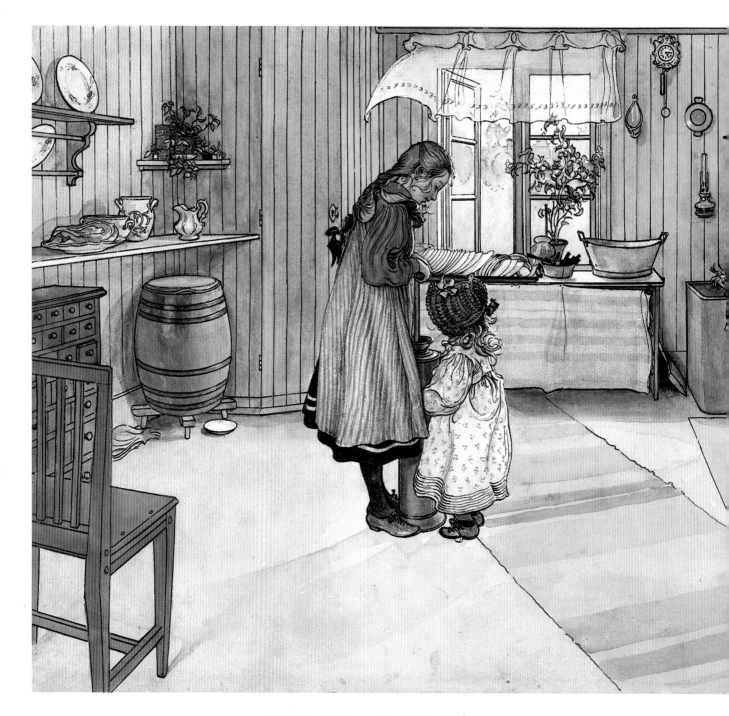

147.[167]. Carl Larsson, The Kitchen, *1898.*
Watercolour, from the Ett hem *series.*
Suzanne and Kersti churn butter; the kitten Hans hunts mice behind the stove.

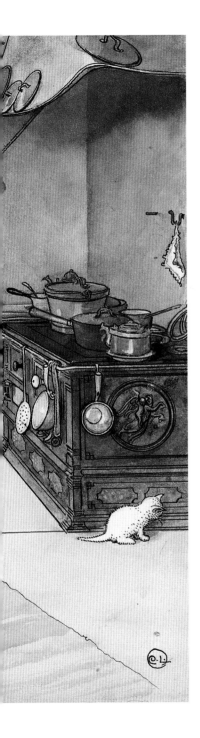

The kitchen

For many Swedes one of the most evocative pictures in the whole *Ett hem* series is that showing the kitchen (fig. 147). This is not because of its décor, for it was, and is (fig. 148), the least artful of all the early rooms, being simply clad in yellow-varnished boards, but because of its atmosphere of country childhoods, with the summer breeze coming through the window. In fact the drawing greatly expands what is a small room, with a modern cast-iron stove and hood put in against the Larssons' instructions while they were away. In *Ett hem* Carl rails against them, and in particular against the stove's meaningless twirls of 'engineer's ornament' and the inappropriate use of Bertel Thorvaldsen's much-reproduced relief roundel of the flying figure of 'night'.[33]

148. *The kitchen has changed very little since the 1890s. The window has been altered, the japoniste cupboard has been brought in from the dining-room, and a modern cooker and plumbing installed.*

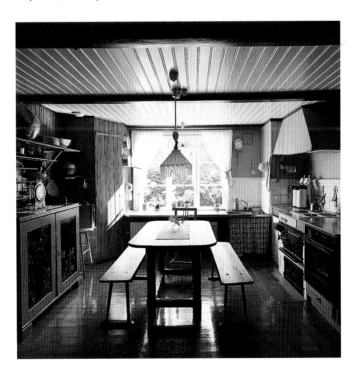

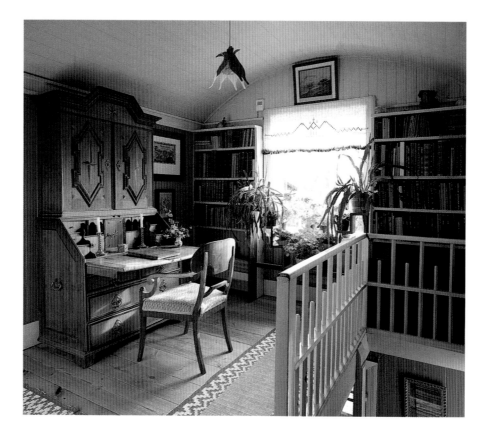

149. Karin's writing-room, looking west.

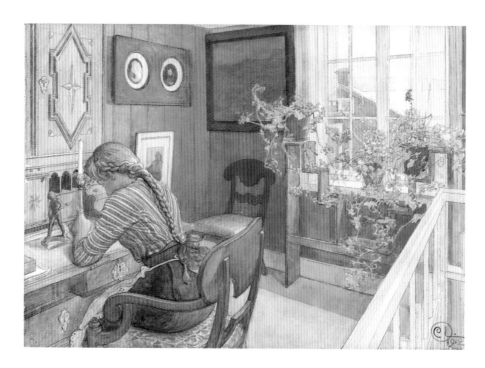

150.[145]. Carl Larsson. Letter Writing, *1912.*
Watercolour.
Ingrid, the daughter of one of the Larssons' servants, writes a letter at the desk in
Karin's writing-room. Under the window is the plant-stand designed by Karin.

Going upstairs

The relatively small rooms at Lilla Hyttnäs meant that no space could be wasted. At the very beginning the landing at the top of the stairs served Carl as a tiny studio. It later became Karin's writing-room, entirely lined out in ochre boarding, with the window subtly emphasized by the gentle curve of the ceiling, and a white railing with high and low uprights (the latter set diamondwise) apparently directly derived from external fencing in the English Queen Anne style (fig. 149) . Below the window, and matching its dimensions and divisions exactly, is a green plant-stand in the shape of an inverted ziggurat (fig. 150). This extraordinary piece, which Karin is known to have designed by 1890 (when it is shown placed in the drawing-room; see fig. 130), has often been described as an early example of functional form. While it is certainly highly practical, its unadorned geometry would probably have been impossible without the example of the stepped constructions of Japanese design. The boarded walls are now hung with pictures by the Larssons' contemporaries, and the shelf over the door to Carl's bedroom is laden with corals and other exotica (fig. 151).

When the Larssons arrived at Sundborn the upper part of the house contained three rooms in the roof space, arranged *en enfilade*, lit at the sides by small windows and reached from the landing through what was to become Carl's bedroom. At the north end was an undecorated storeroom open to the rafters; the other two rooms were low-ceilinged bedrooms, recently redecorated with patterned wallpaper, one with a large upright window at the southern end. In transforming them the Larssons created a contrasted pair of rooms like those on the ground floor below, but this time very much freer of historicizing references. The first room to be tackled was Carl's bedroom, apparently in 1893 after the completion of the ground floor.[34]

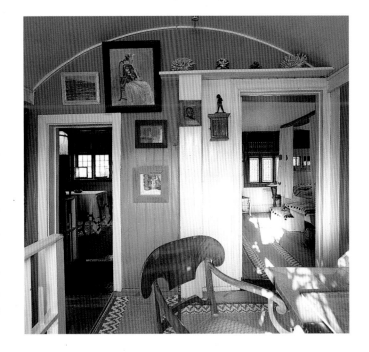

151. *The east end of the writing-room. On the right is Carl's bedroom, on the left the library.*

Carl's bedroom

For himself Carl designed the most stately and architectonic room in the whole house (fig. 152). Almost entirely free of movable furniture, it relies for its effect on painted wooden structures of great subtlety of design. The bed is most unusually placed at its centre, with four posts (fig. 153). Unlike a conventional four-poster, however, it actually touches the ceiling, the unevenness of which is disguised by the upper frame. Attached to the sides of the bed are practical additions for storing a chamber pot, for sitting on when dressing and for a bedside light. It is partially enclosed by curtains and a ceiling cloth embroidered by Karin. Around the top of the plastered walls run red painted bookshelves in the manner of frieze, backed by a cove lined in blue paper and supported by curved brackets and colonnettes, the latter echoing those at one end of the bed. The walls, ceiling and most of the bed are white, while the floor is scrubbed wood. This light colouring was most necessary, for the Larssons made a dark room even darker by the insertion of lilac blue, green, yellow and white glass with sixteenth-century-type leading into the altered east window and the taking in of the window to the west into the studio space. The latter was not entirely removed, however, but formed into a small, square, shuttered opening into the studio. This was both a curiosity and highly practical, allowing Carl to view his bigger paintings and mural cartoons from a greater distance. Around the opening is painted an oak-leaf garland, perhaps in ironical reference to the triumphantly successful paintings below, while on the adjacent wall is a built-in cupboard painted with huge arching hinges, one of Carl's most dramatic conceptions (fig. 154). These may have been added, together with the curious

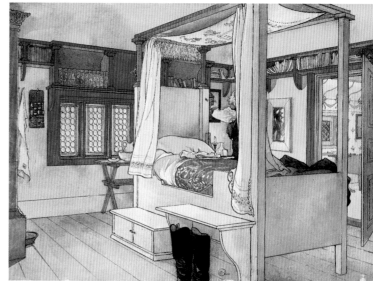

152.[147] Carl Larsson, Father's Room, 1894-7. Watercolour, from the Ett hem *series. Almost invisible, but nevertheless at the centre of the picture, is Carl fixing his collar. He has shown the room a good deal lighter than it really is. Beside the pistol is the inscription 'Note: not loaded'. As in most of the rooms at Lilla Hyttnäs, heat is provided by a tiled stove, seen on the left.*

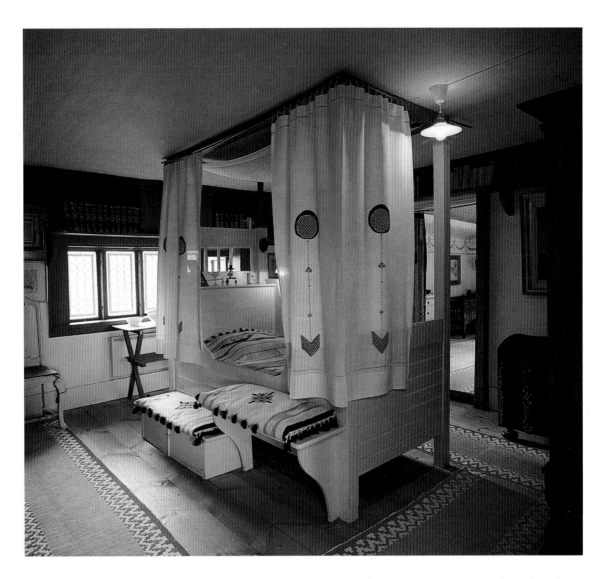

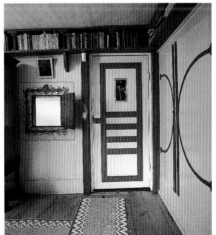

153. Carl's bedroom from the door to the writing-room.

154. Carl's bedroom, looking west.
The small window looks into the workshop below

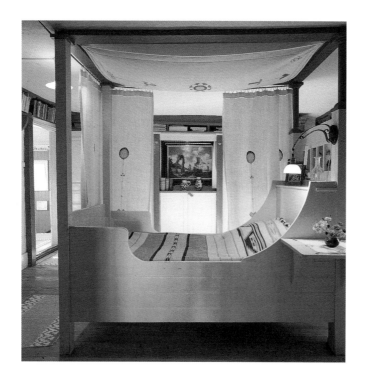

155. *Carl's bed from the door to Karin's bedroom.*

156. *Carl Larsson.* My Bedroom, *1909. Watercolour. Reproduced in* Åt solsidan, *1910.*
It is interesting to compare this atmospheric (and correctly lit) view with the sharper drawing made earlier (fig. 152). The door has been removed; light streams in from Karin's room, through her 'Rose of Love' portière.

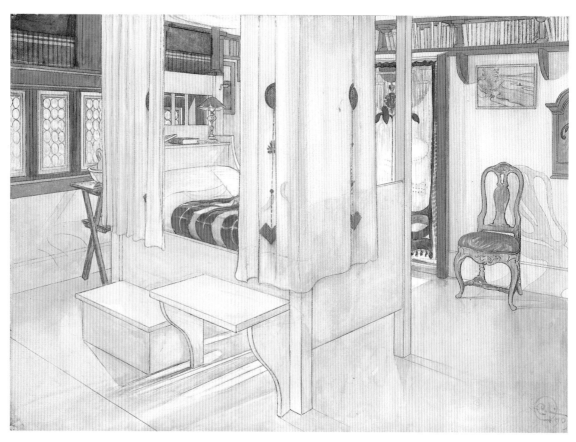

abstract paintings on the door panels, in 1906. It was perhaps at the same moment that the bed was modified to accommodate a shelf at its head and its side shaping made less rectilinear (figs 155–6). At about the same time the door to the adjacent bedroom was removed and replaced with an open-weave portière to let in more light. Called the 'Rose of Love', it was woven by Karin.

Modern commentators have detected puzzlingly patriarchal messages in the design of Carl Larsson's bedroom (and bed). How could this perfect father have set himself up in such splendid isolation while his wife and small daughters had to sleep all together next door? Could it have been a reaction to his crowded and vermin-ridden childhood? Carl claimed he did not know it was healthy to have the bed in the middle of the floor. In fact, as so often at Lilla Hyttnäs, the design emerged from a number of different considerations, including practicality, historical atmosphere, modernity and sheer show.

In practical terms the room presented the same challenges as the dining-room below. With three doors, one giving the only access to the bedroom next door, it could never be truly private and only one wall could take a bed. If the room was to be anything but a corridor, something dramatic had to be done. It is interesting that the Larssons' contemporaries failed to see the radical nature of the solution. Used to the conspicuous comforts of the usual bourgeois bedroom, they noticed only the room's simplicity. Radicals like Ellen Key praised it, while others compared it unfavourably to a servant's room.[35] Carl revelled in its plainness, claiming that 'in my simple bed, on my straw mattress, I sleep well and deeply, like a king in his state bed'.[36] He had, of course, solved the practical problem by creating his own version of a state bed. Its closeness to beds by British designers such as Charles Rennie Mackintosh and Baillie Scott was simply the result of similar aesthetic forces at work, for these British designs came

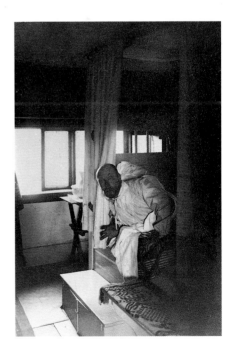

157. Carl Larsson in bed, c. 1906?.

too late to influence Larsson, who was indebted to ideas nearer home. With its boarded shaped sides, posts and textile curtains it resembles a Swedish cottage bed, except that such beds are built against the wall for warmth and convenience. By pulling his bed to the centre of the room he could turn it into a four-poster; that it was intended to recall old examples, albeit in an abstracted and consciously modern form, is confirmed by the rest of the room. Plastered and whitewashed and with its painted garland and a leaded-light window contrived to suggest a great depth of wall, it is evidently intended to echo a sixteenth-century castle interior.[37]

Karin's and the little girls' room

On seeing that the Larssons had taken down the ceiling in the bedroom room next door, Karin's aunt Emmy Bågenholm said that she would rather sleep in a prison cell.[38] The Larssons, however, wanted more air, for which they would happily sacrifice the gentility of a ceiling. This room for Karin and the children was consciously contrasted with Carl's domain next door: while his room was vertical, dark, architectonic, historicizing and largely free of movable furniture, Karin's, horizontal in emphasis, had a sunny and permanently festive atmosphere and was filled with movable furniture (fig. 158). Everything above the old ceiling level, and all the woodwork, was painted light green, and the walls were whitewashed. At the start all the beds were painted green. Karin's, which was made for the room, was given privacy by a simple striped curtain on a pole. By 1909, with the Larssons in permanent residence, Karin had a broad cot-like built-in bed backed by a walk-in wardrobe, painted white with yellow details (fig. 160). These changes, the elimination of the pine-top pattern on the walls, and the addition of the 'Rose of Love' portière and cheerful red-checked curtains and bedcovers, were in line with the more simplified ordered style characteristic of Lilla Hyttnäs after 1900. The ceiling rafters, boxed-in for greater visual effect, led the eye to the square small-paned window, its impact increased by reducing its size from the aunts' original. Window shutters frame it on either side and give a focus to the whole room; each folds in the middle to form a heart in the centre when closed (fig. 159).

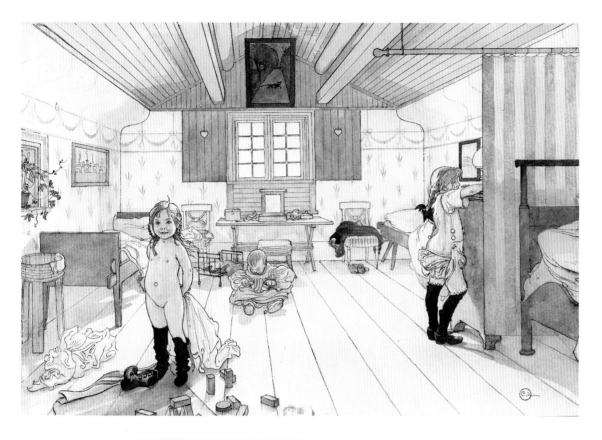

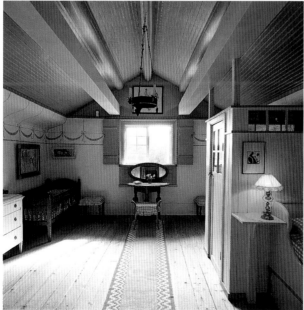

158. *[159] Carl Larsson.* Mother's and the Little Girls' Room, *1897. Watercolour, from the* Ett hem *series.*
This picture of Karin's bedroom has become a symbol of the informality of Swedish summer living. For Carl, in the text of Ett hem, *it symbolized a return to normality, the moment the children were allowed to sleep with their mother after her serious illness in 1897. The furniture mixes chairs from the drawing-room with simple folk pieces.*

159. *Karin's bedroom, looking north.*

Although used inside a room, they are of external type; their use in this context was perhaps suggested by a similar pair by Baillie Scott shown in *The Studio* in 1895.[39] Unifying the room like a permanent party decoration, and curving graciously over the beam-concealing cove, is a painted ribboned garland, culminating in flowers over the door. The whole scheme was a present to Karin, painted for her nameday in August 1894. The painted pattern of green pine-tops was no doubt added at the same time.

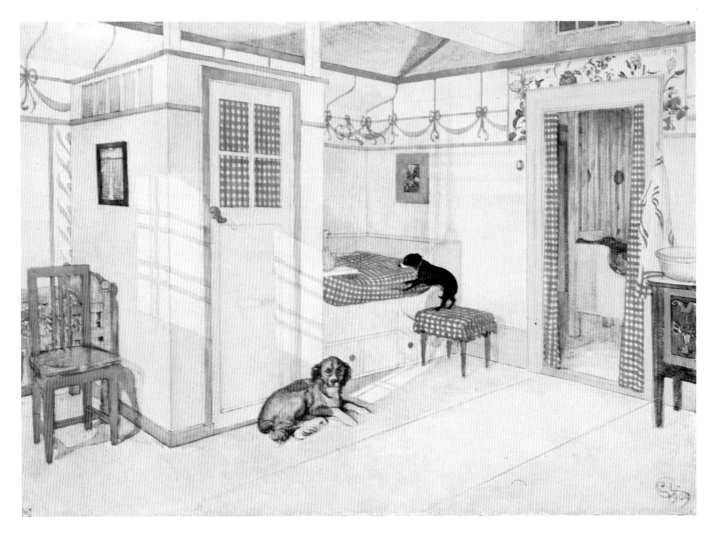

160. Carl Larsson. Joupjoup and Kiki.
Reproduction in Åt solsidan, 1910, of a watercolour of 1909.
The Larsson's two dogs in Karin's bedroom,
by 1909 fitted with a new built-in bed.

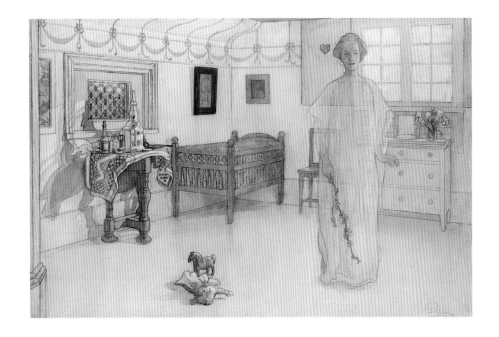

161.[162]
Carl Larsson.
The Home's Good
Angel, 1909.
Watercolour.
Reproduced in
Åt solsidan, 1910.
By 1909 the
children were too
big to sleep with
Karin, but the beds
she designed for
them were still in
the room.

The small studio and library

At the other end of the cottage, balancing Karin's bedroom, was a
storeroom, entered by a door on the other side of Carl's room. In the later
1890s the Larssons turned it into a small studio, in which they also sat in
the evenings and from which Karin could listen out for the small children
in her own room. Carl's vignette in *Ett hem* (fig. 162), which greatly
exaggerates the room's length, shows a plain arrangement with a boarded

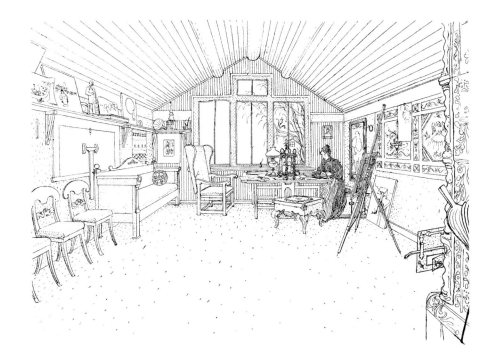

162.[155].
Carl Larsson.
The small studio,
looking north; a
vignette in Ett hem,
1899.

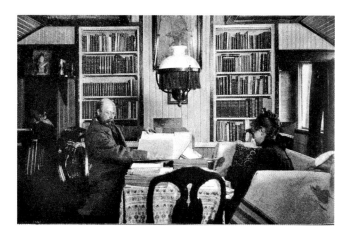

163. Carl and Karin Larsson in the library, 1903. The earliest view: at this stage only the Japanese prints had been put on the ceiling. Photograph from Hvar 8 dag, 31 May 1903.

ceiling, simple shelves, an enlarged north window (see fig. 229), and a clever system by which the side window shutter lets down to form a well-lit table, presumably for etching and drawing. After 1901, when the new wing was added to the north end of the old cottage, the room was turned into a cosy cabin-like library, with yellow boarded walls, bluish-green shelves and a dark broad-boarded floor (figs 163, 166). The Larssons retained or cunningly adapted many of the original features (including the shelves), but blocked the door to Carl's bedroom and made new ones to Karin's writing-room and the Old Room. The room is lit by a leaded window to the east, the old end window being boarded up and partially filled with shelves, as is the blocked door. The roof beams are boarded in a series of planes to accommodate Japanese prints and photographs of Italian art and architecture. Kept in place by movable frames, these were intended to be interchangeable (fig. 165). The room is dominated by a rectangular kitchen table, entirely covered in a thick, white, woollen cloth with a striking insect motif by Karin woven at the end. Concealed under a cloth at the other end of the table is the red Rococo sofa shown in many of Carl's paintings (fig. 224), but on view is a set of Rococo chairs (given by Karin's mother), a fine Rococo commode and a modern armchair, the last the only piece of furniture with sprung upholstery in the whole house.

Such a concession to comfort is a reflection of the great importance that Carl attached to this little room, with its thousands of books and magazines, both Swedish and foreign, on art and design, literature, history and many other branches of knowledge. It was of course a resource for his work, but the library also had a deeper meaning, for he felt it was a shrine, a still centre from which to explore mankind's highest achievements. It was evidently its role as a window on the world that led the Larssons to house more Japanese works of art in the library than in any other room; these included prints, some specially framed (fig. 164), as well as a mask and sculpture.

164.[74] Utagawa Kunisada, View of Hakone, c. 1840. Colour print from woodblocks, displayed in a Larsson frame in the library – the combination of Dalarna blue with the exotic subject is typical of the Larssons' approach.

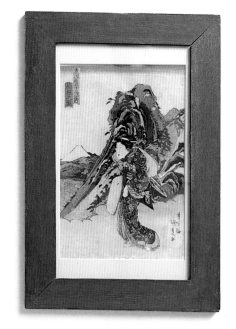

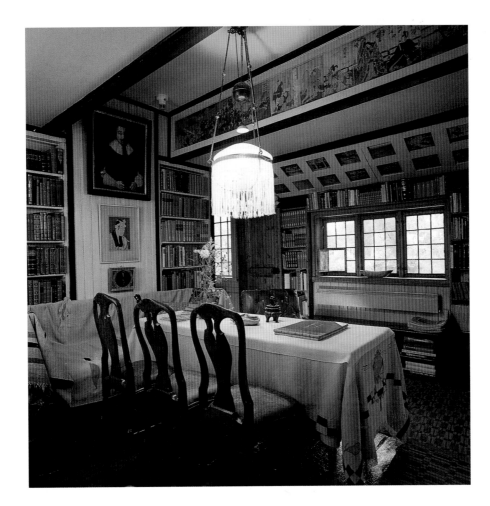

165. The library.

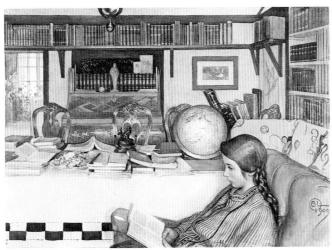

166. *Carl Larsson*. The Library.
Reproduction in Åt solsidan *(1910),*
of a watercolour of 1909.
Kersti reads a novel in the library.
The door on the left leads to Karin's
writing-room and the stairs.

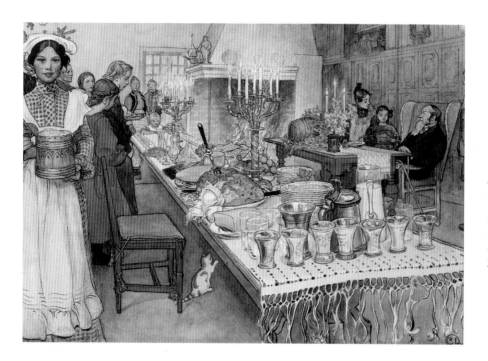

167.*[129]. Carl Larsson.*
Christmas Eve, *1904. Watercolour,*
reproduced in Spadarvet, *1906.*
Carl Larsson's best-known Christmas
scenes are set in the new studio. On
Christmas Eve Carl's father is brought
food seated in the great leather armchair.
In the foreground is the maid Martina.
The table, hugely stretched by a trick
of drawing, groans with the traditional
buffet meal, the whole composition
symbolizing the end of the agricultural
year shown in Spadarvet.

The new studio

The addition of a big studio to the old cottage almost doubled the size of Lilla Hyttnäs but at first made only one new room. It was inaugurated on New Year's Eve 1899 and was from the start a family and social room as well as a space big enough, at twelve by nine metres, to accommodate work on several mural cartoons at once. As a social space for the now permanently resident family it took over some of the functions of the old studio, including Christmas festivities, music-making and balls (figs 167–8). To Carl it was a 'temple of Art'[40] and as such became both a working studio and a display space for his own work, notably the cartoon (made in 1899) for the fresco at the Norra Latin grammar school, showing the schoolboys at military prayers. Installed by 1908 and provided with a white wooden 'altar' at the centre, it dominates the room and gives it a church-like atmosphere, enhanced by the motto in dignified roman script running around the top (fig. 169).[41]

168. *The everyday use of the studio by the children is well shown in this photograph of 1905. On the wall is Carl Larsson's great painting* Gustav Vasa's Triumphal Entry into Stockholm, *made for the National Museum, Stockholm.*

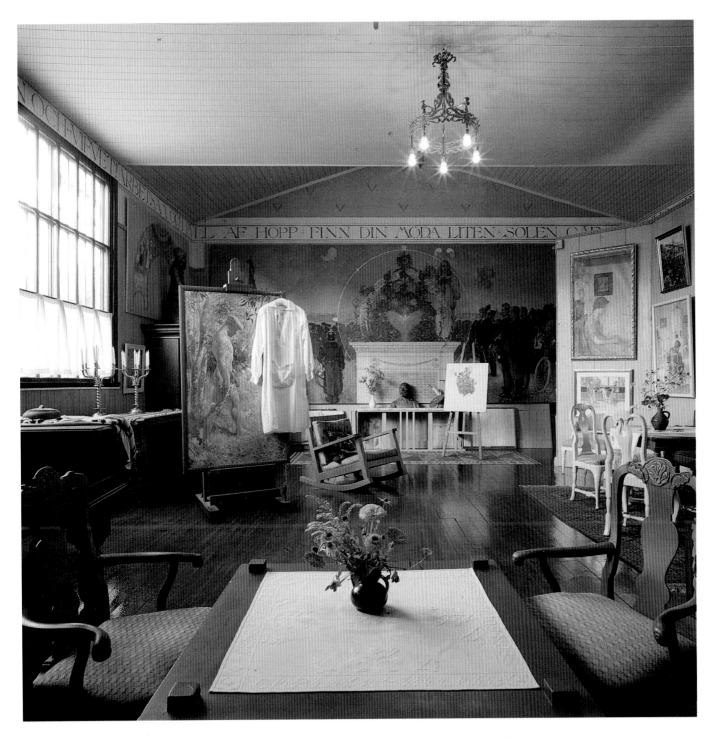

169. *The east end of the studio. Carl's smock hangs from the easel.*

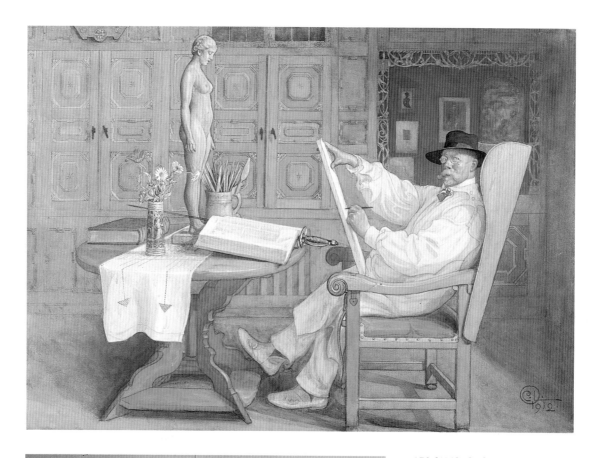

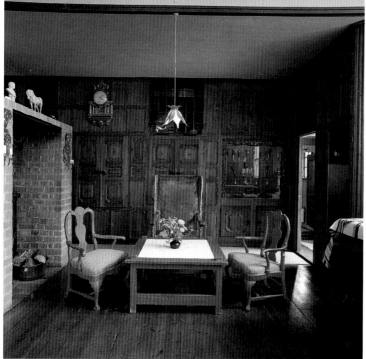

170.[132]. *Carl Larsson. Self-portrait, 1912. Watercolour.*
Carl draws a figure by his friend Anders Zorn. The place in the great Bible is marked by a rapier. Such details, as often in Carl Larsson's self-portraits, seem to be in some way symbolic.

171. *The west end of the studio. The low table was designed by Karin; the chairs are 17th and 18th century.*

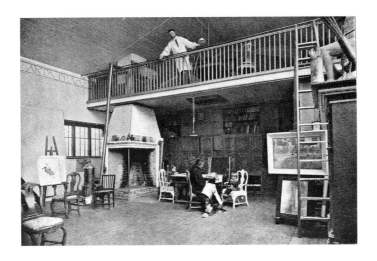

172. The studio in 1903. Carl stands on the new gallery, while Karin works on a textile. Photograph from Hvar 8 dag, *31 May 1903.*

Like most of the rooms at Lilla Hyttnäs this studio underwent several changes, gradually becoming smaller as the difficulties of heating and the need for extra rooms made themselves felt. In its early stage it was divided (like the first studio) into two distinct areas, for study and leisure activities and for painting, the former being at the west end marked by the free-standing fireplace and the installation of a set of late seventeenth-century panelling from Schleswig-Holstein (figs 170–1). To plan its installation Carl made a diagram in paint and canvas, the only surviving design drawing for any of the work at the house (fig. 173). It makes clear that the panelling was also functional, concealing storage cupboards and providing areas for the display of curiosities, which eventually included a 'museum' of Lapp artefacts.

The closing-in of the room began in 1902, when the panelling was topped by a balustraded gallery for the etching press and from which Carl could inspect the large mural cartoons laid out to be painted on the floor (fig. 172). Eight years later the fireplace was greatly enlarged and a screen wall built for the hanging of large cartoons (fig. 174). In 1903 the gallery was filled in to become a children's bedroom, the 'lower dovecote', while in 1910 most of the rest of the roof was lowered to create the 'upper dovecote', lit by the former upper part of the studio window. The 'lower dovecote' still contains its *art nouveau* wallpaper, an interesting example of the use of this type of wall covering by the supposedly wallpaper-hating Larssons.

173.[133]. Carl Larsson. Design for the installation of the panelling in the new studio. Pencil and oil on canvas.

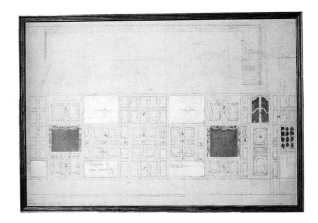

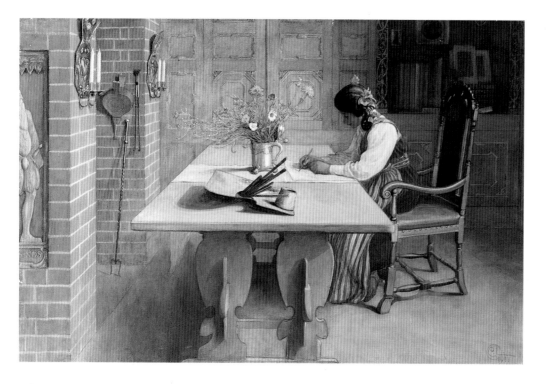

174.[144]. *Carl Larsson.*
Hilda, *1911. Watercolour.*
Partially reproduced in Andras
Barn, *1913.*
One of the Larsson children's
English cousins, Hilda Bather,
draws in the studio at a
beautiful vernacular table.
She is dressed in a local folk
costume, from Delsbo. Before
her is the enlarged studio
fireplace.

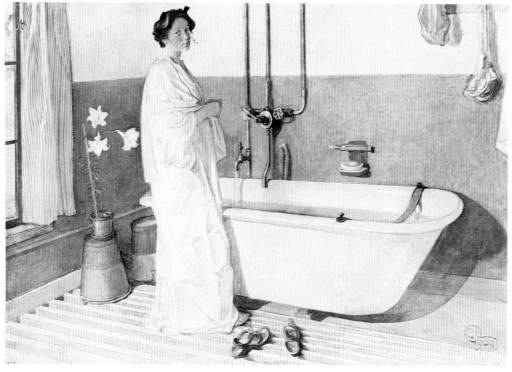

175. *Carl Larsson.* Lisbeth.
Reproduction of a watercolour
of 1909, in Åt solsidan, *1910.*
Modern plumbing came to
Sundborn in 1902. Here Lisbeth
prepares to bathe in the first
bathroom. The elegant Japanese
composition of the painting
distracts us from the room's
bare functionalism.

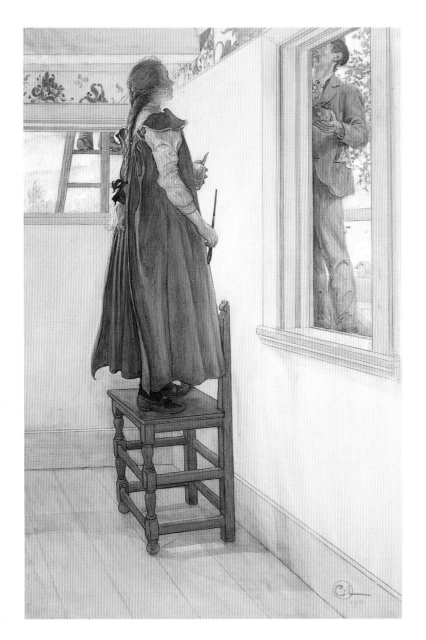

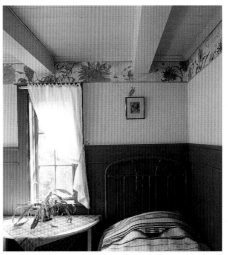

176.[166] Carl Larsson. Suzanne and Another, 1901. Watercolour.
Suzanne paints the floral frieze in her room, while on ladders (it is on the first floor), the painter Carl Oscar Persson and another work on the outside of the new building.

177. Suzanne's room.

The Old Room and others

The family's permanent move to Lilla Hyttnäs in March 1901 was marked by the building of an infill completing the corner between the new studio and the old cottage. Most of its rooms, including a bedroom for the boys later turned into a bathroom (fig. 175), were highly practical and minimally decorated. The Larssons' eldest daughter Suzanne ornamented her own room with a charming floral frieze in her father's style (figs 176–7). Next to it on the upper floor, but usually reached via the library, is the last major addition to the interiors at Lilla Hyttnäs, the Old Room. Intended for guests, it was also, according to Carl, a place in which to put to practical use all the old things they had collected (figs 178–9).[42]

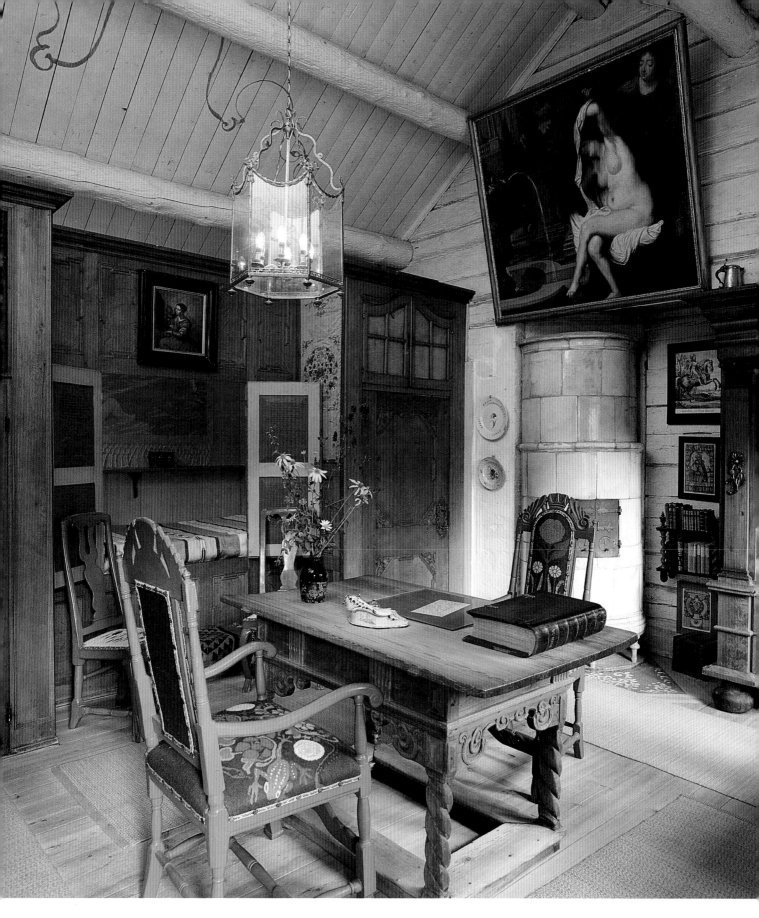

178. *The Old Room, looking north-west.*

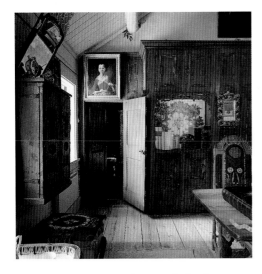

179.
The Old Room, looking south. The door leads to the library.

It thus brought together many of the earliest objects formerly elsewhere in the house, including the Baroque table from the dining-room (and workshop) and a set of blue-painted Baroque chairs. New to the house were the Flemish pictures and an enormous German Baroque cupboard of the type common in contemporary historicizing dining-rooms[43] but here used by Karin for her linen (fig. 180). The setting for these objects is the oldest-looking and most impressive room in the house. It is, however, a complete piece of make-believe, with its massive but non-functional ceiling beams and lime-washed logs, and two of its walls constructed from the left-overs of panelling from the new studio, into which is built a box bed with doors (figs 181–2). On one of the ceiling slopes is painted, perhaps with a touch of irony, 'only the truly old is eternally young', while the other slope, visible from the bed, is inscribed in German: 'Put your trust in God alone'. The inside of the bed is painted a warm pink in marked contrast to the rest of the room with its quiet tones of white lime and unpainted wood in different shades, so unlike the bright colours in the rest of the house. In this antiquarian interior, seated in the great chair and reading passages from the old Bible on the table, Carl could transport himself back to the period of Sweden's greatness.

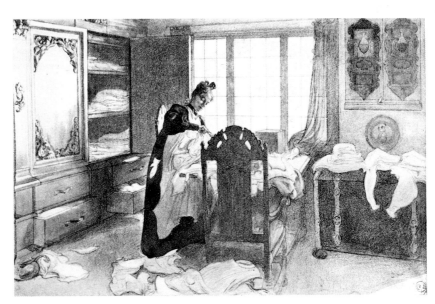

180. *Carl Larsson.* Karin by the Linen Cupboard, *1906. Watercolour. From Nordensvan 1920.*
The German linen cupboard is so big that the Old Room must literally have been built around it. The cupboard was formerly in Carl Larsson's Gothenburg studio (see fig. 22).

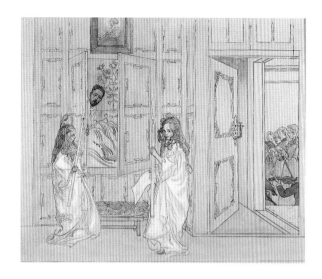

181.*[163] Carl Larsson.* Morning serenade for Prince
Eugen in Sundborn, *1902. Pen and ink and wash.*
The visit of his fellow artist Prince Eugen to Sundborn
marked the pinnacle of Carl Larsson's social success.
As shown in this drawing (given to the prince), the
occasion was celebrated with a morning call from choir
and violin; the song was composed by Carl. The prince's
name headed the list of guests inscribed on the doors
of the box bed in the Old Room, a permanent record of
the many celebrated visitors to Sundborn.

The Old Room represented a shift in
the Larssons' attitude to the past, which
was becoming increasingly conventional
as the earlier rooms of the house were
given a more modern tone. The trend was
to culminate in 1912 with the addition to the new studio of an extension,
into which was installed a complete painted interior of 1742 rescued from
a house at Lilla Aspeboda near Falun (fig. 183). As Carl's retreat from the
never-ending stream of visitors to Lilla Hyttnäs (as well as a guest room
and summer bedroom), this small room, out of context and isolated like a
folk-museum display, shows how far the Larssons had travelled both
aesthetically and politically since the daring artistic house of the early
1890s, with its ideal of family living.

In that respect it is interesting to compare both these rooms with an
earlier attempt at the folk idiom, the fitting out of the upper part of the
härbre or storehouse in the garden as a summer bedroom for the maids,
shown in *Ett hem.* The Larssons there created a fresh modern version, in

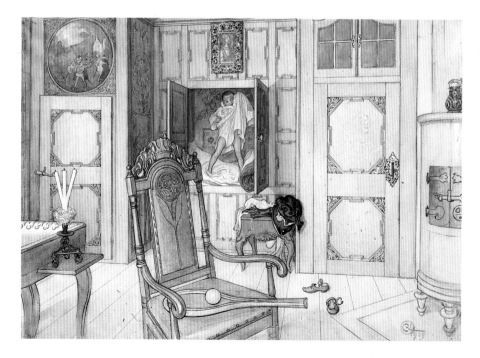

182.*[164] Carl Larsson.* The Old Room, *1909. Watercolour. Reproduced in* Åt solsidan, *1910.*

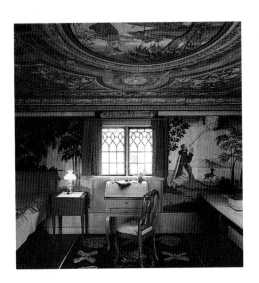

*183. The Lilla
Aspeboda room.*

red and green, of the main room of a Dalarna cottage, complete with built-in beds, except of course that here the room was for sleeping in only. Hanging from the roof, perhaps permanantly, but maybe only for the nameday being celebrated, is one of Karin's textiles, dated 1893. It is based on the type of hanging used for temporary decoration in southern Swedish (not local) vernacular houses but its pattern and detail are not from that source (see chapter 3). Like the room it is a modern reworking of the folk idiom, and it fits perfectly with it.

A question of responsibility

The *härbre* bedroom prompts the frequently asked question of the respective roles of Carl and Karin Larsson in the creation of Lilla Hyttnäs. It is clear that most if not all of the painted ornament was done by Carl while certain individual pieces of furniture are known to have been designed by Karin, as were nearly all the textiles. Carl's public attitude to work of his 'idol' was sometimes less than positive, allowing him to describe such pieces as the two children's beds in her bedroom as having been 'ingeniously made out of roof shingles according my wife's ridiculous design',[44] but that was part of a characteristic pose in which he presented the carefully conceived interiors at Sundborn as having been casually and rather economically assembled according to necessity.

In fact Carl had a deep admiration for his wife's work, and there is every likelihood that the aesthetic union that was expressed in Karin's role in approving his work as an artist also carried through to the house. In practical terms, Carl's absences in the 1890s meant that Karin was often in charge of the work on site, but while her letters often mention building work in progress, the complete lack of references to the design process suggests that the whole thing had already taken place. The manner in which the textiles are perfectly integrated in terms of design and colour make it clear that the interiors were the product of an indivisible collaborative effort.

6

KARIN LARSSON

Lena Rydin

For Carl Larsson's sixtieth birthday in 1913, the major Swedish weekly magazine *Idun* paid tribute to him in a special number. Many of Sweden's leading cultural figures wanted to take part in congratulating Larsson. But one of them, the author Elin Wägner,[1] did something unexpected. She paid tribute instead to the artist's wife, Karin:

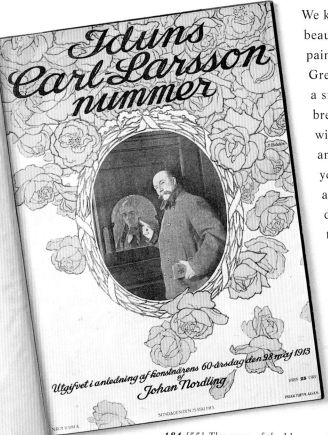

We know no artist's wife so well, not even Rosetti's beautiful model. We follow you from the beautiful painting, where you stand in the verdant garden in Grez par Nemours [later named Grez-sur-Loing], a small white bride with a myrtle bouquet at your breast and a garland in your hand. We see you with Suzanne in your arms, creating an idyll among the brushes, easels and pastels. We see you with Suzanne's brothers and sisters, one after the other and all together. You carry them, dress them, serve them food and mend their torn clothes in the evenings. Your home in Sundborn is not only the work of a good housewife, but also of a good artist, and you are that artist. There are details in the Larsson home which a man could not think of. But you not only take art into the home, you also take the home into art, for you shell the peas and mend the boys' trousers in the studio.[2]

184.[55] The cover of the Idun *special number for Carl Larsson's 60th birthday, 28 May 1913. He is shown pointing to the portrait of his idol, painted on the door of the workshop in 1890; the photograph was taken in 1911.* Idun *was a weekly magazine for ladies and the home.*

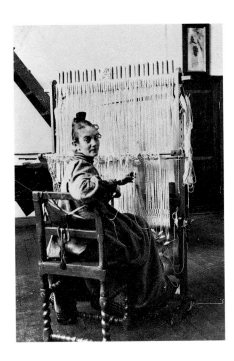

185. *Karin Larsson at her tapestry loom, 1908.*
She is weaving the 'Rose of Love', the portière between the couple's separate bedrooms.
Photograph by Ernst Söderberg.

By this time Karin Larsson had been weaving her modernistic tapestries for the home for over ten years. She wore a highly individual reform dress, and had created a new fashion for children. Her ideas spread rapidly through the distribution of Carl Larsson's scenes of home life. But he was the star, and she the extra.

The idol

Elin Wägner was the first to draw attention to Karin Larsson's artistic achievement. While it was quite a song of praise, the article also pointed out that Karin was known solely through her husband, just as Beatrice was known through Dante and Laura through Petrarch. This laid the basis of a misconception regarding Karin, thus also contributing to the myth that

186. *Carl and Karin Larsson hanging an exhibition at* Konstnärshuset *(The Artists' House), Stockholm, 1907.*
This is rare pictorial evidence of the Larssons' working together; the painting, which she is dusting, shows herself at her everyday work by the linen cupboard in Sundborn, with untidy hair and wearing an apron (see fig. 180).
But she was also a woman of the world; here she is wearing a fashionable hat and one of her beautiful, flowing dresses.

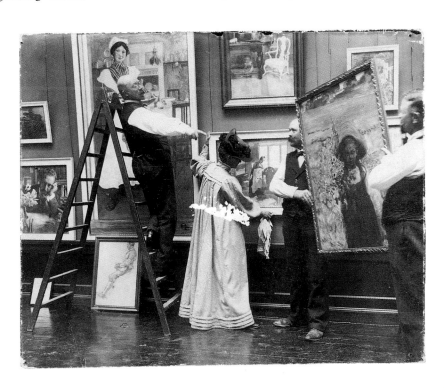

came to surround her. She was portrayed as the male fantasy of the idealized, undemanding woman, made to be worshipped without giving anything in return. This was one of the images of woman loved by the period, and Elin Wägner in fact did Karin Larsson a disservice by evoking it.

The works of art depicting Karin reinforced this image. She was the obvious principal character in Carl Larsson's art. He painted her continually, as if to elicit her secrets:

Perhaps it was precisely because she was of such great importance that it was so difficult to portray her. It was easier to idealize her. Sometimes she is unapproachable and abstract like a madonna, sometimes she is a funny doodle with a bun and a snub nose, but he does not really *see* her. He only sees her significance.[3]

187. Carl Larsson. Azalea, 1906. Watercolour.

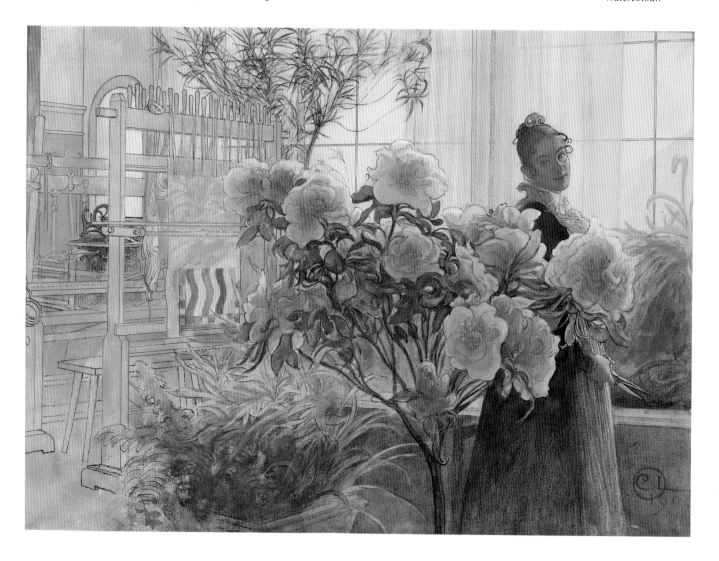

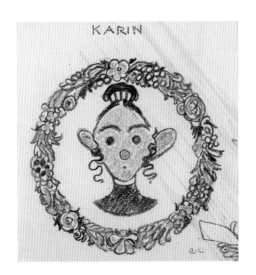

188. *[173]*
Carl Larsson.
Caricature Portrait
of Karin Larsson,
probably 1905.
Charcoal and
pastel.

Beatrice is no model for today. Neither has Karin ever had any feminist followers; the general view is that she gave up her painting and devoted herself to her family. On the other hand she never saw herself as a victim, although she would probably be more esteemed had she done so. On the contrary, her letters to her husband and to her mother Hilda constantly mention joy. How could you make a martyr of Karin, who so often called herself 'the happiest woman in the world'? Attempts there have been, but with unconvincing results.

One thing is crystal clear: the real Karin is concealed behind a series of images from which nothing of her down-to-earth, realistic and humorous personality emerges. Carl's portrayals of her may have enhanced her beauty as a model; but in fact she had both feet on the ground, as is clearly shown in her letters and above all in the story of her life.

189.
Celebrations on
Karin's nameday,
August 2nd 1905,
with Lisbeth,
Carl Larsson, the
model Leontine,
Olga Palm and
Brita. They carry
the caricature
portrait in fig. 188,
drawn to a formula
established by the
early 1890s, and
probably earlier.

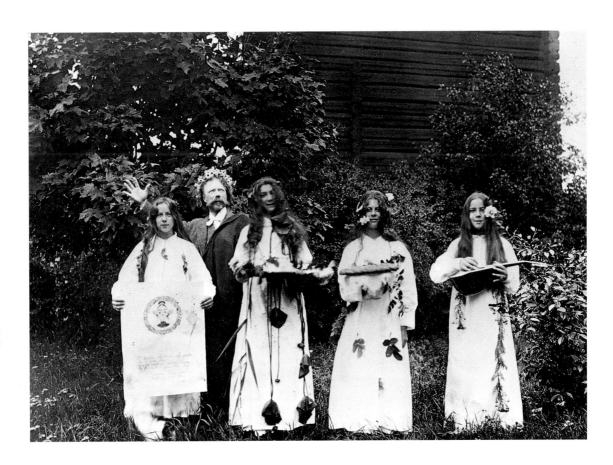

France and Sweden

To understand the nature of their home at Sundborn, we must go back to the summer of 1882, the turning-point in the couple's relationship. The scene is an artists' colony in the small French village of Grez-sur-Loing. The village still looks just as it did then, with reflections of its slowly flowing river sparkling under the old stone bridge. The light shimmers and permeates every leaf, hovers on the small, brightly coloured rowing-boats: soft, vibrant and quite different from the strong, pure Nordic light, which gives the scenery and objects such sharp contours.

A jocular, festive atmosphere prevailed in the artists' colony. Many of those close to Carl and Karin saw the love between them growing, but the summer passed without anything being said. Then one clear, warm day in September, the artists had gone to the nearby village of Montcourt to eat grapes, pausing on their way home at the bridge in Grez.

'Then we fell behind the others ...', Karin Larsson later described in a letter to her parents.[4] Carl's autobiography continues the description: 'Karin put her arm in mine, her little finger brushed against my hand, and I burst out: How I love you!'[5] This was his first declaration of love to her. Throughout life he was to show his feelings towards her openly, and to write love letters when they were separated. Almost twenty years after their marriage he wrote:

> Archaeologists are taken aback when they study cuneiform writing, papyri, archives and birth certificates to discover that the women, who have been greatly loved by men, were always between the ages of forty and sixty. I understand this so well ... Karin is now forty-three, and when she is sixty, my love will be hard to bear, for then jealousy will probably arise.[6]

In September 1882 a letter of proposal was sent express from Grez to Karin's father in Sweden. 'I'll get it over quickly: I love your daughter!', Carl Larsson wrote to the merchant Adolf Bergöö.[7] His prospective father-in-law's reply arrived promptly: 'You write "What am I? Not much yet." You suffice for us provided you are a Man in the full sense of the word.'[8]

The Bergöös in Hallsberg were unusual parents in the late nineteenth century, in an old-fashioned Sweden with rigid values. In middle-class circles, people did not marry without money. But Karin's parents – he with roots in a family of shop-keepers and she from a family of millers and millwrights – had unusually great confidence in their children.

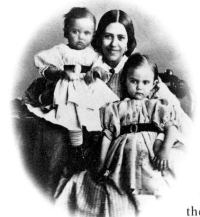

190.
Karin Bergöö (right) with her mother Hilda and her sister Elsa, 1862.

Karin Bergöö was born on 3 October 1859 into a family lacking nothing, either emotionally or materially. Her parents had cultural interests. Her father encouraged the three children to cultivate their talents, and her mother gave them a happy childhood with games and fairy tales. As a child, Karin was a dreamer. But she developed into a strong-willed young woman, who got her own way in studying to become an artist. After attending the Academy of Fine Arts in Stockholm, she wanted to go on to Colarossi's famous art school in Paris. She belonged to a pioneering generation of young women artists in Paris.

She chose her husband with the same self-assurance as she chose her profession, without hesitating in the face of an uncertain future.

In June 1883 Carl Larsson and Karin Bergöö were married in Stockholm. The emotional bridegroom cried and almost dropped the ring. He was thirty, and she was twenty-four. The shy, serious and wide-eyed Karin had conquered the most popular member of the artists' colony, the one who could brighten up even the greyest day. But Karin was aware of the childhood shadow of poverty and insecurity behind his sunny façade.

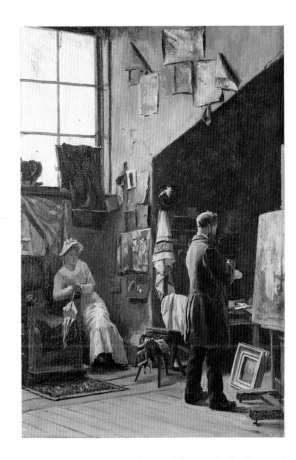

191.[168] Karin Larsson. Professor Malmström's Studio, *c. 1882. Oil on canvas. Karin studied history painting under Malmström, who also designed in the Old Norse style (see fig. 53); Karin's portfolio from her academy days is lettered with her name in the same style.*

192. Portrait of Karin Bergöö at the time of her engagement to Carl Larsson, 1882. This neat girl from a good family in Hallsberg seems an unlikely candidate for an interior design revolutionary.

Their love story is certainly like a tale from Hans Christian Andersen – the boy from the slums, who marries the merchant's beautiful daughter. The meeting with her was an obvious turning-point for Carl Larsson. Success followed in the wake of happiness. And what about Karin? Carl awakened her as a woman, he made her laugh, and she became just as attached to him as he was to her.

After the wedding the couple returned to Grez. When their daughter Suzanne was born in August 1884, Karin put her paintbrushes aside. Not many of her paintings survive, so that it is impossible to determine how talented she really was in this area. Most of them were produced during her studies in Stockholm and Paris, before the marriage. Was it a sacrifice for Karin to give up painting? In a letter to her fiancé she joked: 'My dear idiot! Thank goodness I had the idea of getting engaged to you. It's the best way I could think of to get away from that confounded painting.'⁹ The words of a girl in love should certainly be taken with a pinch of salt, but the fact is that there is no proof whatsoever that Karin missed her painting. It should not be seen through modern, feminist eyes as the wrong decision. The life of a woman painter was tough in the Swedish artists' colony, which at the turn of the century resembled a gentlemen's club. Karin made a strategic choice as a woman, and later found an artistic area in which she was not in competition with Carl. He also did well for himself, by marrying into the sheltered comfort and security of the middle classes.

Perhaps Karin intuitively knew the danger of professional envy, a well-known phenomenon in artists' marriages. She probably understood that Carl needed a central role, both professionally and within the family. As Scott Fitzgerald coarsely and directly expressed it to his wife Zelda, also a writer: 'Our life together is my material'.¹⁰ There is no sign that anything similar was expressed explicitly between the Larssons, but it is a fact that Carl, like others of his time, condemned women artists outright.

As a newly-wed in Grez, Karin felt insecure for the first time: everything was new; she was no longer an independent artist. She certainly knew most things about colour and form, but she had never studied domestic science – she could not even make porridge. She now had to cope with taking care of a child, throwing parties on limited funds and receiving her husband's intellectual friends. Her (probably justifiable) anxiety about being inadequate is seen in cries for help in the letters to her mother. Also writing home, Eva Bonnier (another Swedish woman artist visiting Grez) described how fumbling, clumsy and tearful Karin was at the beginning of the marriage.[11]

But family life developed her. She had to use all her resources. She learned quickly and took short cuts. She picked up the basics of cookery from the women of Grez. She made soups and casseroles in French earthenware pots. Her cooking became so successful that she developed a (perhaps overconfident motto): 'If you only know what it tastes like, you can make it!'

When the Larssons returned to Sweden in 1885, an itinerant life began that was governed by Carl's commissions. Karin packed and unpacked, and they had many different addresses.

An artistic partnership

Karin was not only Carl's wife and model. She was also his best critic, upon whose opinion he relied. When they had settled again in France for a year (1888-9), this time in Paris, Carl Larsson wrote to his mother-in-law Hilda:

She is my darling, my friend and – what is very important to me at the moment – my *colleague*. By that I don't mean the cooking you have touched on with concern, but the contribution she makes to my work. She is 'le bon sens'.[12]

Many years later Martina Eriksson, employed by the Larssons around the turn of the century, described the ritual surrounding a finished work of art. Carl and Karin Larsson would stand for a long time in front of the painting with their arms around one another, and have a conversation about lines and colours, which the young Martina did not understand.

Then they would talk further, and at last the mistress would say: 'Don't touch it any more, Carl – it's fine.' I didn't mean to watch all this. But it was so beautiful that I couldn't help it.[13]

In fact, Karin Larsson's artistic break did not last for more than six or seven years. Her creativity blossomed on all levels at Lilla Hyttnäs in Sundborn – a summer cottage from 1889 and a permanent home from 1901. Carl's muse, so thoughtful and quiet in the watercolours, was in reality a hard-working

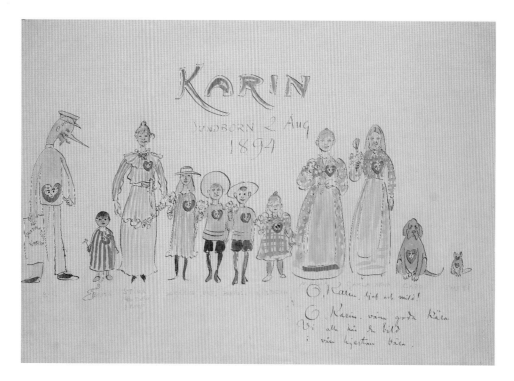

193. *[20] Carl Larsson.* Nameday Picture for Karin Larsson, *1894.*
Carl Larsson made this humorous drawing for Karin's nameday on 2 August 1894. Almost everyone in the picture wears her portrait on their hearts – Carl, the dog and the cat wear it on their stomachs! The line-up includes her sister Stina, Old Anna the cook and the servant Maria.

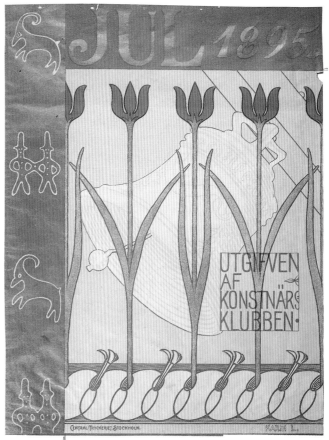

194. *[175] Cover of a Christmas magazine for 1895 for* Konstnärs Klubben *(The Artists' Club), designed by Karin Larsson.*
One of the very rare examples of flat design by Karin in media other than textiles, this cover includes stylized tulips which strongly recall the later railings made for the rooms of the house at Sundborn. The pattern of linked palettes and brushes at the bottom was apparently suggested by a frieze in an illustration of C.R. Ashbee's dining-room in The Studio, *April, 1895.*

woman. How did she find time for anything other than taking care of her large family? Between 1884 and 1900 she gave birth to eight children: Suzanne, Ulf, Pontus, Lisbeth, Brita, Matts (who died in infancy), Kersti and Esbjörn. She was the hub of the Carl Larsson 'business', the central figure in her large family, and the hostess in a constantly open house.

In Sundborn the Larssons developed a way of co-operating: they formed a team and complemented each other's talents perfectly. He was the effusive one, covering walls and furniture with foliage, flowers and proverbs. She was austere and often abstract (fig. 194). The 'Larsson style' was not only a new fashion in interior decoration but signalled a new lifestyle: child-friendly, positive and inexpensive. There was no best room. All the doors were open. The rooms were created for family gatherings. There was a summer atmosphere indoors, even when the snow was whirling outside. Carl's and Karin's vision of a home and the creative joy on which their philosophy of interior design was based permeated every room.

Karin's textiles

According to an old Swedish proverb, the home is the mirror of the soul. In Sundborn, Karin could at last settle down to a quiet life in her own home, in a district where she had played at her grandparents' as a child. She immediately felt at home. She made textiles for the home, created her own fashion for herself and the children, designed furniture and lent a joyful atmosphere to everyday family life.[14] As can be seen in Carl's paintings, she arranged beautiful and original still-lifes of flowers. Everything she did expressed a new way of thinking. She made the little village in Dalarna into her vantage point on the world.

In Dalarna, the Larssons took part in a defiant and independent provincial culture, which has remained strong. Just as a new world had opened up for the couple in France, the old-fashioned province of Dalarna was a radical experience for them. Folk costumes were still often everyday wear. Each village had its own costume. The homes blazed with colour on cupboards, walls and doors. Textile treasures were stored in chests and lofts. Women had a strong position.

During a visit to the village of Bingsjö in Dalarna in the winter of 1890 Karin learned to spin and weave braid, while Carl Larsson painted. 'She is much admired for her aptitude', Carl wrote in a letter.[15] He himself became

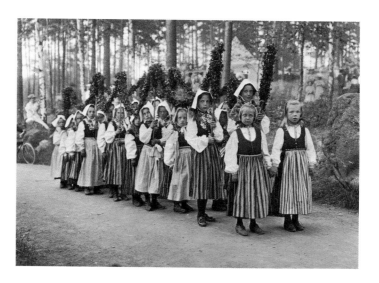

195. Children from Sundborn parish, including Kersti and Brita, wearing the costume invented by Karin, based on that of the neighbouring district of Svärdsjö. Inventing new folk costumes was not unusual at the time; the trend culminated in 1902 with the designing of a 'national' folk costume. Photograph by Olga Rinnan.

one of the advocates of National Romanticism, but even Karin was active in this area. She designed a folk costume for Sundborn, based on one from a neighbouring district (fig. 195). Her textiles contain many local Dalarna features.

By the mid-1890s Karin Larsson's textiles began to crop up in Carl's series of watercolours *Ett hem* (A Home), and her development as a textile artist can be followed from year to year in his work. Ironically, it was through Karin that modernism stole into Lilla Hyttnäs, despite Carl Larsson's dislike of modern art. His watercolour *Nameday in the Storehouse* (fig. 197) shows the extent to which Karin had begun to initiate her own artistic path. Her gift for co-ordination has become visible, expressed through her skill at mixing patterns and colours into a decorative whole.

Carl Larsson was also fond of painting a remarkable cloth, which Karin embroidered in 1897 (fig. 196). The inspiration is unknown, but it is reminiscent of the wrought

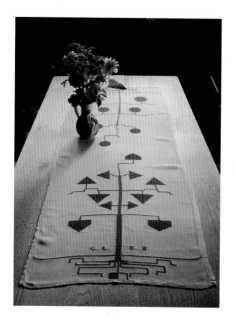

196. [181] The remarkable cloth of 1897 made for the dining-room table showed Karin Larsson's individuality as a textile designer. It is embroidered in a lattice stitch with red cotton. The tree pattern with fruit symbolizes the Larsson family. This photograph shows a copy of the cloth, the original of which is now worn and faded; Lilla Hyttnäs, which is still used by the family, contains many such excellent reproductions of the original textiles.

ironwork of Dalarna. The cloth is embroidered with a coarse, red thread on white linen, and represents the family tree, with the eight apples symbolizing the Larsson children (the differently shaped apple represents Matts, who died in infancy). This is a clear and early example of Karin's abstract style, a style with which she was to experiment and develop both in embroidery and in tapestries.

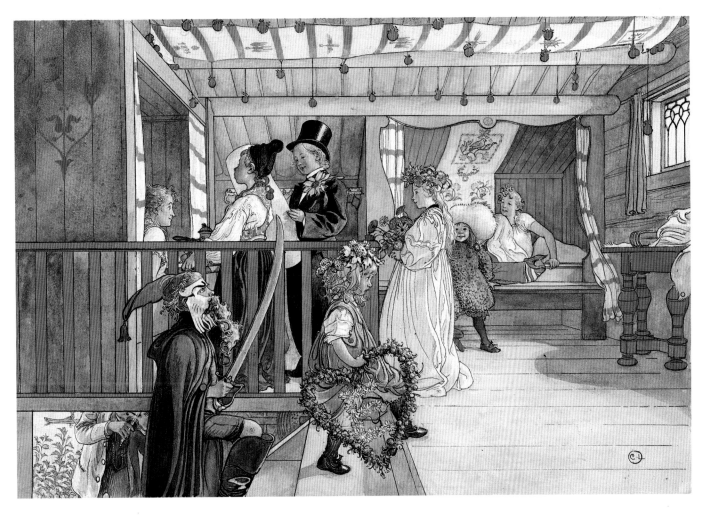

197. *Carl Larsson.* Nameday in the Storehouse, *1898. Watercolour, from the* Ett hem *series.*
The Larssons' maid Emma is visited at 5 a.m. by the children in fancy dress, one of them wearing a costume from Rättvik.
The interior, fitted out in 1893 and used as a guestroom as well as occasionally by the maids, shows that Karin has already taken the first steps along her own artistic path. A folk-influenced canopy dated 1893 hangs from the ceiling, but the motif between the red stripes is embroidered with stylized birds, which appear to be of Celtic origin. The red balls decorating the canopy are her invention. The striped fabric of the canopy is used unembroidered in the bed curtains. The blue-painted woodwork, the red-painted railing and the red table strengthen the happy impression of the room

Artistic maturity

Karin Larsson's most creative period was between 1900 and 1910, during which she produced a number of exceptional textiles. Her individuality was expressed primarily at the tapestry loom. Knowing how pleased he was with beautiful things, she gave most of her work to Carl. She often hurried to finish a cushion or a tapestry in time for Christmas or birthdays, describing herself as 'dreadfully covetous of the minutes' to finish a present. As early as 1892, in a letter to her mother, she relates how pleased Carl was with her Christmas gift of a piece of embroidery: 'No man could indeed be more fond of such things than he. It is really touching to see how he busies himself with it.'[16]

By the time Carl turned fifty on 28 May 1903, he was famous and popular. The whole of Sweden knew how the Larsson family lived. Tourists were already making their way to the house. That year was also significant for Karin in that she began her first major tapestry, an abstract vision of the 'Four Elements' (fig. 199). As so often was the case, the tapestry was intended for a particular place in the house. It decorated the space above the sofa in the brightly coloured dining-room, which was now given a unifying focal point. The abstraction of the subject was advanced for this period, when members of the professional organization Handarbetets Vänner (The Association of Friends of Textile Art) were still mainly doing floral compositions.

Karin Larsson's boldness of design is yet greater in her 'Sunflower' cushion, which she embroidered in 1905 (fig. 200). In an unusual, foreshortened perspective reminiscent of Japanese woodcuts, she divided the sunflower (one of the favourite flowers of the aesthetic period) between the four corners of the blue linen fabric, merely suggesting its whole.

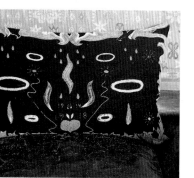

198.[184] Karin's last gift to Carl was a cushion, which he received at Christmas 1918. It was embroidered by Karin and her daughters Lisbeth, Brita and Kersti. The subject, the world on fire, is Karin's picture of the First World War with flames, shellfire and tears, and is very far from the idyll of Sundborn. Karin's insight into the war finds a powerful and sensitive textile expression.

199.[180] Karin began the tapestry the 'Four Elements' in 1903; it was made to fit over the new red sofa in the dining-room, and can be seen in fig. 126. The colours were vibrant, but have faded over the years; this half-finished copy which was being made in 1906 shows their original power. The piece was Karin's first large tapestry, but was already marked by a personal, artistic imagination. Earth, water, air and fire are shown as abstract patterns; the centre motif can be interpreted both as a cross and a maypole.

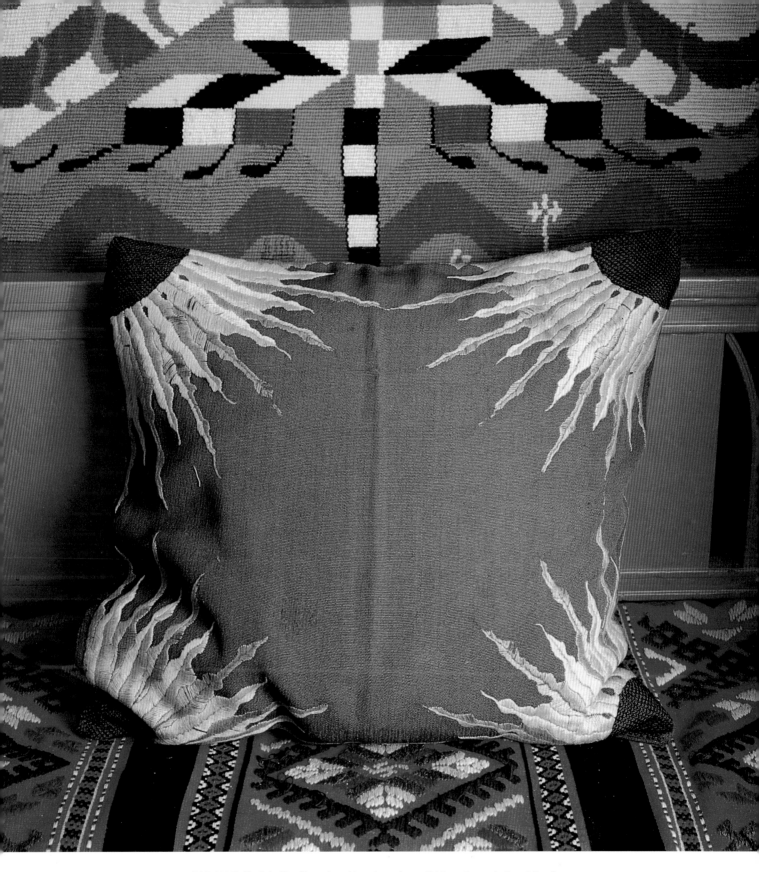

200. *[183] Karin's 'Sunflower' cushion dates from 1905, and was designed for the
centre of the dining-room sofa, placed below the 'Four Elements' tapestry
(see fig. 126). It is sewn on a blue ground in the rep technique with embroidery in
green, yellow and brownish black. Sunflowers were one of the favourite artistic
motifs of the Aesthetic Movement period, but Karin Larsson's
free treatment of the flower in the design is innovative.*

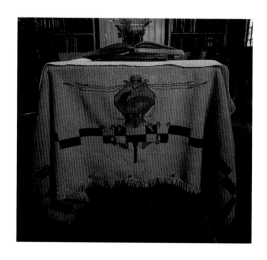

201.[157] The library at Lilla Hyttnäs is like a ship's cabin: dark, warm and cosy. For the rough kitchen table at its centre Karin made an all-enveloping, coarse, white cloth with a colourful, sewn-on border in tapestry technique; it provides a bright focus for the dark room. A brightly coloured, stylized insect clings to a black and white chequered border. She began the tapestry in 1906, and finished it as a Christmas present for Carl in 1909.

The death of Ulf in 1905 brought great grief to the home. None the less, Karin was soon back in full swing at her loom. This time she made a cloth to brighten the library, a dark room on which the family often gathered for reading aloud in the evenings (fig. 201). She wove a piece of tapestry and sewed it on to a coarse, white cloth. The decorative motif of the stylized insect grasping the black and white chequered border was complicated, and Karin was content with only putting it on the visible, short side of the cloth. While Karin was at work on the tapestry one day, her daughter Brita came in eating some fruit. 'Mummy, weave in my pear', she begged. Karin had a sense of humour and was open to unexpected ideas. The pear was duly incorporated.

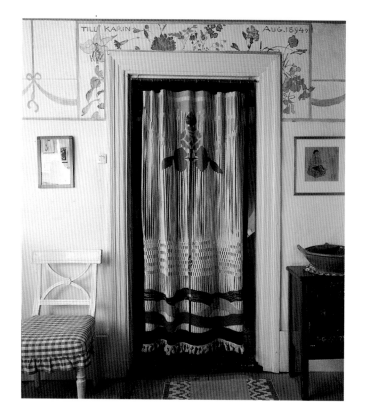

202.[152] The portière the 'Rose of Love' between the couple's separate bedrooms was one of Karin Larsson's boldest, freest and most time-consuming textile enterprises. The challenge was to weave a curtain, which would not reduce the light in the inner, darker room. Karin's solution was a tapestry with a loose warp. The elegantly simple central motif is surrounded by macramé in many different types of interlacing patterns. The wavy lines of the ground give life to the curtain; the stylized rose reaches up from the ground towards the sun. A little serpent, the enemy of love, coils around the stem. But its evil has no chance in this positive textile.

In 1909 an exquisite curtain between the couple's separate bedrooms first appeared in Carl's paintings. In the summer of 1894 he had painted a garland of flowers for Karin's nameday in August. Fifteen years later she responded in the form of an open-weave portière known as the 'Rose of Love' (fig. 202), one of her most remarkable textiles. It required ingenuity and accuracy, since it is visible from two rooms. The wave motif of the 'Four Elements' recurs at the bottom of the curtain, and forms the ground for a rose striving to reach the sun. The enemy of love, a thin serpent, coils around the stem. It is woven and knotted in a macramé technique, which she devised herself. As far as Sweden was concerned, the loose warp was new. What was its source? Karin provided no clues, but the curtain is undeniably reminiscent of the rattling bead curtains in Mediterranean shops.

Karin Larsson was by no means a needlework teacher's ideal pupil. Both her compositions and her technique were sometimes amateurish. She was generous with feeling, composed freely, and changed her mind during the course of her work. She often invented her own stitches. There were jumps in the woven fabric, and the backs of her cushions and cloths were often fairly untidy. Details and symmetry were of less importance to her than a sense of the whole. There is a story that illustrates Karin's approach to her textiles in a nutshell. When one of the women from the village sat weaving rugs for the house in Sundborn, she happened to make a mistake and asked Karin, whether she should undo it. 'Just go on, it doesn't matter', was the reply, 'the hand should be visible.'

Tradition and innovation

Karin was not a rebel. However innovative in her designs, she remained firmly within the bounds of traditional female activity. Her attitude to interior decoration and furnishing is similar to that evoked in Selma Lagerlöf's novels, in which women sit cosily at their embroidery frames, as if complying to Strindberg's view that there is 'no more beautiful sight than a woman embroidering by lamplight'.[17]

In her choice of medium Karin was certainly guided by living in a golden age for textiles. Between 1890 and 1914 old textiles were collected with unprecedented zeal in Sweden, with patterns and techniques that were copied and inspired new ideas. As a result such organizations as Föreningen

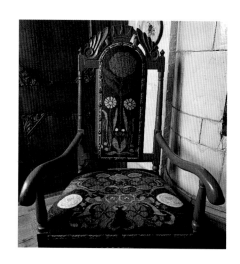

203.[171,172] The Jugendstil-inspired covers on the blue armchairs in the Old Room were woven by Karin Larsson about 1912, but it is uncertain whether Carl or Karin provided the design. The tapestry's flora and fauna are luxuriant and colourful; snakes coil on the seat fabric, and frogs leap out from the background vegetation.

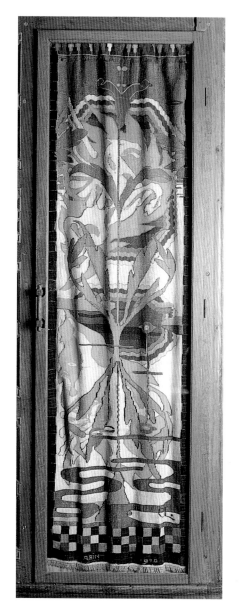

för Svensk Hemslöjd (The Swedish Handicraft Association) were founded, giving rise to the birth of modern textile design and the start of collaboration between artists and weavers.

Karin's only training in textiles was a short course she took in weaving. She was not a novice, however: sewing, embroidery and preparing their own dowry was part of the education of middle-class girls. Among Karin's advantages was that she did not need to struggle for recognition, unlike the textile designers now emerging in Handarbetets Vänner; she could afford to be 'unsuccessful' in her tolerant family and artistic environment, and could devote herself to experimenting and testing her limits in peace and quiet.

Karin Larsson's textile designs have three characteristic features: boldness, abstraction and simplicity. By contrasting geometric shapes with plant forms and combining elements of modernism with the soft, curved forms of *Jugendstil*, she gave her textiles a sense of lightness and movement. Her colours were pure, strong and bright. She had many sources of inspiration, the colours and free forms derived from peasant textiles being particularly clear in her cloths, cushions and woven fabrics. She used stitches from various provinces and took local textile features from several districts; she was evidently familiar with Skåne cushions, Halland embroidery and the four-strand braided fringe and black stitch patterns of Dalarna (figs 205-7). According to her son-in-law Axel Frieberg, in his book *Karin*, she also got ideas for designs from her dreams. Nature was

204.[189] Both Carl and Karin Larsson collaborated on the woven tapestry hanging 'Pegasus', inspired by the ancient myth about the winged horse, made in 1910. Its design seems to have been a joint effort, but she wove the tapestry, which is signed 'CL' and marked 'Karin'. The strong colours, the climbing flower and the chequered pattern in the background are typical of Karin's textile style, while the naturalistic horse is more characteristic of Carl's hand.

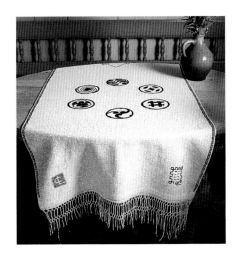

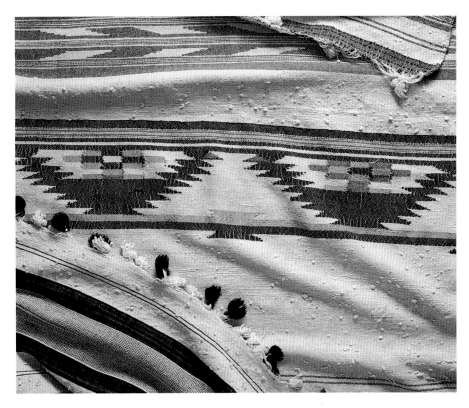

205. *The decorative but also strict and direct approach of Japanese art seems to have inspired Karin in two different linen cloths, one of which is shown here. Her black and white embroidery is a Western interpretation of Japanese mon or family badges. But there is also evidence of the influence of traditional Dalarna models in the delicate three-strand braided fringe, which edges the cloth.*

206.[154] *No one knows who gave Karin the idea for the Sundborn blanket. She designed the pattern and colours (white-grey-black-orange) in an American Indian style in 1901. The intention was that the women of Sundborn could weave these to make a little money. According to an oral tradition, the black and orange pattern on the upper part of the blanket represents baskets of oranges.*

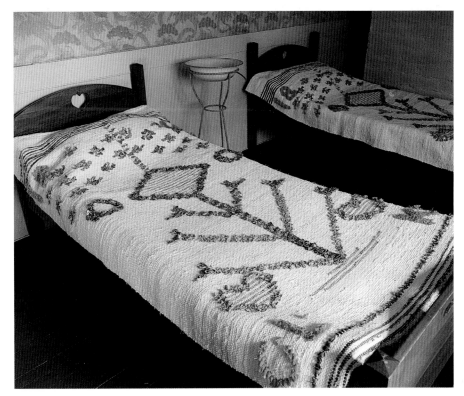

207.[188] *The design of the bedspreads at Lilla Hyttnäs, shown here in the lower dovecote above the new studio, was composed by Karin in the late 19th century. The bedspreads combine Swedish tradition with modern textile design. They may represent a tree of life or more probably a Swedish maypole. The textile technique is traditional, such weaving with rag inserts coming from Hälsingland, in northern Sweden.*

another source of inspiration. As she put it in her diary: 'From a field of clover, gone to seed, I got the design for a 'clover rug', which I shall weave this winter.'[18] This is one of her rare allusions to a specific derivation for her ideas. Another reference in her diary, written after she had finished her daughter Kersti's trousseau in the late autumn of 1920, says:

I am now weaving rag-rugs with threads of many memories. Here are red stripes from the little girls' red coats, which I made and in which Father often painted them. The white rags were once baby clothes. A blue-spotted strip is from the dress in which I posed as a model, with the children running naked among the trees at Bullerholmen.[19]

Besides dreams, nature and the textile heritage, then, Karin drew on her memory for inspiring images: the aesthetic joy of France, trips to Italy, works of art at museums in Europe, art books and avant-garde publications from England and Germany, to which the couple subscribed. Most significantly, she synthesized the traditional and the modern, absorbing influences both from the Swedish peasant tradition and Continental designers in the forefront of modernism. An example of the latter is her use of a fashionable chequered design, similar to those in the furniture, textiles and other objects of Josef Hoffmann and Koloman Moser in Vienna and Jessie R. Newbery in Glasgow.

Karin's clothes and furniture

Karin did not confine herself to weaving and embroidery. By 1890 she had designed a remarkable plant stand (fig. 212). She designed a chandelier and beds (figs 208–9); in 1906 she designed a rough, heavy rocking-chair (figs 210–11) and a square table for the new studio, pieces in which the function was obvious and the construction was not concealed. According to a Larsson family legend, the local cabinetmaker, who produced the original pieces of furniture, was so ashamed that he delivered them after dark. The chair and table resembled the late *Jugendstil* furniture which was being designed in Sweden and elsewhere in Europe, particularly in Munich, at that time. They were clearly home-made, but the style was new and avant-garde, quite different from the otherwise decorative furniture in the home.

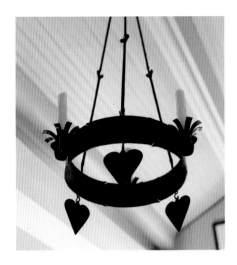

209.[170] *The children's beds designed by Karin first appear in views in 1902, replacing a disparate collection used before the house was permanently occupied. Cot-like but quite large, they have side bars made of thin wooden roof shingles and are painted in a fresh green. They were the only one of Karin's designs to be mentioned by Carl in his writings as having been conceived by her.*

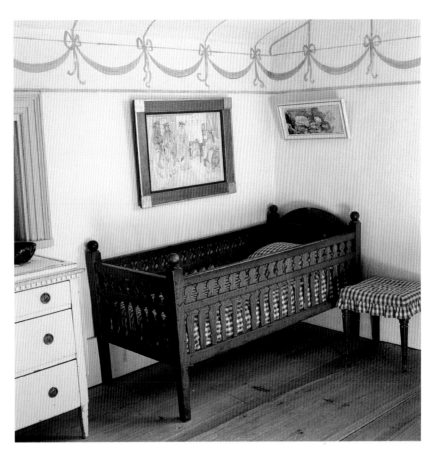

208.[192] *The Larssons were very particular about lamps, finding many contemporary shop-bought designs particularly offensive. Carl designed simple and beautiful shades for electric bulbs in the shape of cactus flowers in thick, red-painted paper to hang over the dining-room table. Karin designed a wrought-iron chandelier inspired by the circular examples of the 12th and 13th centuries. The heart-shaped hanging decorations and the divided candleholders are her own addition. It is now in her bedroom at Lilla Hyttnäs.*

210.[190] *Karin Larsson's colour schemes were neither restrained nor cautious. The almost shockingly massive modern rocking-chair, which she designed for the studio in 1906, was painted in a strong red colour, which has become yellow with age (see fig. 211).*

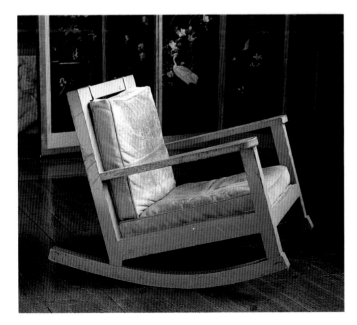

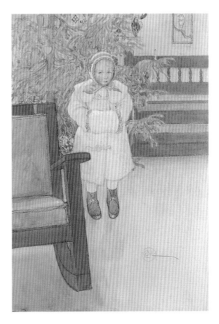

211.[191] *Carl Larsson.* Girl with Rocking-chair, *1907. Watercolour.*

As regards clothes, discreet Karin Larsson was just as conspicuously modern as in her textiles. In Carl's paintings from the early 1890s onwards, she wears dresses in a flowing style so distinctive that it has acquired the status of a Karin Larsson model. One reason for her chosen style of dress could be her numerous pregnancies. Nevertheless, it is surprising that she dared to go against the accepted fashion. A dress reform association was founded in Sweden in 1885, but its fine ideals did not influence public fashion. The cut of clothes around the turn of the century, which accentuated a tiny waist, required corsets. Karin misled the eye by adopting fashionable details of the period, such as stand-up collars and leg-of-mutton sleeves (fig. 213). This created a modest impression, which made the observer forget that decent women should be corseted; the loosely hanging dresses were associated with 'loose' morals.[20]

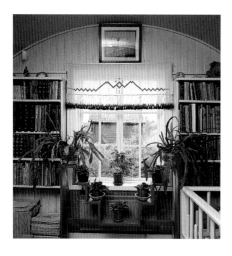

212.[146] The window in Karin's writing-room makes a complete composition. At the bottom is the plant-stand she designed as early as 1890. Its stepped shape is echoed in the embroidery of the linen pelmet curtain, sewn in red cotton. Tassels of different length in light red wool and dark blue cotton hang from the three-strand braided fring

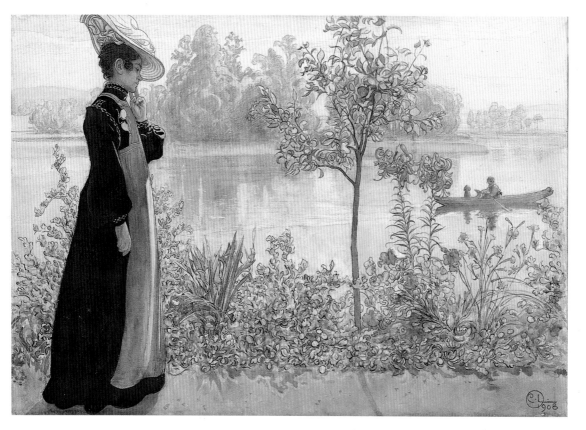

213.[103] Carl Larsson. Late Summer, 1908. Watercolour. Reproduced in Åt solsidan, 1910. 'Karin, walking by the flowerbed along the shore, looks sadly at the the very last blooms of autumn. The next night they were killed by the frost. And then the school began in Falun and we went there' (from Åt solsidan).
Karin is dressed in one of her typical designs. It appears to have been inspired by the dresses in Pre-Raphaelite paintings, but also by work clothes and the comfortable cut of the artist's smock; the loose-fitting style is also reminiscent of Rococo dress design.

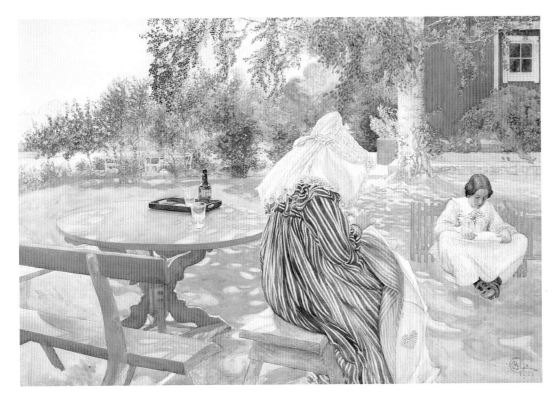

214.[179] Carl Larsson.
Karin and Brita
in the Garden, *1911.*
Watercolour.
On a hot summer's day
Karin mends one of
her own embroidered
bed curtains while Brita
reads. Karin wears a
typically individual
ensemble, a loose dress
and apron (both striped)
and a large cotton
bonnet of the type used
by French countrywomen
in the fields.

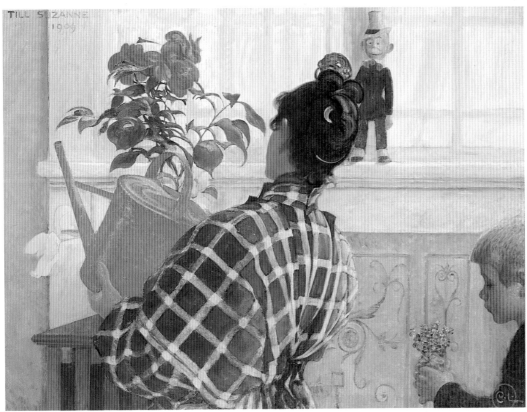

215.(178) Carl Larsson. Karin and Esbjörn, 1909. Oil on canvas. Given to his daughter Suzanne.
Karin, in a romantic dress and with a tortoiseshell comb in her hair, watering flowers, and Esbjörn with a bunch of
violets; they are watched by Carl, in the form of his alter ego clown doll standing on the window-sill. The scene
takes place in the family house in Falun. Karin's love of flowers led her to transform the poor piece of land in
Dalarna into a beautiful, old-fashioned garden.

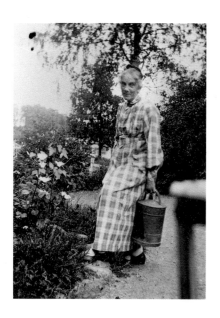

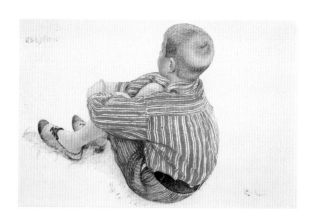

*216. A summer picture of
Karin Larsson in Sundborn,
in the early 1920s.
Her style of dress remains her
own. The checked, cotton dress
was not what ladies in their
sixties wore at that time.*

*217. Carl Larsson. Esbjörn,
c. 1908-9. Watercolour.*
*For a long time children were dressed like small adults, but around the turn of the century more
comfortable children's fashions began to appear. Karin was in the forefront, designing appropriate and
individual clothes for her children. Esbjörn's clothes here are a good example of her style, with shirt
and trousers in two different stripes. The co-ordination of different patterns was characteristic of her
approach, both in clothes and in interior decoration.*

Karin also created comfortable clothes for the children, suitable for
family life in the country (fig. 217). She used simple, robust fabrics and
was fond of mixing patterns in a modern way. She did not fall for fashion
trends, such as sailor suits. As she put it in letters to her mother: 'I'm going
to dress our children in the English style, it looks so practical';[21] and: 'I
have found some grey velvet in Falun, like the workers in France use, and
have cut out three dresses and two coats for my daughters today.'[22]

A surviving heritage

The textiles still at Lilla Hyttnäs show that Karin left nothing to waste:
everything is patched, mended and re-used. She made a long cushion, for
example, from her daughters' blue coats, which she embroidered beautifully
with garlands of flowers. There are large and small items, monograms for
bedlinen, tray cloths, humorous animals embroidered on napkins, clothes,
cushions and woven textiles. They remind one of weekdays and
celebrations. The past is brought to life through the fragments: crayfish
parties, coffee parties, summer breakfast in the garden, supper in the
dining-room. The meals, in which traditional Swedish food alternated with
French delicacies and home-made pasta, were central in the life of the
Larsson family.

In Carl Larsson's watercolours of the home, time stands still as far as
Karin is concerned: she is eternally young and wide-eyed while the children
grow up and leave home. As Carl encountered setbacks in artistic life and
became unwell, the couple seldom left Sundborn. But their love was

constant. They remained like teenagers in love throughout life. If Carl loved Karin so much, why did he never mention her publicly as his inspirer and collaborator? They both recognized that they had created the home in Sundborn together, but he consistently took a dominant attitude in public. It was his home and his work. In this respect, he was a man of his time.

On her husband's death in 1919, Karin could all too easily have become an inconsolable widow. But she was a realist. She continued a dialogue with Carl through her diary, in which she noted family events in an unsentimental way. She visited each child in turn, staying with the one who most needed her help at the time. She mended and sewed clothes for her grandchildren, also making textiles for her children. These were less bold than her textiles and embroidery for the home in Sundborn. She returned there each summer, surrounded by her loved ones. One winter's evening, in February 1928, when Karin Larsson was staying with her son Esbjörn at his farm in Södermanland, she telephoned her daughters before going to bed. That night she died peacefully, sixty-eight years old, without a lot of fuss, just as she had lived.

Karin's contribution

Karin Larsson's art was relatively unknown during her lifetime. Attention was first drawn to her work more than fifty years after her death in a few publications of the 1960s.[23] Her textiles were seen with fresh eyes, and the amateur Karin was suddenly ranked among the foremost early textile creators. One of her great admirers is the well-known Swedish textile designer Professor Edna Martin, who summed up Karin's achievement thus:

> Karin Larsson was Sweden's foremost trendsetter. She has influenced us enormously with her style of dress, her children's clothes and her vision of an enjoyable everyday life. She was an exceptional artist, a pioneer in Swedish textile design. Her textiles set the tone. I never cease to be amazed by her.[24]

The time has come to erase the dreamy image of Karin Larsson, and to allow the real, energetic artist to emerge. Above all, she is to be found in her colourful textiles, where she could not hide her true personality, her femininity, her boldness and her strong emotions.

7

THE LARSSON APPROACH
TO OLD FURNITURE

Elisabet Stavenow-Hidemark

When Carl Larsson paid his first visit to Sundborn with his father-in-law, he painted a portrait of one of Karin's aunts seated at her bureau in the drawing-room (fig. 219). The painting shows the white-painted, cross-backed chairs with the blue and white striped covers, and simple, striped rag-rugs on the floor. When Carl Larsson's father-in-law gave him the farmhouse the old furniture naturally came in handy notwithstanding the total remodelling of the interior which took place around it.

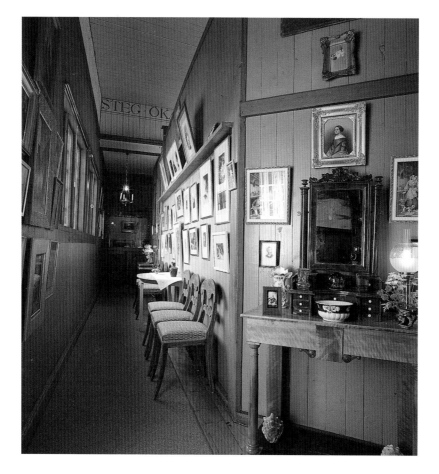

218. The 'Holy Corner' in the new studio at Lilla Hyttnäs, with the few things inherited by Carl Larsson from his grandmother's and from his childhood home. They include a Biedermeier chiffonnier and a ceramic bowl, in which Carl had his children baptized. The passage beyond is hung with prints by his friend Anders Zorn.

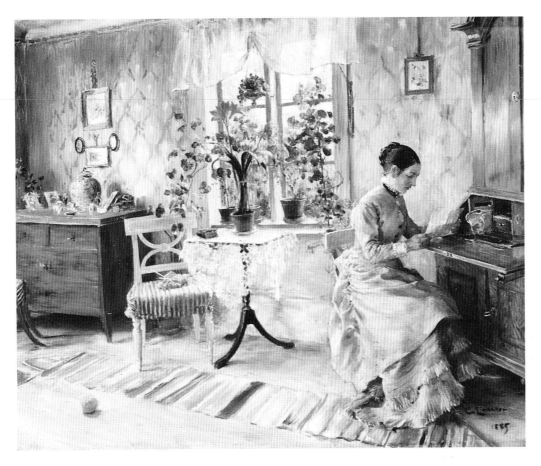

219.[118] Carl Larsson. A Woman in an Interior, *1885. Oil on canvas.*
This is Carl Larsson's earliest picture of the drawing-room at Lilla Hyttnäs, painted on his
first visit, and showing one of Karin's two aunts, who still lived there. There is a middle-class,
refined, but old-fashioned atmosphere in the room, far more refined than the exterior of the
building at that time. For their own arrangements the Larssons took over the furniture,
including the white Gustavian chairs with the striped covers, as well as the narrow rag-rugs on
the scrubbed floors. All the rest was either covered up or swept away.

Carl Larsson described his first impressions as follows: 'everything indoors was neat and tidy, the furniture was of the simplest type, but old-fashioned and hard-wearing, inherited from parents, who had lived in a property in the neighbourhood'; the cottage, he wrote, was not 'worth very much, and the furniture even less'.[1]

The inheritance came from Karin and her solid, middle-class background. Carl did not have much from his old home, but he revered the few things he inherited from his mother and grandmother, and called the place where they were arranged 'the holy corner' (fig. 218). The interest he took in procuring furniture for the home and endowing it with memories of a great Swedish past may probably be seen as compensation for his social origins.

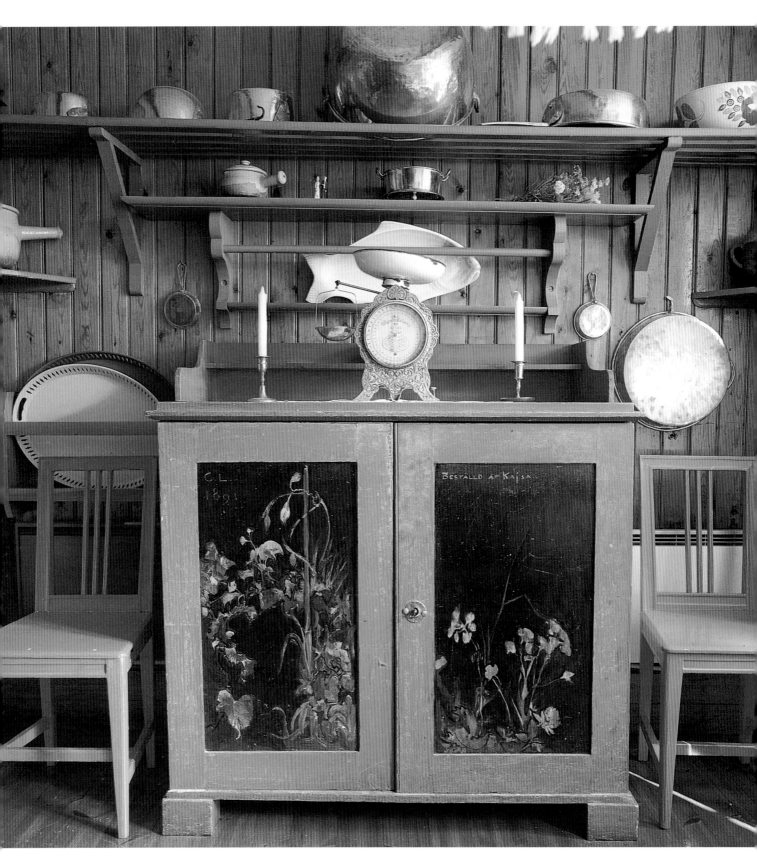

Carl Larsson could make a work of art out of even the simplest piece of furniture. The very plain cupboard, which at first stood in the dining-room, was painted in China red, and the door panels were black-lacquered and decorated with growing flowers, in a clearly Japanese-inspired, asymmetrical composition (fig. 220). This piece of furniture expresses much of the young Carl Larsson's freedom and inspiration.

Carl and Karin Larsson filled their house with old furniture, bought or given at different times. Nearly every room has a piece of furniture radiating a Baroque exuberance and a feeling for constructional clarity characteristic of peasant master craftsmen. Many of the heavier pieces of furniture probably belonged to mine shareholders, well-off land-owning farmers with a share in the local mine and arable land. Several corner cupboards with mouldings on the doors came from farmers' homes in Dalarna. Such furniture was inexpensive at that time, and Larsson sometimes bought furniture in such bad condition that it had to be restored by his handyman. On the other hand, most of the old furniture bought for the home was well-made, of solid materials and good craftsmanship, stable and intended for practical purposes. These items are a reflection of Larsson's nationalism, an expression of his pride in Sweden's period as a great power in the seventeenth and early eighteenth centuries.

Historical but not antiquarian

In Carl Larsson's case, an interest in history did not mean an antiquarian approach. He treated furniture freely. He did not alter it, but wherever he saw a smooth surface, he tended to decorate it. The furniture thus acquired a double perspective: it belonged both to the past and to his own time. He took furniture and made it his own with a portrait of a child or a beautifully lettered inscription – his own or Karin's name, or stating the intended function of the piece of furniture.

Because this did not happen according to a firm plan, it always has the charm of the unexpected. There is a definite feeling of spontaneity. This is

220.[113] The simplest piece of furniture could become a work of art. This cupboard was painted by Carl Larsson for the dining-room in 1891. He signed and dated one door and inscribed the other 'Ordered by Kajsa' (i.e. Karin). The asymmetrical flower painting is Japanese in feeling. In 1903 it was moved to the workshop, and finally ended up in the kitchen.

equally true of the doors of the house. He must have felt that their smooth panels demanded decoration: Karin on the sliding door to the workshop (1890), his daughter Brita on the drawing-room door (1900), little Esbjörn in the dining-room (1906) (fig. 221) and Kersti on the door to the library (1907).

Artist's colours were naturally used in the decorative parts, but where a whole piece of furniture was painted, thick, glossy oil paint was used. The latter now comes as a shock to anyone with a professional responsibility for old furniture, but Carl Larsson obviously wanted that effect.

Repainting cupboards

The Larsson home contains many solid, heavy and richly ornamented cupboards of different sizes from the late seventeenth and early eighteenth centuries. Carl would pick out their sculptural details and emphasize them with contrasting colours. A cupboard on feet, with the inscription IPSO HEND 1694, is depicted in a watercolour showing the workshop when it was still his studio (fig. 225). The front of the cupboard is made up of Renaissance strapwork ornament, black framing and infill panels. It now stands in Carl Larsson's bedroom. The door panel within the richly moulded frame has been decorated with the lettering 'KARINS LINNESKÅP 1897' and a charming full-length portrait of his daughter Brita (fig. 223). In an article in *Svenska hem i ord och bilder* (Swedish Homes in Words and Pictures) in 1916, Carl Larsson himself described it as 'an old peasant cupboard, in which I keep my loose collars'.[2] In fact, he was having a dig at the magazine's readers, whose expensive and conventionally over-furnished homes were usually featured in the magazine.

Karin soon brought to the house a new and larger linen cupboard, of a so-called 'Hamburg' type, which stands in the Old Room. In 1906 Carl painted her sorting linen next to this piece of furniture, which is built-in, veneered and appears to support one of the roof beams (fig. 180).

There is also an old wall cupboard (which formerly hung in the Stockholm flat) in the background of this painting (fig. 222). It was once a spice cupboard.[3] Behind the richly sculptured doors, there are lots of small drawers. He boldly painted it so that each individual motif is picked out: green walls, red fittings and ochre guilloche patterns surrounding the red and brown pine cone in high relief. The text states that it was intended to 'put old rubbish in' and includes family names.

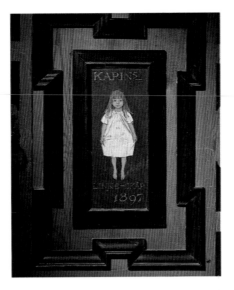

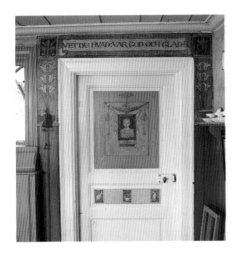

221.[117] *A portrait of Esbjörn on the dining-room door, painted in 1906. Above it is the inscription 'You know what? Be good and cheerful'.*

223.[148] *Detail of a cupboard dated 1694, now in Carl's bedroom, showing a portrait of Brita in carefully initialled linen, dated 1897. It is inscribed 'Karin's linen cupboard'. The cupboard in its unaltered state can be seen in the first studio in fig. 139.*

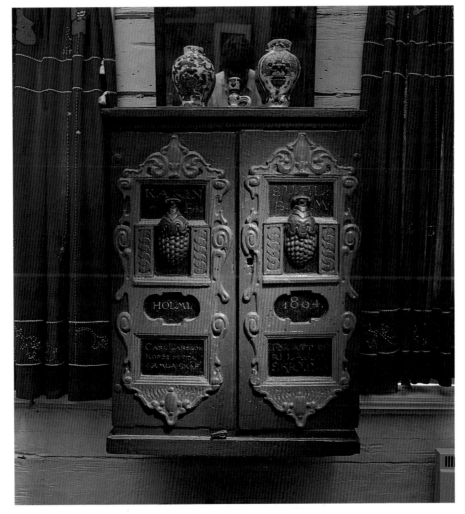

222.[165] *A small 17th-century hanging-cupboard carved in high relief. It was bought by Carl Larsson in Stockholm, and painted by him with glossy oil paint in brilliant colours. The text, expressed in appropriately ancient form, is divided into six cartouches and gives Karin's maiden name and the initials of the children, including Matts, who was born in November 1894 and died in January 1895. It concludes 'Holmia [Stockholm] 1894' and 'Carl Larsson bought this old cupboard to put old rubbish in'. It is seen in fig. 3 in 1895, hanging against the panelling in the dining-room-cum-studio in the Stockholm flat, and in fig. 180, showing the Old Room where it still hangs.*

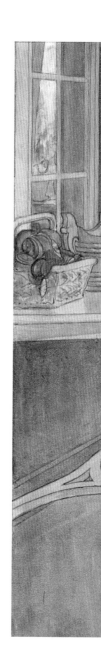

The workshop contains a large, blue cupboard, painted in a shade usually known as Dalarna blue. It was probably once the base of a larger piece in two halves. The cupboard is first seen in one of Carl Larsson's paintings in 1914.(fig. 225) With its weight, ornament in low relief and spherical feet, it is a typical piece of Baroque furniture, probably from Dalarna. Originally it had black mouldings against a wood-coloured ground. It now stands luminously at the back of the room against the ochre, matchboarded wall and green mouldings.

In the corner to the left of the sideboard there is a small wall cupboard with a three-sided front, a door with two panels and a garland at the top. This cupboard is painted in a deep green, and the garland and panels have a red ground decorated with a heart and a flower. Swedish peasant cupboards are certainly rich in colour, but not these colours – they are Carl Larsson's own.

A table

Among Carl Larsson's best-known watercolours is *Sunday Rest* (1902) (fig. 34). Karin is sitting with folded hands on the sofa in the workshop, but she is barely visible: only her hands, part of her dress and the newly ironed, white apron are shown. Her hands are resting on a solid Baroque-style table with spiral-shaped legs. Carl evidently respected the craftsmanship of this table, as he left it undecorated and included it in many of his pictures (fig. 224). Like most of the old furniture, it was moved around the house, and it now stands in the Old Room, where it tends to merge into the background.

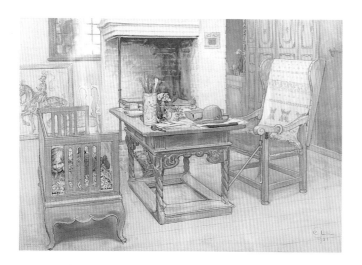

224.[193] *Carl Larsson.* Hide-and-Seek, *1901. Lithograph, made by the magazine* Idun *under Larsson's supervision to sell to readers, after a watercolour of the same year. The Larssons' daughter Kersti plays in the new studio, lying in a red-painted sofa which mixes neo-classical and Rococo styles. Beside it is a magnificent Renaissance-style table in unpainted wood. With its spiral-shaped legs and heavy framework at floor level, it is an excellent example of Dalarna-made furniture from Sweden's period as a great power in the 17th century. The remarkable 17th-century leather-upholstered armchair (with a reclinable back) is also found in many pictures, a seat of honour, generally reserved for Carl Larsson himself.*

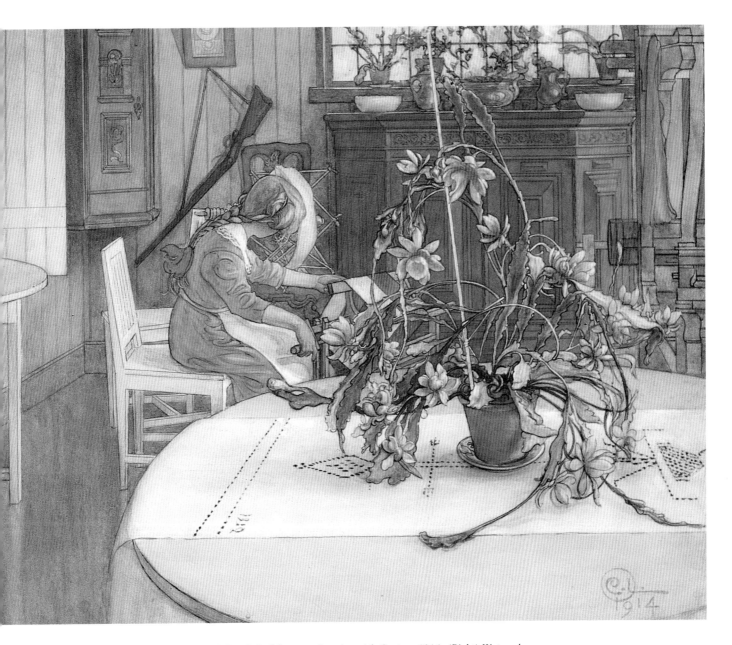

225.[127] Carl Larsson. Interior with Cactus, 1914. (Right) Watercolour.
The workshop is seen here with a newly acquired cupboard in the
background. It is characterized by the powerful idiom of the Baroque, and
is probably a piece of mine shareholders' furniture from Dalarna.
Originally it was of unpainted wood with black mouldings. The thick, blue
oil paint is totally foreign to such a piece, but it is certainly beautiful
against the ochre wall and the green mouldings.

Seating

The Larssons' home contains a number of chairs of urban character, particularly late Baroque and Rococo pieces. These are characterized by a baluster-shaped splat with a keyhole-shaped opening. In the early eighteenth century, Baroque chairs were usually either left unpainted or painted brown (fig. 226), while Rococo chairs were painted ochre, blue-green, warm rose or brown. There are many chairs of this sort in the house, either painted in a considerably stronger shade than was usual in the eighteenth century, or in white, which was not used at all. The paint is not the thin, matt of the eighteenth century, but often a thick, glossy oil. The chairs in the workshop are painted a strong, medium blue (fig. 227); others are in a warm green. The high-backed chairs in the large studio are glossy

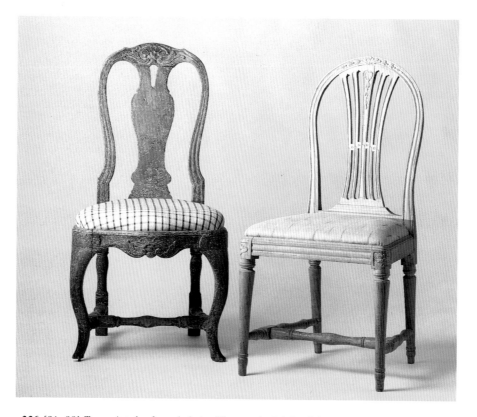

226. *[81, 88] Two painted softwood chairs. That on the left is of the 1760s, that on the right of about 1800, by Carl Johan Wadström, a well-known Stockholm chairmaker. Swedish chairs from the second half of the 18th century were often painted. The Rococo chair to the left was originally thinly painted in ochre, and shortly afterwards painted in indigo blue. The other chair was pink from the start. All the upholstery is modern.*

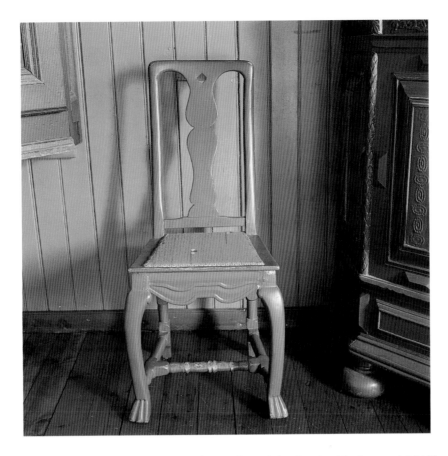

227. A late Baroque, early 18th-century chair in the workshop is painted in the same bright blue colour as the sideboard in the same room. The ochre panelling and Karin's orange-coloured woven fabric for the seat enhance the colour effect. Originally a chair like this would have been left unpainted or would have been painted brown.

white, and the armchairs are a matt, warm red. This bright colour scheme was at first unique to the Larssons, but it spread like an epidemic among those who had come to love Carl Larsson's picture books and wanted to achieve the same effect. The chairs must also be seen in relation to the wall behind; the contrasts of blue against ochre, green against yellow, red against green epitomizes the Larssons' approach to decoration. The red furniture is now felt to be particularly characteristic of Carl Larsson, and it should be noted that he used this colour in various warm shades: a brownish red, a slightly orange-coloured red and Chinese red; these would change shades with repainting, as was the case with the well-known dining-room furniture.

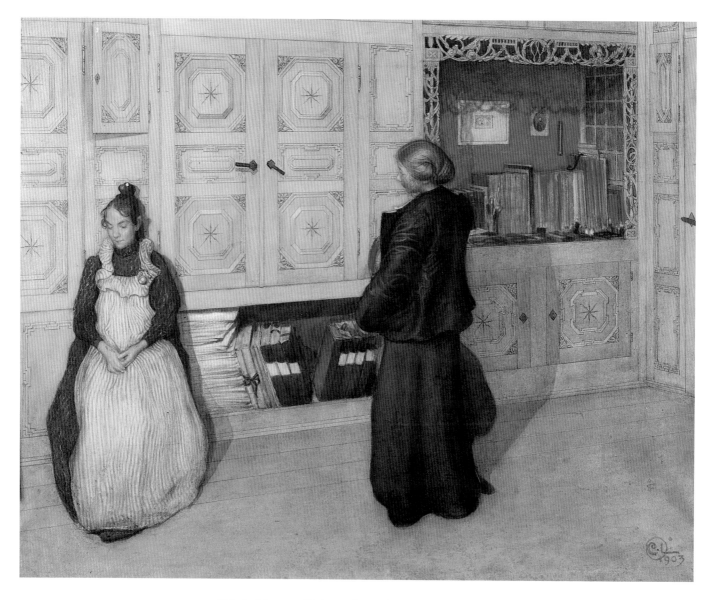

228. *Carl Larsson.* Mother and Daughter, *1903. Watercolour.*
There is something of Sweden's former grandeur about most of the Baroque furniture at Lilla
Hyttnäs, but this panelling, which Carl Larsson was very proud of, is from
Schleswig-Holstein. Part of it was put up in the Stockholm flat in the 1890s; at Sundborn it was
used to fit up the new studio (shown here)and the Old Room (fig. 182).

The carved panelling

Carl Larsson was evidently proud of the richly carved panelling from Schleswig-Holstein, a piece of work in the Renaissance tradition from north Germany which he bought at a high price, unseen, from a Danish antique dealer.[4] He does not seem to have minded that it was not Swedish: he appreciated its fine craftsmanship and elegant carving. Part of the panelling was first installed as a feature in the combined dining-room and studio on Glasbruksgatan in Stockholm. After the family's move to Sundborn, the panelling was divided between two walls with a built-in box bed in the Old Room, and a large, often depicted wall in the new studio (fig. 228).

Artistic licence

Carl Larsson's attitude to furniture was full of contradictions, as it was to so much else. He loved good craftsmanship, but he himself built or ordered sofas whose workmanship might be decorative yet comparatively crude. While many of his acquisitions expressed his pride at being Swedish, he often altered the furniture, repainted chairs, and added paintings and texts to the cupboards. From an antiquarian point of view, such a course of action is to be condemned, but Carl Larsson's artistry makes him an exception to the rule. He introduced something cheerful, personal and self-willed into his environment without which posterity would be the poorer. There are opportunities to study items of furniture in their original state in museums. At Carl Larsson's home the furniture he painted or altered so boldly offers an opportunity for other forms of delight.

8

TRANSLATION AND TRANSFORMATION: CARL LARSSON'S BOOKS IN EUROPE

Cecilia Lengefeld

Carl Larsson's international fame as Sweden's best-known artist has had a decisive effect on that country's image abroad in the twentieth century. Crucial to this process has been the mass publication of colour reproductions of the watercolours of his home at Sundborn. Through his illustrated books in particular, Larsson reached a large and devoted public in Scandinavia and Germany during his lifetime, and in the rest of Europe, the USA and Japan from the 1970s.

Ett hem

Larsson made his name on the Swedish book market with the lavish edition of *Ett hem* (A Home) in 1899, with illustrations and text by the artist (fig. 229). This publication was based on a series of twenty watercolours on which Larsson had been working since the mid 1890s, and which had been

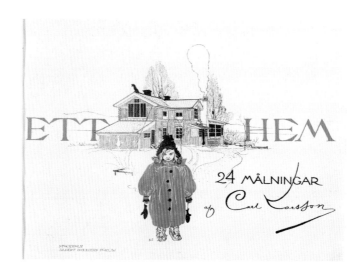

229. *[42] After Carl Larsson. Title-page of* Ett hem *(A Home; 1899). Coloured line block after a pen and ink drawing made in the winter of 1899.*
The drawing shows Lilla Hyttnäs from the north-west with Kersti in the foreground. This is the only view to show the house in this state, just before the new studio was built.

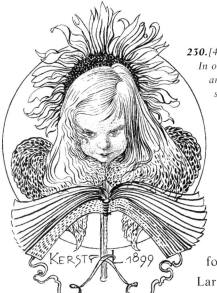

230.[43] After Carl Larsson. Kersti, *vignette in* Ett hem, *1899. Line block.*
*In one of Carl Larsson's rare essays in outright symbolism, prominently placed on
an end-leaf facing the half-title of the book, Kersti is shown as a winged
secular angel backed by a sunflower halo. She reads a book, presumably
intended to be* Ett hem *itself: Sundborn is heaven on earth.*

exhibited at the Art and Industry Exhibition in Stockholm
in 1897. The interiors of his home in Dalarna, with members
of his family occasionally used as models, provided an
entirely new type of subject, a combination of modern
architectural drawing and genre painting of the past with a
focus on family life. It was a significant personal triumph for
Larsson that the National Museum in Stockholm acquired the
watercolour series two years later.

The Stockholm publisher Karl Otto Bonnier (1856–1941), who had
made a name for himself by promoting contemporary Swedish literature,
immediately interpreted Larsson's paintings as a manifesto for a new ideal
of life and living. Intent on innovation both in the content of books and
their design, Bonnier (not Larsson) had the idea of reproducing the
watercolours with the aid of the latest printing techniques, in an elegant,
large-format, modern, *de luxe* edition. Larsson began the text on Christmas
Eve 1898.

Bonnier and Larsson had been collaborating continuously since the
1870s, as the artist's main source of income for over twenty years was from
illustrating magazines and books, and designing book covers. He was the
most prolific book illustrator of the period in Sweden (some thirty
commissions for different publishers between 1874 and 1894), and was
particularly in demand for his pen-and-ink
drawings and wash drawings to illustrate
Swedish classics. Having specialized in
eighteenth-century dress and interiors, as in
Anna Maria Lenngren's *Samlade skaldeförsök*
(Collected Attempts at Poetry, 1884), Larsson
also showed his strength in a contemporary

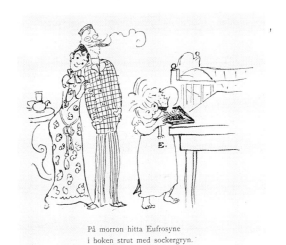

På morron hitta Eufrosyne
i boken strut med sockergryn.

*231. Carl Larsson. Illustration, drawn in Sundborn in 1890,
to the conclusion of Larsson's poem 'ABC', first published in
the periodical* Svea *(1891) and reprinted in his book* De mina
(1895). Line block.
*In this poem, and others about the antics of 'Eufrosyne',
published at about the same date in* Svea, *Carl Larsson
introduced his family to the reading public.*

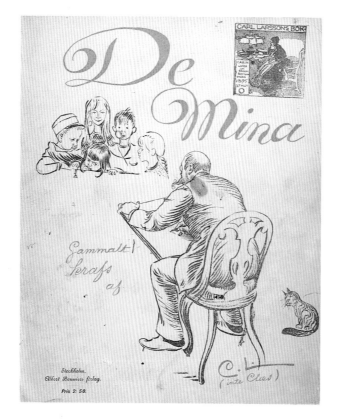

232.[48] Carl Larsson.
Title-page of De mina, *1895.*
Line block.
De mina *(My Loved Ones) was named*
after the painting of the same name
painted in 1892 (see frontispiece),
which it reproduced in colour as a
frontispiece (see fig. 6).
A small volume containing a disparate
collection of pieces, chiefly previously
published, it was the first book on the
Larsson family. It was billed in Svea
as 'This Christmas's funniest book'
but was a commercial failure. This is
the Larssons' own copy, with Carl's
book stamp showing 'Karin reading
about Gordon' in 1895.

work, Viktor Rydberg's novel *Singoalla*, published by Bonnier in 1894 (fig. 36). For this he produced wash drawings whose flowing lines show the influence of *Jugendstil*. The edition was highly praised, yet represented the last time Larsson made the complete illustrations for another writer's text.

For the *Ett hem* project of 1899, Bonnier increased the number of watercolours to twenty-four,[1] asked Larsson for pen-and-ink drawings to serve as vignettes, and above all persuaded him to write an accompanying text. The artist, who was certainly enthusiastic about the idea itself, was not particularly willing to act as a writer. He was probably thinking of his début as an author on the book market with *De mina* (My Loved Ones) – also published by Bonnier (1895) – whose satirical *causeries* had not been a success (fig. 232).

Larsson gradually overcame his insecurity as a writer, but not without encouragement by letter from Bonnier: 'Your text is excellent!'[2] But ultimately Larsson's text proves to be uneven compared with the consistent artistic freshness and fairly unambiguous message of his watercolours. He intended his prose mainly to be a vehicle for interpreting the language of his paintings. The introductory sentence explains the aim of the book: to provide an 'informative text to accompany these paintings of my dear home in Dalarna'. He sought to demonstrate how anyone could quite informally 'leave an artistic and personal mark' on his own home, without previous knowledge or much money, but endowed with a little dexterity. The very simplicity and individualism of the interior design was Larsson's guiding principle. He objected to the current taste, which dictated mass-produced period furniture. He sharply criticized 'the draperies of persons of rank, hung ridiculously over doors, in corners and behind pictures, their display stands with cheap trash, and their artificial flowers with ribbons, dust and microbes!'. After this diatribe, Larsson indicated desirable models, which had gone out of fashion with the progress of industrialism: the modest household goods of Swedish country people, which they had made, woven, painted and sewn themselves.

In order to avoid being heavy-handed, Larsson lightened the text. He interspersed it with anecdotes about himself and his family, looked back on his poor and joyless childhood, eulogized patriotism, gave good advice on bringing up children, and finally provided glimpses of happy family celebrations. However, the nature of a pattern book for modern interior decoration is never lost in this miscellany, particularly as the illustrations are mainly devoted to this theme.

Karl Otto Bonnier

Bonnier was a significant example of a certain type of publisher who had an increasing influence on cultural life in turn-of-the-century Europe. As a 'cultural publisher' typical of the period, he was keen on making a personal mark on the publication programme. In the *Ett hem* project, his creative input meant that he produced an avant-garde work of art in book form, in close collaboration with Larsson, for whom he was also playing the unusual role of mentor. As a result of Bonnier's approach, the design followed avant-garde English models in using modern layout and typography as well as art printing paper; the final product was far from usual, even for this publishing house. Above all it was expensive, chiefly due to the costs of producing masters for the colour reproductions. It was not surprising that Bonnier, with the aim of reducing costs, wrote to his foreign colleagues encouraging them to publish parallel editions of *Ett hem* in translation.

As is evident from Bonnier's archives, the firm's international contacts were numerous and extensive. Bonnier sent proofs of Larsson's pictures to Germany, Denmark and England; the London publisher William Heinemann also received an English version of the text. Although Bonnier praised the book as 'very valuable',[3] the desired result abroad was not forthcoming. 'Damned Englishman' was Larsson's comment in a letter to Bonnier.[4] Heinemann's rejection also affected Larsson's personal connections in England: Karin Larsson's sister, Stina, was married to an Englishman, Frank Bather (a geologist at the Natural History Museum in London), and the Bathers were shortly to visit Sundborn. In the same letter to Bonnier, Larsson promised with a flash of humour: 'I shall get my own back on Bather for the other rascal.' Several years later Heinemann's lack of interest still irritated Larsson, as is revealed in a letter to his friend Thorsten Laurin, a print collector: 'When the English publisher read my text, he rejected it, and said that it did not suit English purposes – or something of the sort'.[5] It is significant, as we shall see, that Larsson singles out his text as the inhibiting factor.

Larssons and Spadarvet

In Sweden *Ett hem* was published in an edition of 3000 copies in time for Christmas 1899. Each book cost 12 kronor, a price that prohibited immediate sales success. But Larsson's ideas and the book's design were positively received in the press by modern-minded critics. Despite the fact that the edition was still in print three years later, Bonnier proposed a 'sequel'. A *de luxe* book of similar format, with text and illustrations by the artist, was published for Christmas 1902. Entitled *Larssons* in an edition of 4500 copies at 15 kronor, the new book was centred on family life rather than a personally created home environment (fig. 233). Bonnier's agreement with Larsson included world copyright for the text and reproductions, as had been the case with *Ett hem*. But this time the publisher did not try to benefit from foreign rights, although he had not abandoned the idea. The obvious solution was to concentrate on Germany, where Nordic writers were having great commercial success at that time.

Larsson therefore made his foreign début in Germany. However, the German translation of his next publication, *Spadarvet* (1906) (figs 234, 235), with its twenty-four watercolour reproductions, was not a success.

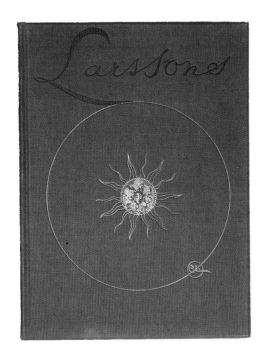

233.[51] *Carl Larsson. The cover of his book* Larssons *(1902). Nothing could better express Carl Larsson's view of his family than the design stamped in gold on the cover of* Larssons. *He is the earth circling a sun containing Karin surrounded by the children. Significantly, he is indicated by his signature alone: above all he is an artist.*

234.[45] *Carl Larsson. Drawing for the title page of* Spadarvet: Mitt lilla lantbruk *(Spadarvet: My Little Farm; 1906). Pen and ink and watercolour.*
Larsson bought the farm called Spadarvet in Sundborn in 1897. It was run by others, but provided accommodation for his family. Here Esbjörn and Kersti (wearing the Sundborn costume designed by her mother), play at farms in a neat garden, perhaps a wry comment by Larsson on his role as a gentleman farmer. The 24 coloured plates of the book take the reader through the farming year, culminating with Christmas at Lilla Hyttnäs (see figs. 40, 167).

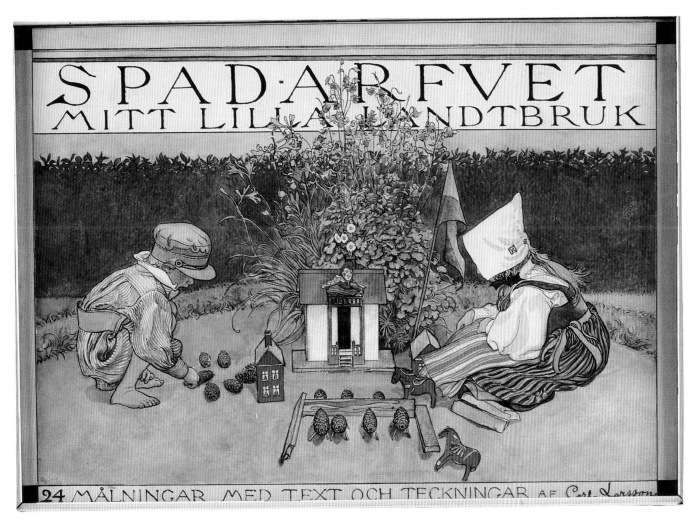

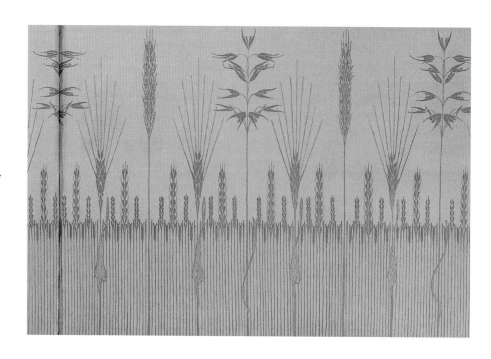

235.[46] Carl Larsson. The endpapers of Spadarvet: Mitt lilla lantbruk (1906). Carl Larsson's superb decorative sense is evident in the detail of all his books. Here a range of cereal crops is formed into an elegant pattern in the Japanese manner. A very similar pattern, used by Eugène Viollet le Duc for a wall covering in Histoire d'une maison, 1873, may have given Larsson his initial idea.

This time the book project, which was centred on the Swedish farmer's work throughout the year, was Larsson's own idea. Nostalgic reflections on peasant culture were guaranteed a certain response in Sweden, where a patriotic, at times passionate, song of praise to the morally superior peasantry was in line with a current interest in the native roots (*hembygd*) and the concept of Swedishness. This was not the case in Berlin, where *Bei uns auf dem Lande* was published by Bruno Cassirer in 1907, in an edition of 500 copies at 20 Deutschmark; the translation, by Ida Jacob-Anders, followed a protracted and at times sluggish correspondence between the publishers, in which Bonnier was always the driving force.

Bonnier did not consider himself to have a monopoly of ideas with regard to creating books, and discussed with Cassirer at the planning stage the idea of replacing Larsson's text with an essay on the artist written by a German art critic.[6] It would not have been difficult to find a suitable journalist, since as an exhibitor Larsson met with a positive response in the newspapers of the German art centres, while Cassirer as the publisher of a modern art journal had every conceivable contact. But, in the end, Cassirer did not bother to adapt the book's content to 'German taste'. This was one of the reasons why the German public was unsympathetic in its attitude. Adjectives such as 'strange', 'chatty' and 'old-fashioned' were characteristic of several reviews, for instance those in the *Vossische Zeitung* and *Neue Freie Presse* (December 1907). Sales were disappointing: barely 130 copies were sold in eighteen months.

German developments

Meanwhile Ellen Jungbeck-Grönland, a Swede living in Düsseldorf, was translating *Ett hem* and *Larssons* on her own initiative. Feeling homesick, as she later admitted in a letter to Larsson, work on the artist's texts was 'a great and real joy' to her.[7] This expatriate's initiative was to be the prelude to one of the really great sales successes on the book market in the German Empire. It is therefore sad that only the barest facts are known about Jungbeck-Grönland herself. She grew up in Småland and was married to a German publisher in Düsseldorf, but was not one of the large group of more or less professional translators who introduced Nordic literature in Germany: she is not known to have translated more than Larsson's two books.

Interesting information on Jungbeck-Grönland's role in the German book project emerges in her above-mentioned letter to Larsson: she 'discovered' her compatriot, and to her delight she 'succeeded in finding a publisher'; but it was the publisher who knew how to transform her translations into a real success. She complained to Larsson that she 'had wanted two volumes, one of *Ett hem* and one of *Larssons*, each picture and each line of text deleted broke my heart'.[8] Cuts and alterations were not, however, a painful process for the publisher Karl Robert Langewiesche (1874–1931). Such editorial changes in artistic originals were part of the daily routine at the publisher's editorial office in Düsseldorf, from which came one bestseller after another.

Jungbeck-Grönland must have been in contact with Langewiesche by 1908. At the end of December, the latter was writing to Bonnier asking what he and the artist might think of a 'German work with illustrations by Carl Larsson'.[9] A busy correspondence between Düsseldorf and Stockholm ensued during the first half of 1909; the book was to be published that Christmas. In January Bonnier had given his consent to a collage of Larsson's Swedish editions, adapted to the German market: 'You can choose just as you like from the three albums'.[10] The result was an inexpensive book in a reduced format with sixteen colour reproductions. By heavily cutting and pasting Jungbeck-Grönland's translations, Langewiesche produced a Larsson book which would appeal to the Germans. The artist's interior design ideas gave way to an idyllic, almost religious image of a happy, sunny home centred on children. Larsson's allusions to the bad taste of 'persons of rank' and similarly critical comments were simply deleted. Not only the truncated text but Langewiesche's choice of illustrations emphasized instead the harmony of family life. All pure interior design subjects were missing in his Larsson book; Larsson's wife and children were brought to the fore.

Das Haus in der Sonne

It would be unfair to compare Langewiesche's sales with those of Cassirer without taking several factors into account. Langewiesche's book with the ingenious title *Das Haus in der Sonne* (The House in the Sun) cost only 1.80 Deutschmark (fig. 236). But the sensationally low price was not the only explanation for the fact that the first print run of 40,000 copies sold like hot cakes. *Das Haus in der Sonne* was produced as one of an already well-known series of popular books which Langewiesche advertised with great ingenuity. Furthermore, he excelled at devising book titles with sales appeal. He knew that *Das Haus in der Sonne* would have associations with current aspirations for family life, health and a 'simple' life in the country; the Larssons' fair-haired, lively family suited this collection of ideas. The book had an overwhelmingly favourable reception ('You don't discuss Larsson – you love him!'[11]) Particularly in the provincial press, Larsson was presented as the perfect farmer and 'Teuton', occasionally with racist overtones.

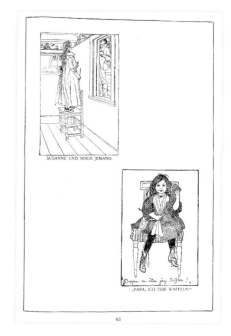

236.*[54, 60] Page from Carl Larsson,* Das Haus in der Sonne *(The House in the Sun, Düsseldorf and Leipzig, 1909).*
In Germany Das Haus in der Sonne *was the first best-seller in translation from Swedish, selling 100,000 copies by 1912. The success continued, though at a slower pace, and with a break during the Second World War It was probably not the book's message which bothered the Nazis, but rather that the original publisher Karl Otto Bonnier was a Jew.*

While *Das Haus in der Sonne* made its triumphal progress through German homes in one edition after another, the question arises as to how Larsson himself reacted to the manipulation of his message. It could conceivably have shocked him. Bonnier did not formally need to ask the artist's permission for changes, and he did not do so. In fact, Bonnier forgot to inform Larsson about the publication at all. Several copies of the finished book arrived by post straight from Düsseldorf, with a very friendly letter from the publisher: 'Perhaps you will be somewhat pleased with this German edition with your illustrations, and perhaps your wife will be

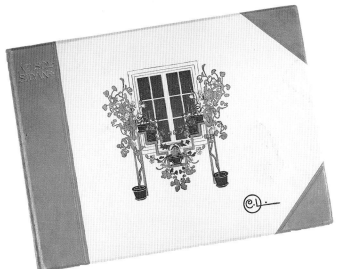

237.[53] After Carl Larsson. The cover of Åt solsidan *(On the Sunny Side, 1910).*
The cover shows the window and plant-stand in Karin's writing-room, with the evening sun, shown in gold, pouring in. In Åt solsidan, *as in* Ett hem, *the reader was shown the house at Sundborn and the Larsson's house at Falun in a series of colour plates. The preceding commentary, which lacks the design-reforming slant of* Ett hem, *is decorated with vignettes and laced with Larsson's own thoughts on life, art and politics. Like* Ett hem, *the book was later published in a smaller, cheaper format.*

pleased with the amusing copy, which my wife Stefanie herself has bound for her'.[12] Larsson, who understood German, was certainly not offended. He proved to be entirely in agreement with his 'transformation' and to accept the demands of fame. 'I am happy, flattered and moved', he began his letter of thanks (in German) to Langewiesche. 'I read my silly text aloud [to Karin], and we thought that it was much better than in Swedish'.[13]

When visiting Germany in 1913, the artist enjoyed being recognized and – as he wrote home – being a 'famous man'.[14] In the German Empire, Larsson's popularity was to continue undiminished until his death in 1919, by which time Langewiesche had sold almost 200,000 copies of *Das Haus in der Sonne*. However, the German public took no notice of the later picture books, which Bonnier published: *Åt solsidan* (On the Sunny Side; 1910) (fig. 237) and *Andras barn* (Other People's Children; 1913), which were translated into German and turned down by Langewiesche. Bonnier launched the former under the title *Lasst Licht hinein* (Let the Light in) from his Leipzig branch and published it as a *de luxe* edition in 1911 (fig. 238). *Anderer Leute Kinder* (1913) was marketed by Cassirer with unknown results. Neither of the books provoked any appreciable response in the press. The conclusion may therefore be drawn that Larsson's books needed to be 'edited' to suit 'German taste' before they could be appreciated in the German Empire.

238. Carl Larsson. Title-page of Lasst Licht hinein *(Let the Light in, 1911). Half-tone after a watercolour.*
The title-page of the German edition of Åt solsidan *repeated the Swedish publication exactly, reproducing the watercolour* The Carpenter and the Painter *(fig. 136).*

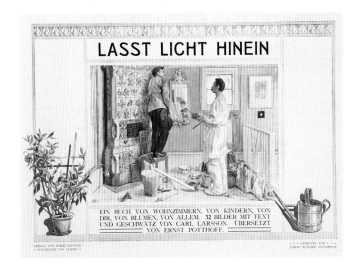

Exhibitions in England

During Larsson's lifetime *Das Haus in der Sonne* contributed more substantially to his reputation than any of his other publications, making an impact not only on Germany but elsewhere in Europe. The book title was re-used for quite different groupings of Larsson watercolours, exhibited as 'het huis in de zon' in Amsterdam (1912) or as 'la casa al sole' in Rome (1911). As a book, however, the success in Germany was not repeated elsewhere.

Larsson had extremely limited success in England. His biographer Georg Nordensvan maintained in 1912 that the artist had no expectations whatsoever of achieving success there.[15] The magazine *The Studio* had occasionally reproduced individual watercolours (1896, 1903, 1905 and 1907) and had published an article by the Swede Sunny Frykholm in 1904 with six illustrations from the Sundborn milieu.[16] He had been praised by the Dane Georg Bröchner in *The Studio* (1907 and 1910), but nobody in England was prepared to act as an 'impresario' for Larsson, to promote him energetically and systematically, as was the case in Germany, Italy and the USA.

The Swedish print collector Thorsten Laurin, who not only acquired Larsson's entire output of prints but established and looked after the artist's network of contacts with art dealers in Germany, also made a concerted effort in England. According to a letter to Larsson, he sent photographs 'of your latest paintings' to *The Studio* in August 1910.[17] It may therefore be assumed that a 'studio talk' the following month, signed 'T.L.', was by Laurin. He was also very probably responsible for the contact with the British Museum. A notice in *Svenska Dagbladet* reveals that 'the Director of the British Museum's Print Room, Campbell Dodgson, has acquired 17 etchings by Carl Larsson on behalf of the Museum'.[18] Dodgson was one of England's most prominent connoisseurs of modern graphic art, but the Larsson etchings were acquired for his private collection, although they later passed to the Museum.

In 1905 two Larsson watercolours were lent from the Thiel collection to an exhibition at the New Gallery in London.[19] In 1911 it was Laurin who helped Larsson make a much more public appearance on the English art scene: he was co-organizer of an *Exhibition of the Work of Modern Swedish Artists* at the Public Art Galleries in Brighton, which was 'the first exhibition of its kind ever held in this country';[20] there were fifteen watercolours and six etchings by Larsson. Laurin also arranged for the exhibition to be shown at the Walker Art Gallery in Liverpool that autumn. It is uncertain whether the exhibitions resulted in any purchases. The reviews primarily reflect uncertainty regarding the exhibits, and the non-committal 'art criticism' is concerned mainly with a description of the exotic motifs. A journalist who was at the opening of the exhibition in Brighton cautiously praised Larsson as 'the popular artist' whose watercolours were 'remarkable for their elegance and joyous character'.[21] And *Stockholms dagbladet* quoted a comment in the *Liverpool Courier* on Larsson's watercolour *In Mother's Bed* (signed 1908) (fig. 239), which was evidently noticed only because 'A king is much the same anywhere, but two children lying on a bed are something quite different in Stockholm from what they are in Liverpool, and we are much obliged to him [Larsson] for showing them to us.'[22] The watercolour, which cost £167 according to the catalogue, was sold in 1912 by a Stockholm dealer for 2250 kronor; in the same year it was shown at the American Art Galleries in New York.

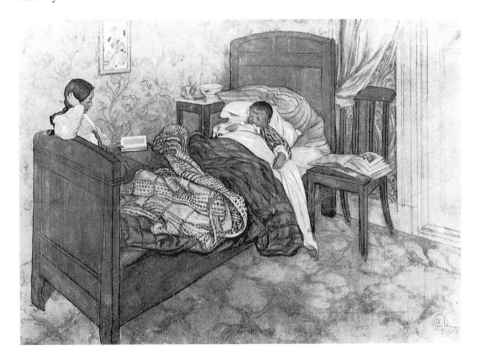

239. Carl Larsson. In Mother's Bed, *1908. Watercolour. Reproduction in the catalogue of the*
Aquarellausstellung des Sächsischen Kunstvereins *in Dresden, 1908.*
Depicting Kersti and Esbjörn, this watercolour is an excellent example of how several of Larsson's works of art travelled to international exhibition centres. Before the painting was shown in Brighton and Liverpool in 1911, it had toured Germany (Dresden 1908 and Berlin 1910-11). In 1912 it was sold in Stockholm for 2250 kronor, and was exhibited later that year at the American Art Galleries in New York.

Reproductions in Europe

British publishers were similarly disinclined to take Larsson on, so that England was not an interesting market for Bonnier either. By contrast, he received enquiries almost weekly from Germany, Austria, France and Holland, from art dealers who wanted to offer reproductions of Larsson's watercolours for sale. This was not surprising in view of his exhibitions, particularly in Germany, where major and minor galleries had put on some twenty-five shows of his work. Neither was it surprising that Europe's art dealers approached Bonnier, whose foreign business almost exclusively concerned reproductions. The firm advertised its 'rich stock of Swedish original illustrations' in the publishing trade's most important directory (published in Leipzig). But Bonnier pursued a deliberately restrictive policy with his copyright. He did not want to sell individual motifs, as he said in a letter to Langewiesche, since he felt that this would be detrimental to 'big business'.[23] By regulating the flow of illustrations – including postcards – Bonnier hoped to give Larsson's books a better chance on the market. This probably reassured Langewiesche. The publishers' contract prohibited Bonnier from selling cheap postcards with motifs from *Das Haus in der Sonne* in Germany, Switzerland and Austria.[24]

Whether there was any demand at all in England for individual Larsson reproductions is unknown. It is known, however, that Bonnier's efforts to control the publication of pictures in Germany were not always successful. Between 1905 and 1908 eleven reproductions were published in the popular Munich weekly *Jugend* (1908 circulation: 74,000). Larsson's *Iduna* (1901) was even the cover of one of the February issues in 1905 (fig. 240). Ten weeks later the wash drawing *Sleeping Beauty* (1901–2) was reproduced in *Jugend* under the title *Die Spinnerinnen*, accompanied by a sentimental poem by the chief editor Fritz von Ostini (fig. 241).

240. The cover of the magazine Jugend, *February 1905.*
The cover reproduces Carl Larsson's watercolour Brita with Candles and Apples *(1900), which was shown at an international exhibition in Dresden in 1904. It had first been used in 1901 for the cover of the Christmas number of the Swedish magazine* Idun. *The artist's intention with the model's dress (which alludes to Christmas) and props (the basket of apples, which alludes to the pagan goddess Idun) was completely lost on the way from Sweden to Germany. According to Old Norse mythology, the gods recovered their youth by eating Idun's apples. Larsson's creative concept was scarcely intelligible to those who did not know its original use.*

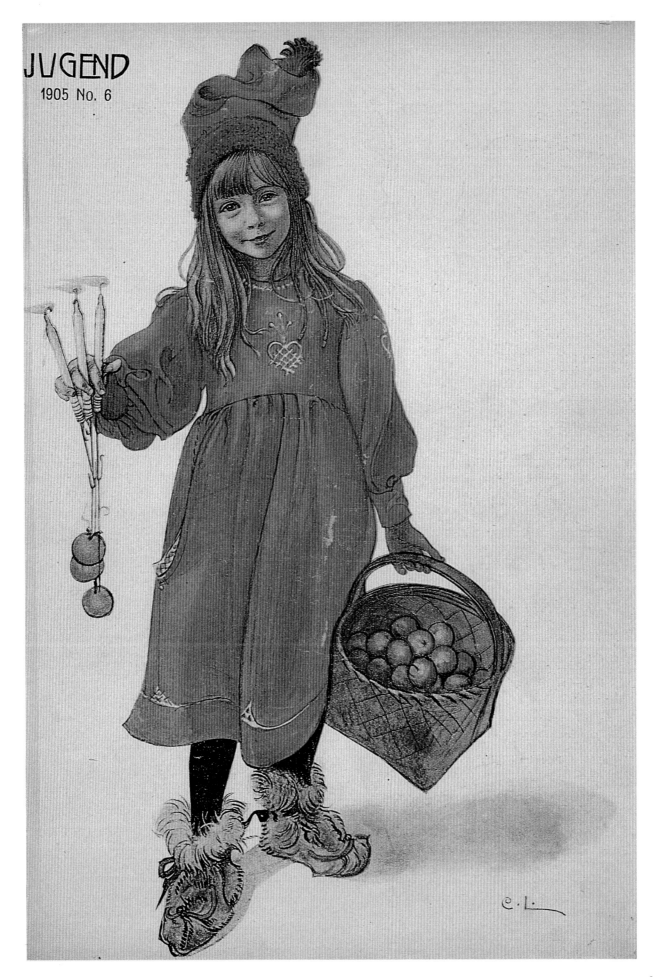

JUGEND
1905 No. 6

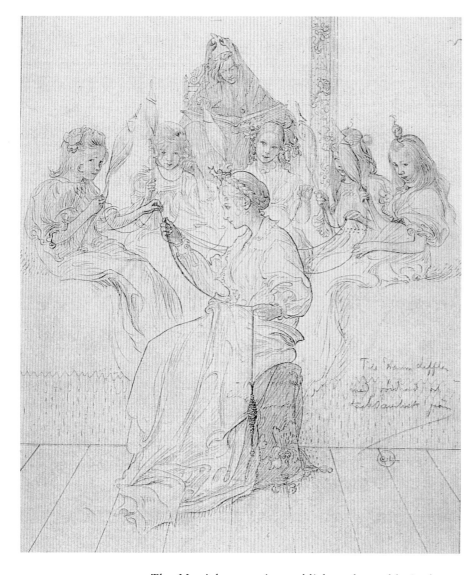

241. Carl Larsson. Die Spinnerinnen, *reproduction in* Jugend, *No. 16, 1905. Carl Larsson's wash drawing was an illustration for 'Sleeping Beauty' in a collection of children's stories translated by Z. Topelius in 1902–3. It was published in* Jugend *without any reference to the original text, and the chief editor Fritz von Ostini imaginatively extolled the languishing young girls' dreams of the future in a poem of several verses. Ostini was one of Larsson's influential admirers in Germany, since he reviewed Larsson's exhibited works very favourably in the Munich daily press (*Der Tag *and* Münchener Neueste Nachrichten*) on several occasions.*

The Munich magazine publisher also sold single reproductions cash on delivery, either framed or unframed. All Larsson's pictures in *Jugend* could be ordered as wall decorations. Bonnier took no notice of this shady trade. Even postcards leaked out (in unknown quantities). In 1911 Langewiesche reacted to this with irritation in a letter to Bonnier. When the artist was consulted, it appeared that he himself was surprised each time the 'lady in the tobacconist's' in Stockholm told him: 'Now you're in *Jugend* again, Mr Larsson!'[25] He scarcely remembered that, naively ignorant of Bonnier's copyright, he himself had given permission to a *Jugend* editor to reproduce the works he had shown in Dresden in 1904. Larsson was inclined to throw away receipts and contracts, and to forget the contents. Even Laurin once tried in vain to clarify a German copyright, but the only reply he received from a distressed Larsson was: 'I probably signed a piece of paper...'. [26] The surviving correspondence is unfortunately not complete enough to reconstruct the full details of these episodes on the fringes of legality.

The tendency to trivialize Larsson and his work, which was evident even during his lifetime, also affected his later status as a reformer in the field of interior decoration. It was a commission to the journalist Lennart Rudström which revived Larsson's reputation. The Bonnier firm republished *Ett hem* (1968), with the well-known reproductions and Rudström's freely invented text, evidently with an eye to a new and trendy market: children. This infantile misrepresentation of Larsson's original message was distributed in Europe and reduced him to a naive father-cum-artist. As a result of the book's success, several other Larsson publications were reworked in the same spirit.

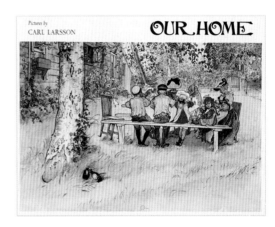

In London, Methuen Children's Books went even further. Under the title *Our Home* (1976) (fig. 242), Olive Jones wrote a fictionalized version of the Larsson story with the eldest daughter Suzanne as narrator. Unlike Larsson's fairly serious, 'informative text' to accompany the illustrations of the home, Jones puts words into Suzanne's mouth to focus on the artist himself: 'My father is the most wonderful man in the world – or in Sweden anyway.' With an undeniable gift for evoking childlike charm, she presents the principal character as a self-absorbed 'Papa'.

How Larsson would have reacted to this type of transformation of his images and their message can only be surmised. Perhaps he would have proudly observed that, by taking his place on children's bookshelves, he was following in the footsteps of Daniel Defoe and Jonathan Swift, whose heroes Robinson and Gulliver have undergone similar metamorphoses. But whatever Larsson might have thought, his new persona – exported even to the USA and Japan – has unfortunately tended to overshadow serious discussions of his importance as the progressive creator of one of the most remarkable artist's homes of the past century in Europe.

242. Our Home, *1976.*
The radical transformation of Larsson's Ett hem *in* Our Home, *through a completely new and child-centred text by Olive Jones, has caused bibliographic confusion. It is described as a 'translation from the Swedish' in the British Library Catalogue.*

9

Carl Larsson's Images: Mass Publication, Distribution and Influence

Elisabet Stavenow-Hidemark

A thin exercise book, beautifully bound in leather, is kept in the library at Lilla Hyttnäs. It contains a school essay entitled 'Father's Studio', written by Ulf, the son who died of a burst appendix at the age of eighteen. Ulf describes the large paintings in Carl Larsson's studio and concludes:

> Besides these large paintings, father has also painted a large number of small, beautiful watercolours, which have been distributed both in Sweden and abroad. Lithographs have been made of some of the watercolours, which the poor have obtained in Christmas magazines to brighten up the dark walls of their bare homes.

Ulf touches here on something important. For while the Larsson picture books were obviously important, it was through the reproduction and distribution of his pictures in other areas that Carl Larsson became a truly popular artist. They appeared extensively as lithographs and half-tone colour reproductions in the fairly expensive Christmas magazines and in the women's weekly magazine *Idun*. Individual prints were distributed through intensive marketing by both Larsson's publishers: Bonnier in Stockholm and Langewiesche in Düsseldorf; to their annoyance, there was also a considerable trade in pirate prints. In Bonnier's case the motive was both commercial and cultural, for he wanted to contribute to educational reform by providing schools with good reproductions of first-rate works of art. The prints themselves were at first largely made in Germany, where four-colour printing had developed more rapidly than in Sweden. This process was a fairly new invention, but great skill in reproduction had already been achieved by the turn of the century.

Evidence of the sale and effect of prints after Carl Larsson is not difficult to find. Ellen Key, who strove to spread culture to the working classes, wrote in her book *Folkbildningsarbetet särskildt med hänsyn till skönhetssinnets odling* (Adult Education and the Cultivation of a Sense of Beauty, 1906) that colour prints of Larsson's pictures from *Ett hem* (A Home) could be purchased cheaply in folders, and were also on sale ready framed at two of Stockholm's art dealers. In 1915 she wrote that 123 'colour prints' by Larsson could be ordered at any bookshop or stationer's for one krona each. This was not without its effect. In a passage which recalls texts by English reformers she wrote:

> In hundreds of small, working-class homes in town and country, the Carl Larsson pictures have displaced the awful oleographs. The Sundborn idylls, with their light, happy atmosphere, have scattered glimpses of beauty and aroused dreams of happiness, where beauty was previously considered to be the prerogative of the wealthy.[1]

It was in fact even more remarkable than this, for Carl Larsson's reproductions reached middle-class as well as working-class homes, crossing social boundaries with their message of family harmony, security and delight in colour and light.

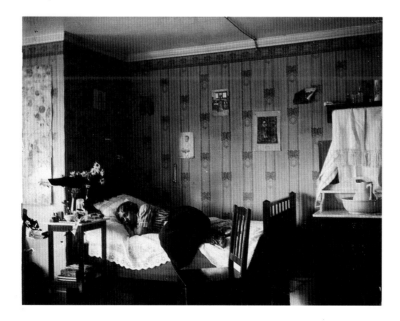

243. A nineteen-year-old girl's room in a middle-class provincial house, 1913. Pinned to the art nouveau *wallpaper is a reproduction of Carl Larsson's* Father, Mother and Child *cut from the 21st Jubilee issue of the Christmas magazine* Jultomten, *1910 (see fig. 126). Photograph by Karl Westman*

Ellen Key was also a supporter of Föreningen för Skolans Prydande med Konstverk (The Association for School Decoration with Art), founded in 1897 by the art historian Carl G. Laurin and his brother Thorsten Laurin; the latter was a friend and vigorous promoter of Carl Larsson. The Association was active on two fronts, both raising funds for monumental paintings by Sweden's best artists in elementary and secondary schools, and obtaining good reproductions. Carl G. Laurin also devoted himself to getting good reproductions into private homes, and Carl Larsson was one of the many artists whose works were distributed in this way.[2]

Carl Larsson's prints

From 1875 onwards Carl Larsson made a total of 112 etched, drypoint and aquatint prints, and four colour lithographs.[3] The subjects of the prints were often portraits of his family, friends and servants, as well as self-portraits. These played their part in communicating the Larsson family and their way of life to a wider circle, and indeed included the earliest printed representation of a family subject (fig. 244). Children appear at the dining-table, playing in the garden or on father's shoulders, many of the compositions being taken from Larsson's paintings. A small number of prints depict subjects against recognizable interiors of the dining-room or drawing-room in Sundborn.

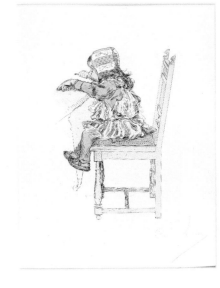

244. Carl Larsson. Lisbeth at the Table, *1894. Etching, issued by* Föreningen för Grafisk Konst *(The Association for Graphic Art). Showing Lisbeth in the Stockholm flat, this was the first published print to feature a member of the Larsson family.*

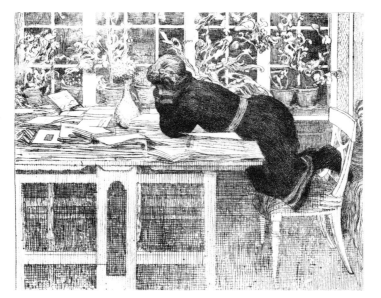

245. Carl Larsson. Brita Reading, *1910. Etching.*

The best-known of these is the etching *Martina with the Breakfast Tray* (1904), derived from a painting (see fig. 43), in which the pretty housemaid is seen in front of the table in the dining-room. The etching *Brita Reading* (fig. 245) is also interesting. Derived from a watercolour, it shows a teenager reading intently, leaning over the gateleg table in the drawing-room; the night sky is dark through the windows, and the whole table is filled with papers and books in disarray.

A vital channel for the distribution of Larsson's prints was Föreningen för Grafisk Konst (The Association for Graphic Art), founded in 1887 to produce prints annually by subscription. In 1888 the Association published its first etching by Carl Larsson, *Profiles* (fig. 23). It was followed by thirteen others, the majority in editions of 500 or more, making Carl Larsson the Association's most substantial single contributor. Three of the four colour lithographs were also published by the Association, printed at various establishments in Stockholm. They included the popular *St George and the Princess* with its fairy-tale atmosphere (fig. 246). It was printed from eight stones in 1896 and reprinted in the following year.[4]

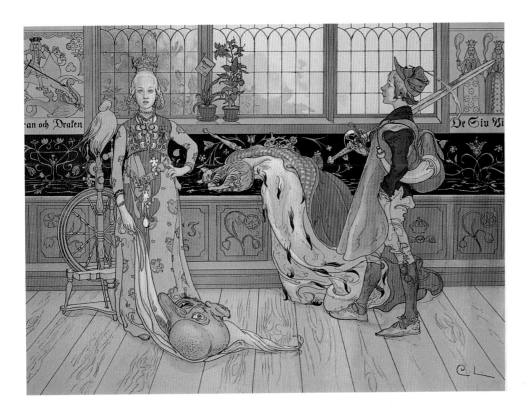

246.[41] Carl Larsson. St George and the Princess, *1896. Coloured lithograph issued by* Föreningen för Grafisk Konst.
The subject is taken from a watercolour, in which the figures are derived from an oil painting of 1893 (fig. 101). They have been placed in an imaginary interior which combines elements of Lilla Hyttnäs with real folk objects, including Dalarna wall paintings which Larsson had in his flats in Stockholm and Gothenburg.

Reproductions

It is difficult to estimate the exact extent of the distribution of Carl Larsson's reproductions, but it was certainly enormous. In middle-class homes the pictures were hung in nurseries, corridors and, of course, in country cottages and summer houses. Most middle-class children born in Sweden before the end of the Second World War probably had a Carl Larsson picture above their beds, at least in the summer cottage (a man born in the 1940s relates that as a boy he always wanted Christmas to be just as in Carl Larsson's pictures, but had to admit with disappointment that it never quite was). In working-class homes the pictures were hung in the only room. The reproductions were sold unmounted in narrow, white frames (fig. 247), of a type fashionable in radical circles. Carl Larsson's original watercolours for *Ett hem* were framed in this way in the National Museum, as were Strindberg's oil paintings.

The largest and most magnificent of Carl Larsson's reproductions was the lithograph *Viking Raid in Dalarna* (taken from a watercolour of 1900, of the same size as the original: 61 cm x 103 cm; fig. 83). Such a reproduction was expensive and was found only in schools and middle-class homes. Interestingly, one of Larsson's daughters had the reproduction above the living-room sofa in her first home in the 1920s (fig. 248).

The influence of Larsson's images

Although the direct influence of Larsson's images is now greatly reduced, they have certainly had a profound effect on Swedish design and interiors since the turn of the century. At the start they led many people to paint their furniture red, green or white, and to arrange it against plain walls in contrasting colours. Even old mahogany furniture was painted over. This was an early instance of do-it-yourself, and the paint manufacturers were quick to offer suitable colours.

Carl Larsson's popular images were, of course, a key factor in the growing trend towards brighter and more colourful interiors, and the use of fewer textiles and lighter curtains which began in the years around 1900. This trend coincided with aesthetic aspirations from many other directions, in the early twentieth century, including especially the German Werkbund, in which Hermann Muthesius was one of the leading figures. Muthesius had absorbed the basics of the Arts and Crafts movement in England, and had spread its aesthetic through his major work, *Das englische Haus* (1904–5),

247. *[194, 195] Carl Larsson.* You know what? Be good and cheerful, *1911.* *Colour lithograph after a watercolour. Set in the etching workshop at the Larssons' house in Falun, the scene shows a grumpy Esbjörn and smiling Kersti, to whom the title, first used on the walls on the dining-room at Lilla Hyttnäs here clearly refers. The frame and brass label engraved with the title and 'Carl Larsson' were standard.*

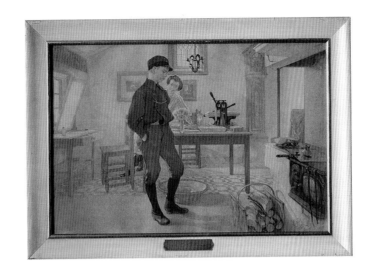

248. *Kersti in the farm Spadarvet, 1920s. Above the bench hangs a colour lithograph of the watercolour* Viking Raid in Dalarna.

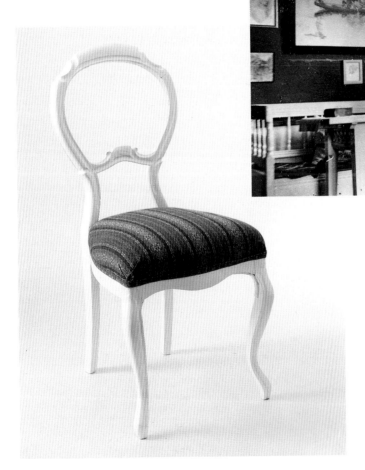

249. *The painting of furniture was one of the main effects of the Larsson influence in the early 20th century. This chair comes from a set of the 1860s which was originally painted brown to resemble mahogany. Although not in the Gustavian style of the Larssons' white furniture, the set had by the 1920s been painted white and given new covers. This example has been restored, but with an unused sample of the original cloth.*

and in a large number of articles, read by the German-speaking world, which included Sweden.

At the same time many other forces were working to change the home in such areas as health, national identity and art. The Swedish handicraft movement and the local folklore movement (both ideologically influenced by England) provided a national focus. Carl Larsson's role in these developments was recognized even while they were happening. As early as 1910 the art and cultural affairs writer August Brunius could write an article entitled *Carl Larsson och en nationell möbelstil* (Carl Larsson and a National Style of Furniture); Carl Larsson and his world were considered the height of Swedishness.[5]

Unrestricted reproduction

Inevitably, the mass reproduction of Carl Larsson's images eventually turned them into icons. They showed a lifestyle to aim for, but they had become symbols, simply part of the background. In 1969, fifty years after Carl Larsson's death, the copyright on his images expired according to Swedish law. Sweden was inundated with Carl Larsson reproductions, now given a new lease of life, and the postcard market was flooded with cropped Carl Larsson motifs. Biscuit tins and Christmas plates were decorated with motifs from the kitchen or dining-room in Sundborn. You could – and still can – buy trays, ashtrays, table-mats and many other items with the well-known images, often poorly reproduced. This degree of overexposure has made it even more difficult to appreciate the qualities of the originals. Larsson was even invoked in the names of brand-new products intended to convey rural security; a dinner service with a creeper in red and green is, for example, called Sundborn. In Sweden advertisements using Larsson images constantly crop up for prefabricated houses, home insurance or rustic furniture – in fact anything where ideas of security, cosiness and Swedishness are useful in promoting sales. For many of those who grew up in the 1970s and 1980s the images have as a result become meaningless and commercial.

The record attendances at the major exhibition held at the National Museum in Stockholm (and in Gothenburg) in 1992 showed, however, that Carl Larsson's paintings, seen in the original, still had a strong hold over the Swedish public. In terms of the direct influence of the images on design, changes are also afoot. The actual interiors at Sundborn, and especially the Gustavian legacy, with the sun on the gateleg table in the Sundborn drawing-room, the chairs with their covers, and the flowers in the window are again seen as symbols of security and tradition. IKEA has mirrored this shift in its recent venture into eighteenth-century reproduction furniture.

More internationally, too, the Larsson influence is back. The winter 1992–3 issue of the international book on future trends *Influences* carried a feature on Carl Larsson, including a self-portrait and watercolours of the Sundborn interiors, shown against a background of William Morris patterns. Headed 'Sundborn: The Swedish Paradigm', the article considered that 'decoration, handcrafts and simplicity were combined with light, color, comfort and joy. This Swedish reinterpretation of Art Nouveau has its place in today's aesthetics.'[6]

More than a century has elapsed since Carl and Karin Larsson created their home, yet it can still charm and impress the visitor as well as convey a convincing artistic strength. Carl Larsson's images of those interiors and their inhabitants are still distributed and loved.

10

THE LARSSON DESIGN LEGACY: A PERSONAL VIEW

Lena Larsson

An early visit

I first visited Sundborn and Lilla Hyttnäs as a teenager in the 1930s. The place was run down, and the Larssons were dead. Carl Larsson's gloomy autobiography *Jag* (Myself) had just been published. No refurbishment for visitors had begun. I felt a special atmosphere in these quiet, ghostly rooms. I had worked as an apprentice cabinetmaker, and was to become an interior designer by profession. Everything there seemed inviting. The little, white bridge over the glittering water, the friendly entrance.

I had attended a mixed school with Carl Larsson's pictures on the walls. Our first headmistress, Anna Whitlock, moved in Ellen Key's circle, and had visited the Larssons at Lilla Hyttnäs. The rooms were well known to me, as were the welcoming colours and the amusing mottoes above doorways and on cupboards. The flowerpots were empty, but something was still sprouting. The plant-stand on the landing was in a pure, modernist style, but the interiors were a striking contrast to the pure, white modernist rooms which I had seen at the Stockholm Exhibition of 1930. But the contrasts strengthened one another. I became particularly aware of this some years later, when I studied under Carl Malmsten, a typically Swedish cabinetmaker and prophet of craft who admired Carl Larsson's feeling for the home.

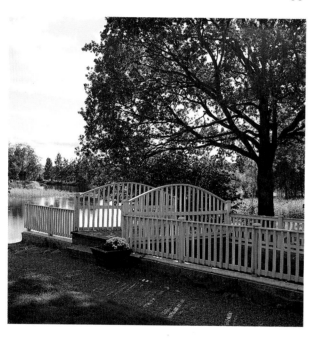

250. *The bridge over the boat dock at Lilla Hyttnäs.*

Larsson and Malmsten

In my book *Heminredning* (Interior Decoration), written with Elias Svedberg and first published in 1947, I compared Carl Larsson's *The Lazing Corner* (fig. 133) with Malmsten's *Living Room* of 1944:

... this is not an ultra-modern interior that you see, but so charming and friendly in all its simplicity. It seems so natural to sit down on the sofa with its robust, blue and white striped cover, which suggests a finer cover underneath. Look at the striped, home-woven rag-rug, at the table with the pipe and reading matter within reach, and the graceful potted plant on the panelled wall. The window needs no curtains – you must admit that it would spoil the whole composition of the wall more than the ivy, which allows nature outside to continue into the room ...

And so to the more recent Malmsten room, with space for everyday life and the whole family around the round table, room for paperwork at the bureau, and a comfortable place for sewing. Notice how the panelling of the cupboard doors is profiled to give the doors a more lively surface, and how the colours complement each other.[1] (fig. 251)

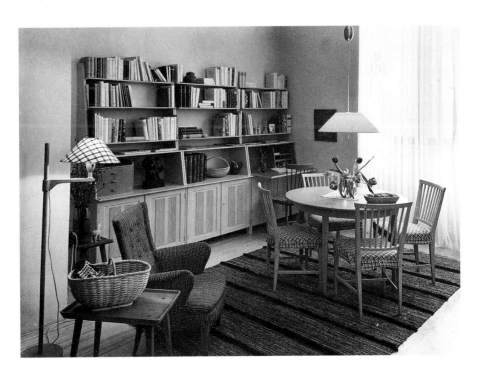

251. Interior with furniture by Carl Malmsten, shown in an exhibition at the National Museum, Stockholm, 1944.
The designs and details of Malmsten's furniture are often based on the Swedish peasant tradition. The furniture range Vardags (Everyday) seen here was designed in the 1940s for Kooperativa Förbundet (The Swedish Co-operative Wholesale Society). The modular storage system was a prototype for many Swedish postwar designs; the chairs are still in production. Photograph by Arne Wahlberg.

Certainly, there are obvious links in the feeling for the home and the appreciation of space, despite the rooms being separated by fifty years. Both rooms have a traditional, Swedish origin in their evocation of the Gustavian style with sparse furnishing, a simple, pale colour range, and furniture with an obvious craft character.

In 1907 the nineteen-year-old Carl Malmsten got hold of a Carl Larsson book for the first time. Malmsten was unhappy at his ordinary school, and wanted to devote himself to creative work. He became a furniture craftsman and designer. In the 1910s and 1920s he made both grand furniture for the new Stockholm Town Hall and simple, now classic, everyday furniture, which is still in production, much of it mass-produced.

Malmsten handed on the Larsson design legacy in simple, everyday, family furniture, traditionally constructed and made to stand up to wear and being moved around. But while the Larssons constantly furnished their own growing home, and had good craftsmen within easy reach, Malmsten worked for a market with increasingly high standards in the home.

Carl Malmsten also had a large family. This was one of the reasons that he began to use pine, with a slightly heavy construction and a beautiful stained finish. The furniture was hard-wearing with strong forms. But Malmsten also worked in fine woods, with both inlaid work and sculptural elements as a means of expression. He was a patient designer.

In Carl Larsson's home, on the other hand, the furniture multiplied in an improvised fashion. It is almost as if Carl and Karin used to order a piece of furniture – a stool or a table – in the morning for delivery that evening. The home contained both inherited furniture in Gustavian and Biedermeier styles as well as new, unpretentious, slatted furniture (an early, more complex version of today's craft-shop products, which are often made of whitewood and painted at home by hand). The Larssons moved their furniture all over the house – the slatted, red chairs from the dining-room were often taken outside.

Carl Malmsten worked as an artistic furniture designer, with a self-assured, personal idiom, and a strong feeling for materials and tradition. He took immense care in the creation of a room. A chair with an armrest and a chair without were two quite different pieces of furniture, even though a common design tradition was constantly evident. He was determined not to improvise, his furniture had substance and left its mark.

For all their differences (and similarities) both Larsson and Malmsten have greatly influenced our view of everyday furniture.

Attention has increasingly been drawn to Karin Larsson's influence on the character of the rooms at Lilla Hyttnäs. It was surely she who conceived all the details of space, children and flowers, while Carl recorded them in his colourful, light-filled painting. The rooms he depicted nearly always radiate harmony and idyll – even if the subject is a sickbed. He revelled in the wonder of a sunny atmosphere and a sense of growth. Sometimes a potted plant pushes aside a child's round face, but only to strengthen the connection between growing things. He constantly portrayed his family, relatives, friends and craftsmen – often including children, and seldom a worn face among the adults.

Return to Sundborn

Around 1960 I returned to Lilla Hyttnäs to write a feature for a then popular magazine, *Allt i hemmet* (Everything in the Home), and was able to re-experience the whole rich environment. I now had my own family. I made notes and drawings of such child-friendly details as the clothes hooks in every corner, a drying arrangement for mittens, the renewable lampshades, the books placed high.

Carl Larsson's ability to capture the moment provides constant nourishment for the visual sense. This is fortunate, as the house itself is fairly muddled. Despite the large number of children, there was no nursery. Suzanne had her own room as an adolescent. She is portrayed standing on a chair in the room, painting a beautiful frieze.

Everything had to have several functions. The drawing-room window with its plants was both a place for homework and a chess corner. The slatted, red dining-room chairs seem to have moved around more than any other items of furniture, even putting in an appearance in the studio, when Karin was shelling peas. This was extremely unconventional at a time when furniture was generally arranged in fixed groups.

The Larssons lived at Sundborn fairly comfortably, enclosed in their own lifestyle. If a new room was needed, it was just built on. But Carl certainly knew all about overcrowding and rotting rooms packed with mattresses, where you could catch rats with your bare hands.[2] The poverty of his own childhood marked him for ever. He did not want to live like that with his family: '... I hear myself recounting this with awful surprise. I who now insist on sleeping in a grand bed in the middle of the room, alone in my bedroom!'³ This white-painted bed, which dominated the bedroom, was also a modern miracle of comfort, with books and glasses within easy reach. It had a bench for dressing, and still provided eye contact with his wife and children through Karin's beautiful 'Rose of Love' portière.

Carl Larsson was often capable of turning a troubled moment into something creative at great speed. His picture *In the Punishment Corner*, according to him the first of his series in *Ett hem* (A Home) (fig. 134), is a case in point: Pontus 'had been cheeky at the dinner table'; he was sent to the drawing-room, where he sits dejected on one of the cross-backed, white chairs. And Carl Larsson comments: 'Blessed was the moment when I had to go there to fetch my pipe tobacco!'⁴ He also fetched his pencil.

Another example is the picture of Carl Larsson, wielding his paintbrush while lifting one of his daughters onto his shoulders. Naturally, he is standing in front of a mirror. His interiors reflect the movements in the room at the very moment at which they are happening. This feeling for the quickly captured impression is also found in many of his portraits of adults, especially those of Karin.

Few Swedes were as fortunate as the Larssons during the early years of the twentieth century, when housing in Sweden was the second most overcrowded in the West, after Finland. The crisis intensified after the First World War, when urbanization received a new impetus and unemployment was severe. The problems were even more pronounced during the Second World War, when there was a total freeze on housing construction. Carl Larsson's book *Das Haus in der Sonne* (1909) must have seemed almost like a fairy tale during the First World War. It was published in enormous editions, and is said to have comforted the soldiers in the trenches.

Sweden's slow industrialization

During and after the Second World War, when women in Sweden increasingly began to enter the labour market, Carl Larsson's pictures, with their wealth of patterns, were rediscovered and stimulated a reawakening of textile traditions. Many women were still attracted to traditional things and took part in the regeneration. The handicraft tradition was now taken over by the textile industry. This was merely a continuation of the 'golden age' of textiles, which the Larssons had discovered when they moved to Sundborn shortly before the turn of the century.

Craft production and small-scale industrial production were found throughout Sweden well into the 1940s and 1950s. Besides local cabinetmakers, decorators and smiths, there were glassworks in Småland, textile artists in Västergötland and people producing handicrafts and woodwork in Dalarna. The furniture and textile industries in particular continued to build on the simple styles of the eighteenth and nineteenth centuries. A cottage industry could develop into a small industry, with local people taking part in production; most of the goods were sold at markets all over the country.

Lilla Hyttnäs contained no industrially made furniture of the period: no bentwood or spindle-backed chairs, no narrow sofa beds, none of that early mass-produced furniture which Carl Larsson's friend and enemy August Strindberg described as dark and poorly manufactured. Contact with local craftsmen provided the Larsson home with ordinary, basic furniture, which was then painted in bright, cheerful colours.

When I went into business in the 1940s, I was often asked where one could buy 'Carl Larsson furniture'; the answer was that you had to make it yourself. In 1944 Carl Malmsten published a whole set of drawings for general use. The state loan for setting up a home and the accompanying brochure, first published in 1944, were of great importance as models, despite the slightly moralizing, thrifty tone. Åke H. Huldt, then director of Svenska Slöjdföreningen (The Swedish Society of Crafts and Design), presented beautiful pictures of interiors clearly in the spirit of Carl Larsson. This was particularly evident in the second edition of 1948, in which old and new were blended: the new, light birch and elmwood furniture is juxtaposed with light net curtains and the hard-wearing rag-rug; there are potted plants on the window-sills, and the kitchen utensils and china are almost the same as those in Sundborn.[5] (figs 252, 253)

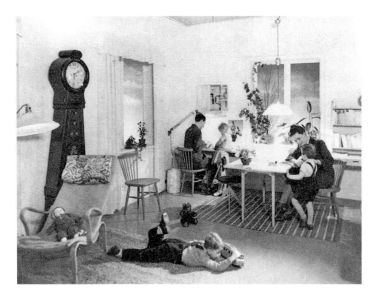

252. Illustration of an ideal room from a brochure published by Svenska Slöjdföreningen *(The Swedish Society of Crafts and Design) and* Sveriges Riksbank *(National Bank of Sweden) in 1948. Such home-loan brochures of the 1940s often showed the whole family sitting together by lamplight, in an interior with an unmistakable Carl Larsson atmosphere. Photograph by Arne Wahlberg*

253. Lena Larsson. The allrum *(multi-purpose living-room) for 'H55', Svenska Slöjdföreningen's exhibition at Helsingborg in 1955. Watercolour by Lena Larsson, 1991.*
The spacious living-room at the H55 exhibition had room for a family with three children to play and spend time together. The example of the multi-function rooms at Lilla Hyttnäs played a large role in developing such ideas. Most of the furniture in the room was ordinary and mass-produced; the post in the centre was intended for coats and often used for children to climb on.

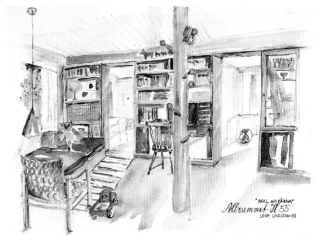

Inspiration for a whole

Carl Larsson furniture was never on sale. It was the rich atmosphere, the mood of the rooms, which was copied from his pictures with their details of everyday life: a stool that has been left behind, a piece of knitting, a tankard, the little white cat licking its paw by the stove. It is surprising that Karin tolerated such an impractical kitchen, with its iron range and water-butt (she did have plenty of help, however); not until the 1940s did the view of both motherhood and housework change radically. Karin's ingenious solutions to domestic problems recur in many of Carl's pictures. Imagine how often a cushion fell to the floor in a family with so many children! Karin did something about it – she made long tapes to tie around the chair leg, as can be seen on the leather dining-room seat cushions.

The Larsson design legacy

The Larsson lifestyle has become part of the Swedish heritage, particularly as regards family life. It foreshadowed a relaxed lifestyle, indoors and outdoors, a novelty at that time. Karin's textiles have given us a new approach to handicraft and needlework. A few years ago, a whole book of aprons and children's clothes from Sundborn was published.[6]

Nearly all Swedes go through a Carl Larsson phase, decorating their homes in red and green, with blue and white striped covers slightly askew, pink geraniums and open doors. Carl Larsson's active, colourful interiors also inspired illustrators of children's books, notably Elsa Beskow as well as such later writers as Astrid Lindgren (the Pippi Longstocking books), Stig Lindberg and Lennart Hellsing. In the Linnea series, Lena Andersson and Christina Björk have created a modern Carl Larsson child, who loves flowers and greenery and is dressed in Karin's children's apron (fig. 254).

Designers and architects have tended to adopt and develop Carl Larsson's furniture and colours in a rather limited way, resulting in a personal blend of style and craftsmanship. Instead, homemakers among the middle classes have tried to re-create his use of colour and style of furniture; their summer cottages often include a narrow glass veranda under a sloping roof.

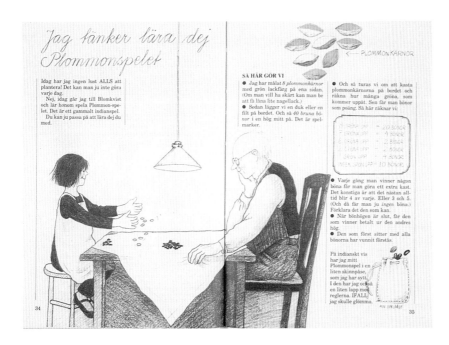

254. *Illustration by Lena Andersson to Christina Björk's* Linnea planterar *(Linnea Plants), 1978.*
The Larsson design legacy recurs in many different fields of Swedish culture. The practical and easy-care clothes of the Larsson children, the apron and sunhat, reappear in one of the popular Linnea books.

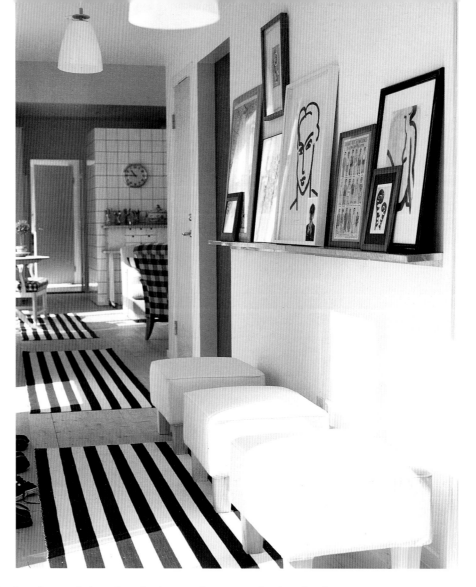

255. *A light IKEA interior with blue and white striped rep-woven carpets inspired by the drawing-room at the Larsson house.*

Several of today's advanced interior designers have sought inspiration in Lilla Hyttnäs. Clear Larsson references are to be found in the bold work of Thomas Sandell. Wood has found a new master in the architect and interior designer Erik Richter (fig. 256). A pupil of Carl Malmsten, he is nevertheless more influenced by the Larssons: 'It is a home which bears the stamp, unique to itself, of the accidental and the playful, a wonderful conjunction in which one feeds into the other... For me the specific characteristics of the home lie in the circumstances behind Karin and Carl Larsson's way of arranging it, rather than in its outer form or design'[7].

Most contemporary young designers – in Sweden and abroad – need to work with new technology and synthetic materials, economical for a hypermarket. It is interesting to note, however, that the multi-national IKEA has a full-page spread in its catalogue of 1996, which is clearly inspired by Carl Larsson. A little girl stands by a large, wooden table top, surrounded by flowers and plants. The colours are reds and greens. The interior is idyllic and full of unlimited possibilities (fig. 257). The Larssons live on.

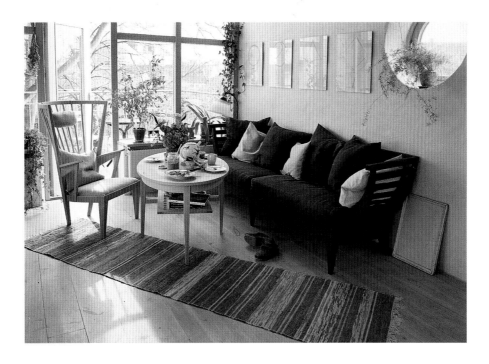

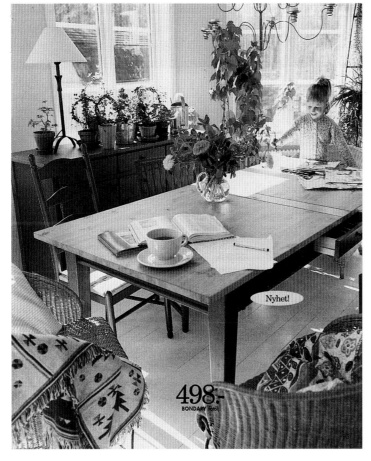

256. *Furniture by Erik Richter, 1994.* *Erik Richter's furniture range* Norrgavel *has given the Swedish furniture market a new look: 'I'm striving towards the Larssons' easy-going, playful and improvised style. Away with lecturing! But it's difficult in the mass-production of furniture.'*

257. *An interior from the Swedish IKEA catalogue of 1996.* *The large, child-friendly table, all the plants and particularly the red and green colour scheme clearly demonstrate that the Larsson tradition is still very much alive today.*

CHRONOLOGY

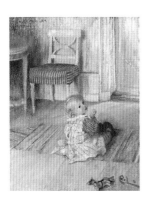

258.[119] Carl Larsson.
Pontus, 1890.
Oil on canvas.
Carl Larsson's children were
models from their earliest
years: here the one-year-old
Pontus sits on the floor
of the drawing-room at Lilla
Hyttnäs.

1853 Carl Olof Larsson born on 28 May at Prästgatan 78, Old Town, Stockholm.

1857 Birth of CL's only sibling, John. The family lives in Grevgatan, in the Ladugård district of Stockholm, thereafter at Grev Magnigränd 7 in a one-roomed flat on the second floor, and at Grev Magnigränd 5.

CL attends the Poor School, later Ladugård Elementary School. Taught under the Lancaster method: appointed a monitor.

1859 Karin Bergöö born on 3 October in Örebro, daughter of Adolf and Hilda Bergöö.

1864 Bergöös move to Hallsberg.

1866 CL enrols in the Principle (preparatory) School of the Academy of Fine Arts on 8 September.

*Cholera epidemic in Stockholm.
Inauguration of the new building of the National Museum, Stockholm.*

1869 CL enrols at the Academy of Fine Arts. Student diploma from the Principle School, one of 12 medallists. Graduates to the Antique School of the Academy proper. Editor of the student newspaper *Pajas* (Clown).

1871 CL at Academy of Fine Arts. Retoucher in the photographic studio of the Roesler brothers.

Illustrator for *Kasper* (Punch). Rents a furnished room near Drottninggatan with A.M. Lindström. Spends summer with his friends Forssell and Wedelin 'in a summer house on the road to Nacka', near Stockholm.

1872 CL in Life School, Academy of Fine Arts. Retoucher in the photographic studio of the Roesler brothers. Illustrator for *Kasper.*
Death of Karl XV; accession of Oscar II.

1873 CL in Academy of Fine Arts. Awarded 25 kronor for life drawing by the Academy. Spends summer at Sickla, outside Stockholm, with Forssell and Vilhelmina Holmgren (by whom he has two children, both of whom die in infancy). Graduates to the Academy's Painting School in the autumn. Karin Bergöö begins school in Stockholm.
Foundation of Nordic Museum, Stockholm.

1874 CL in Academy of Fine Arts. Awarded 150 kronor and commended for *Moses Abandoned by his Mother*. Illustrator for *Kasper* on an annual salary of 2500 kronor.
Foundation of Föreningen Handarbetets Vänner (The Association of Friends of Textile Art).

1875 CL in Academy of Fine Arts. Awarded 150 kronor and commended for *Gustav Vasa Accuses Peder Sunnanväder before the Chapter at Västerås*. Studies etching techniques at Lowenstam's school in Stockholm. Illustrator for *Ny illustrerad tidning* (New Illustrated Magazine) from 19 June. Conscripted.

Adolf Bergöö buys property of Lilla Hyttnäs, Sundborn, in the province of Dalarna, for his widowed mother (d. 1880) and two sisters, Ulla and Maria.

1876 CL in Academy of Fine Arts. Royal medal for *Sten Sture and Queen Kristina* (Ernst Josephson also awarded a medal for the same subject). Illustrator for *Kasper*. Illustrates Hans Christian Andersen's fairy tales. In the autumn paints portrait of Vilhelmina Holmgren.

1877 CL applies unsuccessfully to the Academy for a travelling scholarship. Spring, Vilhelmina Holmgren dies in childbirth with CL's second child. CL travels to Paris on 17 April, studio in rue Capron. Summer in Barbizon. Poverty and suicidal thoughts in the autumn. Paints *Clair obscur*. Karin Bergöö begins in Academy of Fine Arts (without going through the Principle School).

1878 CL passes winter of starvation in Paris. Summer in Barbizon, where he paints Carl Skånberg's portrait, shown at the Paris Salon. Begins 'Giant Painting'; paints *Amor Mercurius*. Applies for the Dahlgren scholarship (awarded to Josephson). Awarded scholarship for 1000 kronor by the Academy. Returns to Sweden. Illustrations in *Ny illustrerad tidning*. Commissioned to illustrate Z. Topelius's *Fältskärns berättelser* (Tales of an Army Doctor).

1879 CL lives at the Brunkeberg Hotel, then with a poor family in Roslagstorg. Friendly with Strindberg. Illustrator for *Ny illustrerad tidning*. Commissioned to paint ceiling and lunettes at the Bolinder mansion, Blasieholmshamnen, Stockholm. Works on *The Suicide's Journey to Hell*. Member of the Student Society of the Academy of Fine Arts, board member and editor of the Society's newspaper, *Palettskrap*. First meets Karin Bergöö at a ball.

1880 CL applies, again unsuccessfully, for the Dahlgren scholarship (awarded to Axel Kulle). Decorative commission at the Bolinder mansion completed. Travels to Paris on 25 November with Josephson. Lives at 53 rue Lepic. Paints *Medieval Jesters*. Illustrator for *Ny illustrerad tidning*.

1881 CL rejected at the Paris Salon. Returns to Sweden on 27 May. Spends summer with Strindberg on island of Kymmendö. Starts illustrating Strindberg's *Svenska folket* (The Swedish People). Returns to Paris: avenue des Tilleuls. Studies at Bibliothèque Nationale. Plans journey to the Orient. Karin Bergöö finishes at Academy of Fine Arts; in April travels to Paris via Dresden, Prague, Vienna, Graz, Venice, Verona and Munich.

1882 CL paints *At the Court Painter's* , which is rejected by the Paris Salon. Ill and suicidal. Moves to Grez-sur-Loing; paints his first intimate *plein-air* pictures. CL and Karin Bergöö engaged in Grez in September. Karin goes to Paris to study in Colarossi's studio.

1883 CL in Grez, Karin Bergöö to Stockholm. Third medal at the Paris Salon for the Grez watercolours; Fürstenberg buys. CL and Karin Bergöö married on 12 June in Stockholm, then back to Grez. In the autumn to Paris: Wilhelm von Gegerfelt's studio at 14 rue Fromentin. CL does watercolours and illustrations for Anna Maria Lenngren's *Samlade skaldeförsök* (Collected Attempts at Poetry). National Museum in Stockholm buys two watercolours. Articles on Carl Larsson by Strindberg in *Svea* and by Nordensvan in *Nornan*.

1884 French State purchases *The Pond* at the Paris Salon. CL finishes illustrations for Anna Maria Lenngren's poems and for *Fältskärns berättelser*. Declines associate membership of the Swedish Academy of Fine Arts. To Grez in March. Daughter Suzanne born there on 11 August.
Strindberg prosecuted for blasphemy for his book 'Giftas' (Marriage), but acquitted.

1885 Family in Grez. CL visits London, where he paints a portrait of Mauritz Lindström and meets Anders Zorn for the first time. Exhibits *Little Suzanne* (fig. 18) at the Paris Salon. Joins the Opponents, a group of 84 Swedish artists calling for the reform of the Academy. To Stockholm in May for the Opponents' exhibition *From the Banks of the Seine* (fig. 20). *The Opponents' Exhibition* on 15 September. November-December CL at Fürstenberg's in Gothenburg. Larssons live in Åsögatan, in the Södermalm district of Stockholm (having stayed briefly with the Bergöös at Linnégatan 5).

Summer, CL travels to Dalarna with Adolf Bergöö; first visit to Sundborn and Lilla Hyttnäs. Adolf Bergöö offers to buy the Larssons another property in Sundborn, but CL refuses. Larssons visit Sundborn as a family in September.

1886 Family at Åsögatan, Stockholm. *The Plein-air Painter* exhibited at the Paris Salon. CL to Paris with Josephson in March. Studies monumental painting in Paris and Italy; visits Italy with Klas Fåhraeus. Returns to Stockholm in May. August, CL to Gothenburg for inauguration of Valand Art Gallery. Teaches at Valand School of Art. The Opponents' demands of the Academy not met; formation of Konstnärsförbundet (Artists' Union) on 18 August. CL a board member of the Stockholm section. First exhibition by Konstnärsförbundet at Blanch's in October. CL makes first etching since attempts in 1875. KL and Suzanne in Stockholm and Gothenburg.

1887 CL to Paris with Fürstenberg. Spring in Grez. Summer at Varberg, near Gothenburg. Paints *The Last Rays of Sunshine*. Takes part in Exposition Internationale at Galerie Georges Petit, 'the greatest honour I could ever have imagined'. Autumn, organizes exhibition by Konstnärsförbundet in Gothenburg, with Callmander. Eldest son Ulf born on 4 April. KL and children in Gothenburg and Varberg.

1888 April CL and KL (without children) to Paris (Boulevard Arago) and (autumn) to Grez: CL to paint Fürstenberg's triptych. Paints proposals for frescoes at the National Museum, Stockholm. Declines the Egron Lundgren medal. Son Pontus born in Paris on 26 October.

Death of Karin's aunt Ulla; her sister Maria leaves Lilla Hyttnäs. In October the property given to the Larssons by Adolf Bergöö.

1889 CL awarded second prize (800 kronor) for three proposals for the National Museum frescoes on 12 January. Larssons return to Sweden in June: CL paints furniture and walls in Bergöös' new house at Hallsberg. CL to Marstrand and Varberg on the west coast in July. The finished triptych shown at the Exposition Universelle in Paris: first-class medal. CL returns to Paris and Grez in the autumn, visits Amsterdam: letter to Viktor Rydberg about art education and craft. Returns to Sweden in December.

From July family at Lilla Hyttnäs. CL stays barely a month. Landing (later Karin's writing-room) used as a small studio. CL returns for Christmas.
Formation of Social Democratic Party

1890 Family at Lilla Hyttnäs (CL also in Stockholm and Gothenburg). February, Larssons visit Bingsjö; in May CL and KL visit Sandhamn for CL to make studies for Sehlstedt's ballads. CL commissioned in the new year to paint the murals at the New Elementary Grammar School for Girls in Gothenburg. New competition for National Museum frescoes announced on 14 June. Member of Svenska Konstnärernas Förening (Society of Swedish Artists).

Adolf Bergöö dies on 13 May: Karin's small legacy helps developments at Lilla Hyttnäs. Dining-room redecorated, first job at Lilla Hyttnäs, inaugurated January. Summer, new studio built and exterior of cottage decorated. Porch added.

1891 January, Larssons move to Stora Glasbruksgatan 15, Stockholm; CL sketches cartoons for National Museum competition, which win first prize. Completes murals at the school in Gothenburg. Autumn, family moves to Gothenburg (live at Fürstenberg's summer house): CL teaches at Valand School of Art, Gothenburg, 1891-2 (and 1892-3). CL leaves Konstnärsförbundet and Konstnärsföreningen on 16 December. Daughter Lisbeth born on 18 February.

Summer at Lilla Hyttnäs. CL given 18th-century pattern book: earliest possible date for work on the drawing-room. Dated decoration on dining-room door and cupboard.
Opening of open-air museum Skansen in Stockholm.

1892 Larssons in Gothenburg. CL travels with Fürstenberg in the spring to Venice via Germany, and then to Paris. Summer, paints *De mina* (My Loved Ones). CL teaches at Valand School of Art, Gothenburg.

Summer at Lilla Hyttnäs. Probable date for work on drawing-room.

1893 CL gives up Valand: spring in Marstrand. Completes illustrations for Sehlstedt's songs. Paints *Sunflowers* and *Mother*, the first pictures to show new Sundborn interiors (the drawing-room). Autumn in Stockholm in Pauli's studio. Daughter Brita born on 10 May in Marstrand.

Summer at Lilla Hyttnäs. Construction of Carl's bedroom, and probably, of Karin's. Dated decoration of the sleeping-quarters in the upper floor of the *härbre* (storehouse). Wood store at the north end of the cottage converted to a summer bedroom for children.

1894 Family move to another flat in Stora Glasbruksgatan 15, Stockholm, this time with two studios. The government approves Carl Larsson's plan for decorating the lower stairwell at the National Museum on 2 February: CL starts work on cartoons. CL and KL travel to Germany, Rome and Paris in the spring: CL to study fresco techniques. August, CL travels in Sweden to make sketches for illustrations to Viktor Rydberg's novel *Singoalla*. CL's first one-man exhibition at Blanch's in November. According to CL, start of the *Ett hem* series of watercolours to keep him occupied during the wet summer. Son Matts born on 24 November.

Summer at Lilla Hyttnäs. Decoration in Karin's bedroom dated August. Fence set up along the river.

Opening of the northern main-line railway from Stockholm to Boden.

1895 Stockholm. CL elected to Statens Inköpsnämnd (National Purchasing Committee), chairman of Konstnärsklubben (Artists' Club). Starts working on cartoons for the National Museum frescoes in May (finished January 1896). Autumn, studies fresco techniques under Pauli in Gothenburg. Christmas, publication of *De mina*. Twelve views of Sundborn, probably including items from the *Ett hem* series, shown in Philadelphia, Chicago, St Louis and Cincinnati. Son Matts dies on 19 January.

Summer at Lilla Hyttnäs.

Nobel prize instituted.

1896 Stockholm. Autumn, completion of National Museum frescoes. CL studies etching under Axel Tallberg. Develops an eye complaint, which casts a shadow over the rest of his life. Daughter Kersti born on 31 March 1896.

Summer and Christmas at Lilla Hyttnäs. Wash-house built. Glazing on studio roof replaced by tiles.

1897 January-April, KL seriously ill with pneumonia at Lilla Hyttnäs; returns to family in Stockholm in April, back to Sundborn in May. CL decorates the foyer of the newly built Opera House in Stockholm with a painted ceiling and a number of lunettes (completed in December). Exhibition of *De mina* (My Loved Ones) and 20 of the *Ett hem* watercolours under the title 'A Home in Dalarna' at the Art and Industry Exhibition in Stockholm. Publication in *Idun* of Ellen Key's 'Skönhet i hemmen' (Beauty in the Home), mentioning the watercolours.

Summer at Lilla Hyttnäs. In March, with money from National Museum frescoes, CL buys the farm Spadarvet and the smallholding Kartbacken (for his parents), both in Sundborn. KL embroiders dining-room tablecloth.

1898 Stockholm. CL completes the Opera House ceiling. Turns down professorship at the Academy of Fine Arts. Starts drawing for the mural at Norra Latin School, Stockholm (completed 1901). Starts cartoon for a tapestry after *Crayfishing* (*Ett hem* series). The *Ett hem* series shown in Berlin.

Summer and Christmas at Lilla Hyttnäs. Mangling-house built next to wash-house. *Härbre* moved to its present location.

1899 Stockholm. January, KL ill with influenza in Stockholm (*Convalescence*, fig. 33). CL makes working drawings for tapestry. CL writes, and draws vignettes, for *Ett hem*, published at Christmas. Publication of Ellen Key's *Skönhet för alla* (Beauty for Everyone) incorporating a revised version of 'Skönhet i hemmen' (1897).

Summer and Christmas at Lilla Hyttnäs. New building containing a large studio added to the cottage: inaugurated Christmas Eve. The old studio converted to a workshop for the family: part of the ceiling lowered and a platform with column built by the end window.

Föreningen för Svensk Hemslöjd (The Swedish Handicraft Association) founded.

1900 CL first-class medal at Exposition Universelle in Paris for Norra Latin cartoon. Self-portrait (fig. 1). The *Ett hem* series bought by the National Museum. Son Esbjörn (last child) born on 5 May. Joint Christening of all the children in the studio.

Summer at Lilla Hyttnäs. Dated portrait of Brita on the drawing-room door.

1901 March family leaves Stockholm and finally settles at Lilla Hyttnäs. CL completes the Norra Latin School mural, Stockholm. Georg Nordensvan's first book about Carl Larsson published.

South wing built between studio and old house at Lilla Hyttnäs; contains Old Room, Suzanne's room, boys' room (converted to bathroom in 1902), maids' room, larder and kitchen corridor. Back door made on east facade and scullery added to west. The little studio converted to a library. New chairs made for dining-room. 1901-3 railings and new platform in drawing-room and wall panelling scheme simplified. KL designs the 'Sundborn' blanket.

General male conscription introduced. First awards of the Nobel Prize. First electric trams in Stockholm.

1902 Publication of *Larssons*.

Gallery built in new studio at Lilla Hyttnäs. Bathroom installed.

1903 CL's 50th birthday. Mural *Outdoors Blows the Summer Wind* at the Latin Grammar School in Gothenburg. CL accepts the Egron Lundgren medal from the Academy of Fine Arts.

New sofa created in dining-room at Lilla Hyttnäs. KL begins weaving of 'Four Elements' tapestry. 'Lower Dovecote' built over studio.

1904 CL makes new sketch for *Gustav Vasa's Triumphal Entry into Stockholm*, shown in National Museum. Begins work on Spadarvet book.

With completion of power station close to Lilla Hyttnäs, entrance gate is resited and rebuilt, shore line straightened and bridge and boat dock built. The upper floor of the *härbre* is raised. The south front of the cottage is planked over and the workshop roof raised, allowing sleeping-quarters under it. By this date the painted

glass in the dining-room modified, a new cupboard built and the 'sin-cupboard' built in the old kitchen doorway.

1905 CL commissioned to paint ceiling at the new Dramatic Theatre in Stockholm. CL goes to Berlin, Paris and London. In exhibition at the New Gallery, London. Exhibition in Venice with Anders Zorn and Bruno Liljefors. Son Ulf dies on 14 April.

Before 1905 a passage to new studio built outside scullery, forming a balcony outside the Old Room. Between 1905 and 1909 the new studio south window enlarged. KL makes 'Sunflower' cushion.

Union of Sweden and Norway (since 1814) dissolved.

1906 CL paints portrait of Oscar Levertin. Self-portrait *Self-examination* (fig. 41). September, one-man exhibition at Konstnärshuset, Stockholm. The National Museum of Fine Arts accepts the new sketch for *Gustav Vasa's Triumphal Entry*. Publication of *Spadarvet*.

At Lilla Hyttnäs portrait of Esbjörn added to dining-room door. Probable date of changes to Karl's bed and addition of built-in bed to Karin's room. KL begins library tablecloth (completed 1909). KL designs rocking-chair.

1907 CL completes the Royal Dramatic Theatre ceiling *The Birth of Drama*. Buys a house in Falun for the children while at school and to live in the winter. *Svenska kvinnan genom seklen* (Swedish Womanhood through the Centuries) published.

Death of Oskar II; succeeded by Gustaf V.

1908 Strindberg attacks CL and KL in *En ny blå bok* (A New Blue Book), published in May. CL begins to think of *Sacrifice at the Winter Solstice*. Paints 14 watercolours for *Åt solsidan* (On the Sunny Side).

1909 CL paints 14 watercolours for *Åt solsidan*. The finished watercolours shown in Munich. CL travels to Germany. *Das Haus in der Sonne* published in Germany.

Universal Exhibition of Craft and Industrial Art in Stockholm. General strike; workers retreat without gains. Universal male suffrage. Selma Lagerlöf awarded Nobel Prize for Literature. Artists trained under Matisse rejected in Stockholm.

1910 CL buys a cottage on the Larsson family farm Lövhulta in Södermanland. *Åt solsidan* published.

At Lilla Hyttnäs ceiling added to most of the rest of the studio to create another bedroom (upper dovecote), the window made vertical to light it. Studio screen wall made permanent and the fireplace enlarged. KL weaves 'Pegasus' tapestry, designed by CL and KL.

1911 CL's second sketch for *Sacrifice at the Winter Solstice* shown at the National Museum in February. CL takes part in an exhibition in Rome and wins first prize, and in exhibitions in Brighton and Liverpool. The Uffizi Gallery buys *Self-examination* (1906, fig. 41). CL attacks modernism in the first issue of *Konst* (Art).

1912 January, KL visits her sister Stina in Wimbledon (a Christmas present from CL). CL visits Berlin and Dresden. Exhibitions in Helsinki and Åbo, Finland. Awarded the Great Gold Medal in Berlin.

A room from a cottage at Lilla Aspeboda added to the studio at Lilla Hyttnäs.

1913 CL's 60th birthday marked by a special issue of *Idun*. Axel Romdahl's book on Carl Larsson as an etcher published. CL travels to France and Germany. New sketch for *Sacrifice at the Winter Solstice* exhibited at the National Museum in November. The book *Andras barn* (Other People's Children) published for Christmas.

Decision to institute a general state retirement pension.

1914 CL designs poster for the Farmers' Protest March. National Museum committee agrees that CL should complete the decoration of the stairwell, but with a subject other than *Sacrifice at the Winter Solstice*.

Farmers' Protest. In February almost 30,000 farmers from the whole country demonstrate in Stockholm for stronger national defences. The king agrees with their demands.

1915 New sketch for *Sacrifice at the Winter Solstice* exhibited in June. The large oil painting hung for approval at the National Museum.

1916 Inaugural exhibition by Carl Larsson, Bruno Liljefors and Anders Zorn at Liljevalch's Art Gallery, Stockholm. Sacrifice at the Winter Solstice shown at Liljevalch's; National Museum refuses not only to purchase the painting but Zorn's offer to donate it. Autumn, exhibition in Copenhagen.

At Lilla Hyttnäs a building is put north of the house incorporating a stable, a garage and a storehouse.

1917 *The Home Exhibition at Liljevalch's Exhibition Hall, Stockholm.*

1918 CL paints a portrait of Erik Axel Karlfeldt. Christmas, CL given KL's 'First World War' cushion, her last work for him.

1919 CL completes the autobiography *Jag* (Myself), two days before his death on 22 January.

1920 CL memorial exhibition at Liljevalch's.

Social Democrats in government for the first time. 1921: universal female suffrage introduced. 1923: opening of Stockholm Town Hall, designed by Ragnar Östberg.

1928 KL dies on 17 February.

1931 Publication of *Jag*.

1936 Attempts to obtain Lilla Hyttnäs for the state, using lottery money; these eventually break down.

1937 Lilla Hyttnäs open to the public on a regular basis.

1943 Formation of the Carl Larsson Family Association to own and run Lilla Hyttnäs.

1953 CL memorial exhibition at Liljevalch's.

1982 New York exhibition

1992 CL exhibition at National Museum, Stockholm, and Museum of Art, Gothenburg.

SELECT BIBLIOGRAPHY
Compiled by Ann J. Topjon, edited by Michael Snodin.

The standard published bibliography on Carl Larsson is that in the important catalogue of the exhibition entitled *Carl Larsson* held at Stockholm and Gothenburg in 1992, which remains the principal overview of his life and art; it also includes sections on the house at Lilla Hyttnäs. The present bibliography, in which works in Swedish predominate, has been derived from that source, with the addition of material published since 1992, further works on Karin Larsson and Lilla Hyttnäs and a fuller list of Carl Larsson's illustrated work. Unless otherwise stated, entries are in the language of the country of publication.

CARL LARSSON: BIOGRAPHICAL

The standard biography is Nordensvan (1920–1), written without the benefit of the posthumously published autobiography, *Jag* (1931 etc.). Alfons (1952) is based on the correspondence. The essays in *Idun* (1913) are key evidence of the reaction to Larsson among his contemporaries.

Alfons, Harriet and Sven: *Carl Larsson. Skildrad av honom själv i text och bilder* [Carl Larsson. Described by himself in text and pictures], Stockholm, 1952. Abridged, 1977. From 1977 also published in Norway, Finland and Germany.

Idun, no. 21, 25 May 1913. Special Carl Larsson issue, including Laurin, Carl. G.: 'Carl Larsson som målare' [CL as a painter], p. 327; Romdahl, Axel L.: 'Carl Larsson som etsare' [etcher], p. 328; Brunius, August: 'Carl Larsson som hembyggare' [homebuilder], p. 330; Nordensvan, Georg: 'Carl Larsson som skrifvare' [writer], p. 331; 'Ett bref från fru Karin Larsson' [a letter from Karin Larsson], p. 338; Thorman, Elisabeth: 'Carl Larsson som textilkonstnär' [CL as a textile artist], p. 338; Nordling, Johan: 'Hos Carl Larsson i Sundborn' [At home with Carl Larsson in Sundborn], pp. 339-43; Wägner, Elin: 'Till fru Karin Larsson', p. 344; Laurin, Thorsten: 'Carl Larssons bokägaremärken' [CL's bookplates] and 'Carl Larsson inför utlandet' [CL and abroad], both p. 345; Pauli, Georg: 'Carl Larsson i Grèz', pp. 346-7; Jonason, Aron: 'Skolhushållet i Falun', 'Carl Larsson som skämtecknare och gratulant' [CL as a cartoonist and congratulant] and 'Carl Larsson i Göteborg', pp. 348-50.

Larsson, Carl: *Jag* [Myself], Stockholm, 1931. Originally serialized in *Vecko-Journalen*, 1930. Second edition, Stockholm, 1953. Reissued in Sweden, 1969, 1987, 1992. From 1985 also published in Germany, Denmark, Norway, Finland and the United States. [John Z. Lofgren, ed., Iowa City, 1992].

Nordensvan, Georg: *Carl Larsson. En studie*, Stockholm, 1901. Reissued, 1906 and 1908.

Nordensvan, Georg: *Carl Larsson*, 2 vols, Stockholm, 1920-1.

Strindberg, August: 'Carl Larsson. Ett svenskt porträtt med fransk bakgrund', *Svea*, no.40, 1884, pp. 130-45. Reissued as a monograph, Gothenburg, 1971; reprinted, 1980.

Svenskt konstnärs lexikon, Malmö, 1957, vol. III, pp. 465-472.

CARL LARSSON: WORK

The fullest accounts of Carl Larsson's artistic work are Kruse (1906) and the catalogues, both entitled *Carl Larsson*, of the exhibitions held in Stockholm and Gothenburg (1992) and New York (1982). The study by Cavalli-Björkman and Lindwall (1982) is also important. The following are standard works for specific areas: Cavalli-Björkman (1987, portraits), Hjert (1983, prints), Lengefeld (1993, influence abroad, especially in Germany), Svensson (1941, book illustration; see also Lengefeld 1994).

Ahtola-Moorhouse, Leena, Edam, Carl Tomas and Schreiber, Birgitta, eds: *Dreams of a Summer Night. Scandinavian Painting at the Turn of the Century*, London, 1986. Exhibition catalogue, Hayward Gallery, London, 1986.

Cardell, Gunnar: *Carl Larssons målningar i Bergöövåningen* [Carl Larsson's paintings in the Bergöö flat], Hallsberg, 1989.

Carl Larsson. 60 reproduktioner i tontryck efter fotografier af originalen, Lund, 1910 (Små Konstböcker, no. 4).

Carl Larsson. Etsningar, bokillustrationer, Uddevalla, 1976. Preface by Stig Ranström.

Carl Larsson. New York, 1982. Exhibition catalogue, Brooklyn Museum, New York. Also published in England (1983).

Carl Larsson, Stockholm, 1992. Exhibition catalogue, National Museum, Stockholm and Art Museum, Gothenburg. Also published in Germany (1992).

Cary, Elizabeth Luther: *Artists Past and Present*, New York, 1909.

Cavalli-Björkman, Görel and Lindwall, Bo: *Carl Larsson och hans värld*, Stockholm, 1982. Revised edition, 1989. From 1982 also published in Germany, France, the United States, England [*The World of Carl Larsson*, 1983], Italy and Finland.

Cavalli-Björkman, Görel: *Carl Larsson. Porträttmålaren*, Stockholm, 1987.

Gullberg, Elsa: 'Swedish Tapestries', *American Scandinavian Review*, vol. 24, no. 3, September 1936, pp. 233-41.

Haack, Friedrich: *Die Kunst des XIX. Jahrhunderts*, Esslingen, 1918.

Hevesi, Ludwig: *Alt Kunst-Neukunst: Wien, 1894-1909*, Vienna, 1909.

Hjert, Bertil, Gunnel, and Svenolof: *Carl Larsson. Grafiska verk. En komplett katalog*, Uppsala, 1983. In Swedish, English, French and German.

Holmes, Charles, ed.: *Pen, Pencil, and Chalk. A Series of Drawings by Contemporary European Artists*, London, 1911.

Kruse, John: *Carl Larsson som målare, tecknare, och grafiker. En studie* [Carl Larsson as painter, draughtsman and printmaker. A study], Stockholm, 1906. First published in *Die graphischen Künste*, vol. 28, 1905, pp. 53-77.

Larkin, David, ed.: *The Paintings of Carl Larsson*, New York, 1976. Also published in Sweden, England and France (1976).

Lengefeld, Cecilia: *Der Maler des glücklichen Heims. Zur Rezeption Carl Larssons im Wilhelminischen Deutschland*, Heidelberg, 1993.

Lengefeld, Cecilia: 'Stilpluralism och experimentlust: Carl Larssons illustrationer till Friedrich Schillers *Kabale und Liebe* (1892)', *Nordisk tidskrift för bok och biblioteksväsen*, vol. 81, no. 2, 1994, pp. 73-90.

Leonhard, Roland, ed.: *Carl Larsson*, Lahr, 1990.

Lindwall, Bo, ed.: *Carl Larsson och Nationalmuseum*, Stockholm, 1969.

Puvogel, Renate: *Carl Larsson. Aquarelle und Zeichnungen*, Cologne, 1993. English translation published in Germany, 1994.

Romdahl, Alex L.: *Carl Larsson som etsare* [Carl Larsson as etcher], Stockholm, 1913. In Swedish, French and German.

Sahlberg, Evert: 'Bergööska huset. Köpmanssläkten i jugendmiljö' [The Bergöö house. The merchant family in art nouveau surroundings], *Örebrö läns hembygdsförbunds årsbok. Från bergslag och bondebygd*, vol. 21, 1966, pp. 41-55.

Serner, Gertrud: *Carl Larsson i Nationalmuseum*, Stockholm, 1947.

Svensson, Georg: 'Carl Larsson som bokillustratör', *Vintergatan*, 1941, pp. 38-81.

Svensson, Georg: 'Från trästick till fyrfärgsplansch. Carl Larsson som illustratör' [From wood engraving to four-colour plate. Carl Larsson as a book illustrator], *Bokvännen*, vol. 28, no. 3, 1973, pp. 47-66.

Varndoe, Kirk, ed.: *Northern Light. Realism and Symbolism in Scandinavian Painting 1880-1910*, New York, 1982. Exhibition catalogue, Washington, New York, Minneapolis and Gothenburg, 1982-3.

Varnedoe, Kirk: *Northern Light. Nordic Art at the Turn of the Century*, New Haven, 1988.

Wilhelm, Kikue, ed.: *Carl Larsson*, Tokyo, 1985.

Zweigbergk, Eva von: 'Jugend och julkvällen', *Biblis*, 1973, pp. 76-93.

CARL LARSSON: UNPUBLISHED AND PRIMARY SOURCES

Lofgren, John Zameo: *The Illustrations in Ett hem*, Master's thesis, University of Oregon, Eugene, 1972.

Melin, J. Robert: *Familjen Bergöös hem, resultat av ett provinsiellt möte på 1880-talet mellan Carl Larsson-Ferdinand Boberg*, Master's thesis, Art History Institute, Stockholm, 1974.

Correspondence and other manuscripts relating to the Larssons are in Stockholm at the Royal Academy for the Fine Arts, Royal Library, National Museum Archive, Thiel Gallery and Albert Bonniers Förlag. Further collections are held at Gothenburg University Library, Uppsala University Library (family correspondence, transcriptions at Lilla Hyttnäs) and Zorn Museum, Mora. The account book is at Lilla Hyttnäs. Thorsten Laurin's large collection of press and other cuttings dealing with Carl Larsson is at the Art Library of the National Museums, Stockholm. The library at Lilla Hyttnäs contains most of Larsson's published and illustration work as well as numerous magazine articles.

KARIN LARSSON

Andersson, Ingrid: *Karin Larsson. Konstnär och konstnärshustru* [Karin Larsson. Artist and artist's wife], Stockholm, 1986.

Anon.: 'Hos Fru Karin på Spadarvet. Bland gyllene solrosor hos en stor målares maka' [At home with Mrs Karin at Spadarvet. Among golden sunflowers at the home of a great painter's wife], *Vecko-Journalen*, no. 42, 1925, pp. 25-6.

De drogo till Paris. Nordiska konstnärinnor på 1800-talet, Stockholm, 1988.

Frieberg, Axel: *Karin. En bok om Carl Larssons hustru* [Karin. A book about Carl Larssons wife], Stockholm, 1967.

LILLA HYTTNÄS

The chief contemporary accounts are Larsson's own *Ett hem* (1899) and *Åt solsidan* (1910, see below). Other important early descriptions are by Bröchner (1906), Key (1897, 1899), Larsson (1916), Näsström (1937), Pauli (1903), Wåhlin (1900) and the contributors to the Carl Larsson issue of *Idun* (1913, see above). For later analyses of the house see Facos (1996), Granath and Hård af Segerstad (1959), Lengefeld (1996, and 1993 above), Rydin (1992, 1994) and Zweigberk (1968). Bergwall (1977) discusses the books in the library, Larsson (1914) is on the Lilla Aspeboda room. The house is set into its cultural and architectural context by Eriksson (1990), Grandien (1987) and Stavenow-Hidemark (1964, 1971). Of the many articles on art and design of the period that refer to the house, published in Swedish and other magazines since the 1950s, only a few are cited here.

Bergwall, Sten-Ove: 'Carl Larssons bibliotek i Sundborn', *Bokvännen*, no. 3, 1977, pp. 37-47.

Blanche, Thore: 'Hemmets målare' [The home's painter], *Idun*, no. 8, 24 February 1900, pp. 113-14, 116.

Breuer, Robert: 'Häuser, die kunstler sich bauten', *Aren*, no. 6, 1910, pp. 650-6.

Bröchner, Georg: 'Some Northern Painters and their Homes', *The Studio*, vol. 38, 1906, pp. 19-24.

Brunius, August: *Hus och hem. Studier af den svenska villan och villastaden* [House and home. Studies of the Swedish villa and villa district], Stockholm, 1911.

Calloway, Stephen: *Twentieth Century Decoration, 1900-1980*, London and New York, 1988.

Cumming, Elizabeth and Kaplan, Wendy: *The Arts and Crafts Movement*, London, 1991.

Eriksson, Eva: *Den moderna stadens födelse. Svensk arkitektur 1890-1920* [The birth of the modern town. Swedish architecture 1890-1920], Stockholm, 1990.

Facos, Michelle: 'Definitively Swedish: Carl Larsson's Home in Sundborn', *Scandinavian Review*, Autumn 1993, pp. 62-7.

Facos, Michelle: 'The Ideal Swedish Home: Carl Larsson's Lilla Hyttnäs', in Reed, Christopher, ed.: *Not at home: the suppression of domesticity in modern art and architecture*, London, 1996, pp. 81-91.

Forsslund, Karl-Erik: *Sundborn. Med Dalälven från källorna till havet*, part 3, Stockholm, 1931.

Fredriksson, Marianne: 'Ska vi göra som Larssons...' [Shall we do it like the Larssons...], *Allt i hemmet*, no. 12, 1959, pp. 27-9.

Gale, Ian and Bryant, Richard: *Living Museums*, Boston, 1993.

Granath, Karl-Erik and Hård af Segerstad, Ulf: *Carl Larssongården, Sundborn*. Sundborn, 1959. Reissued, 1964, 1969, 1973, 1974, 1979. Also published in Germany (1975) and the United States (1978).

Grandien, Bo: *Rönndruvans glöd. Nygöticistiskt i tanke, konst och miljö under 1800-talet* [The rowanberry's glow. Neo-gothic thinking, art and environments in the nineteenth century], Stockholm, 1987.

Hall, Thomas and Dunér, Katarina, eds: *Svenska hus. Landsbygdens arkitektur-från bondesamhälle till industrialism*, Stockholm, 1995.

Hardy, Hathaway: 'Historic Houses. Carl Larsson's Lilla Hyttnäs', *Architectural Digest*, vol. 40, no. 9, September 1983, pp. 184-92, 200, 202.

Key, Ellen: 'Skönhet i hemmen' [Beauty in homes], *Idun*, no. 50, 1897, p. 4 et seq.

Key, Ellen: *Skönhet för alla* [Beauty for everyone], Uppsala, 1899. Four essays, including an extended version of 'Skönhet i hemmen'. One more edition in 1899. 3rd ed., 1904, extended and changed, partly as a result of visits to Sundborn. Reissued, 1908, 1913, 1939 (22,000 copies in all).

Klein, Barbro and Widbom, Mats, eds: *Swedish Folk Art. All Tradition is Change*, New York and Stockholm, 1994.

Larsson, Carl: 'Nils Bengtsson? Reinkarnationskåseri', *Julstämning*, 1914, unpaginated.

Larsson, Carl: 'Carl Larssons hem i Sundborn skildrat af honom själf', *Svenska hem i ord och bilder*, vol. 8, 1916, pp. 155-65.

Leach, Henry Goddard: 'Sweden. A Nation of Craftsmen', *The Craftsman*, December 1912, pp. 295-305.

Lengefeld, Cecilia: 'Carl Larsson-gården i Willingshausen', *Byggnadskultur*, no. 3, 1991, pp. 46-8.

Lengefeld, Cecilia: 'Carl Larsson: Ett hem i Europa. Scenografi och inredningskonst', *Konst og kultur*, vol. 79, no. 2, 1996, pp. 126-33.

Lind, Th.: 'Carl Larsson. Hjemmets og børnenes maler', *Hver 8 dag*, vol. 13, no. 52, 29 September 1907, pp. 982-4.

Linn, Björn: 'Rationalism tried and retried', *Studio International* (USA), vol. 195, November/December 1982, pp. 47-50.

Lofgren, John Z.: 'Carl Larsson's House', *American Preservation*, vol. 3, January 1980, pp. 39-46.

Näsström, Nils Gustaf: 'Solskenhemmet i Sundborn', in *Dalarna som Svenskt Ideal*, Stockholm, 1937, pp. 113-32.

Pacey, Philip: 'Family Art. Domestic and Eternal Bliss', *Journal of Popular Culture*, vol. 18, part 1, Summer 1984, pp. 43-52.

Pauli, Georg: 'Carl Larsson. Med anledning af 50-årsdagen den 28 Maj 1903' [Carl Larsson. On the occasion of his 50th birthday], *Hvar 8 dag*, vol. 4, no. 35, 1903, pp. 550-4.

Rabén, Hans: *Det moderna hemmet*, Stockholm, 1937.

Rheims, Maurice: *The Flowering of Art Nouveau*, New York, 1966.

Rydin, Lena: *Den lustfyllda vardagen. Hos Larssons i Sundborn*, Stockholm, 1992.

Rydin, Lena: *Carl Larsson-gården. A Home/Ett Hem/Ein Heim*, Malung, 1994. In Swedish, English and German.

Sharp, Dennis: 'The House as Home. The House of Swedish Artist Carl Larsson', *Building Design*, no. 874, 26 February 1988, pp. 24-5.

Stavenow-Hidemark, Elisabet: *Svensk jugend*, Stockholm, 1964.

Stavenow-Hidemark, Elisabet: *Villabebyggelse i Sverige 1900-1925*, Stockholm, 1971.

Teall, Gardner: 'The House in the Sun. Illustrated by Paintings and Drawings of Carl Larsson', *The Craftsman*, vol. 19, December 1910, pp. 230-40.

Vessby, [Johan] Hadar [Johansson]: *Hos Carl Larsson i Sundborn*, Uppsala, 1930.

Westman, Lars: 'Alla är vi på något sätt Carl Larssons barn' [We are all in some way Carl Larsson's children], *Vi*, no. 51-2, 1967, pp. 43-7.

Whyte, Frederic: *A Wayfarer in Sweden*, London, 1926.

Wåhlin, Karl: 'Carl Larssons "Ett hem i Dalarna"', *Ord och bild*, vol. 9, 1900, pp. 273-6.

Widman, Dag: 'Carl Larssons hemideal', *Svenska hem i ord och bild*, vol. 41, 1953, pp. 216, 218.

Wollin, Nils. G.: 'Swedish Interiors', *American Scandinavian Review*, vol. 11, no. 8, August 1923, pp. 484-9.

Zweigbergk, Eva von: *Hemma hos Carl Larssons* [At home with the Larssons], Stockholm, 1968. Reissued, 1979.

BOOKS WRITTEN AND ILLUSTRATED BY CARL LARSSON

De mina. Gammalt krafs af C. L. [My loved ones. Old scrawls by C.L.], Stockholm, 1895. Reissued, Gothenburg, 1975.

De mina och annat gammalt krafs av C. L. [My loved ones and other old scrawls by C.L.], Stockholm, 1919. Versions published in Sweden (1975, 1983) and Germany (1978).

Ett hem [A home], Stockholm, 1899. Facsimile (with new plates from the watercolours), 1992. Reissued 1904, 1910. Reissued in Sweden in smaller format, 1912, 1913, 1917, 1920. From 1968 many versions with new texts for children published in Sweden, Denmark, Norway, Finland, Holland, Germany, France, Italy, the United States, England [*Our Home*] and Canada.

Larssons [The Larssons], Stockholm, 1902. Facsimile 1986. Reissued, 1910; in smaller format, 1919. Reprinted in Sweden (1986) and Germany (1978).

Spardarfvet, mitt lilla landtbruk (modern form: *Spadarvet, mitt lilla lantbruk*) [Spadarvet, my little farm], Stockholm, 1906. Reissued in smaller format, with black-and-white plates, 1919. Reprinted in Sweden, 1940. German translation as *Bei Uns auf dem Lande*, Berlin, 1907; reissued, 1977, 1982. From 1966 many versions with new texts for children published in Denmark, Finland, Italy, France, Holland, Germany, the United States, England [*Our Farm*] and Canada.

Das Haus in der Sonne [The house in the sun], Düsseldorf and Leipzig, 1909. Text and pictures selected from *Ett hem*, *Larssons* and *Spadarvet*; many later reissues in Germany. Also published in Italy (1981) and Holland (1975 and 1980).

Åt solsidan [On the sunny side], Stockholm, 1910. German translation as *Lasst Licht hinein* [Let the light in], Stockholm and Leipzig, 1911. Reissued in smaller format, 1914, 1915, 1917, 1920, 1986. From 1978 also published in Germany, Holland and the United States.

Andras barn [Other people's children], Stockholm, 1913. German translation as *Anderer Leute Kinder*, Berlin, 1913; many later reprints. Reissued in Sweden, 1980. From 1978 also published in Germany (in smaller format), Denmark and Finland.

OTHER TEXTS WRITTEN AND ILLUSTRATED BY CARL LARSSON

Several reproduced in *De mina*, 1895 and 1919.

'Pennteckningar' [Pen drawings], *Palettskap*, special Grez issue, 1 November 1882.

'Bellmansfantasi', *Norden, Skandinavisk revue*, 1886.

'Carl Larssons bidrag' [Carl Larsson's contribution], *Nornan*, 1886, p. 185.

'Från Stockholm till Messina', *Svea*, no. 43, 1887, pp. 79-108. Reissued as monograph, Stockholm, 1948 and 1973.

'Björns saga. Eller, Susanna och gubbarna' [Björn's story, or Susannah and the elders], *Ur dagens krönika*, vol. 8, no. 7-8, 1888, pp. 569-82. Reissued as monograph, Stockholm, 1976.

'Gammalstämning' [The good old days], *Svea*, vol. 45, 1890, pp. 62-74.

'Nordanskog. Ett sommarminne' [A recollection of summer], *Jul*, 1890, pp. 14-16.

'ABC. Teckningar och rim af Carl Larsson' [ABC. Drawings and rhymes by Carl Larsson], *Svea*, no. 26, 1891, pp. 204-6.

'När Sankte Lucas kommer...' [When St Luke comes...], *Nornan*, 1892, pp. 61-3.

'Svenska kvinnan genom seklen' [Swedish womanhood through the centuries], *Idun*, Christmas number, 1907.

'Ett svenskt pantheon', *Ord och bild*, vol. 17, 1908, pp. 27-9.

Za 7 dnej [In seven days], no. 10, 13 March 1911, pp. 16, 20 (illustrations for short stories).

'Fädernas torva' [The earth of the ancestors], *Bondetåget*, 1914, pp. 43-4.

'Nils Bengtson? Reinkarnationskåseri', *Julstämning*, 1914, unpaginated.

'Samvetsfrågor' [Matters of conscience], *Julstämning*, 1918, p. 35.

OTHER PUBLICATIONS ILLUSTRATED BY CARL LARSSON

Pajas [Clown], Stockholm, 1869 (journal, various illustrations).

Kasper [Punch], Stockholm, 1871-80 (journal, various illustrations).

Gustafsson, Richard: *Sagor* [Tales], Stockholm, 1874. Reissued, 1875-82.

Ny illustrerad tidning, Stockholm, 1875-80 (journal, various illustrations).

Hyltén-Cavallius, Gunnar Olof and Stephens, George: *Svenska folksagor* [Swedish folk tales], Stockholm, 1875. Drawings by Egon Lundgren, retouched on wood by Larsson. Reissued in 2 vols, 1915-16.

Gustafsson, Richard: *Svenska taflor och berättelser* [Swedish pictures and stories], Stockholm, 1876. Reissued, 1917.

Topelius, Zakarias: *Boken om Wårt land*, Helsinki, 1875.

Andersen, Hans Christian: *Sagor och berättelser af H.K. Andersen* [Tales and stories], Stockholm, [1876]-1877. Second edition, 1890; 'jubilee edition', 1955. Also published in the United States (1887).

Goethe, Johann Wolfgang von (trans. Carl Snoilsky): *Goethes ballader*, Stockholm, 1876.

Thyregod, Christien Andersen: *Från herregård och bondby* [From manor house and village], Stockholm, 1876.

Thyregod, Christien Andersen: *Fyra valda berättelser*, Stockholm, 1876.

Segerstedt, Albrekt: *Nio sagor*, Stockholm, 1877.

Palettskrap, Stockholm, 1878-c. 1882 (journal, various illustrations).

Gerard, Claude: *Soldaten blå. Historisk skizz från Gustav IV Adolfs tid* [Soldier blue. A historic sketch from the time of Gustavus IV Adolf], Stockholm, 1879.

Sätherberg, Herman: *Blomsterkonungen. Bilder ur Linnés lif* [The flower king. Pictures from the life of Linnaeus], Stockholm, 1879.

Thomasson, Pehr: *Troheten i Norden. Historisk skizz* [Loyalty in the Nordic Countries. Historical sketch], Stockholm, 1879.

Nordostpassagen, Stockholm, 1880. Reissue of an article from *Ny illustrerad tidning*.

Reuter, O.M.: *Karin Månsdotters saga*, Helsinki and Stockholm, 1880.

Wettergrund, Josefina (Lea): *Valda berättelser af Lea. Ur minnet och fantasien.* [From memory and imagination], Stockholm, 1880.

Wettergrund, Josefina (Lea): *Valda berättelser af Lea. Tant Ullas höstblommor.* [Aunt Ulla's autumn flowers], Stockholm, 1882.

Wallin, Johan. *Dödens ängel* [The angel of death], Stockholm, 1880. Second edition, 1887. German edition, undated. Also published in Sweden and England (1955) and the United States (1910).

Fehr, F.: *Evighets blommor. En samling religiösa dikter av nyare svenska författare* [The flowers of eternity. A collection of religious poems by recent Swedish authors], Stockholm, 1881.

Strindberg, August: *I vårbrytningen-dikter och verkligheter* [At the break of Spring – Poems and Realities], Stockholm, 1881 (cover illustration).

Tegnér, Esias: *Nattvardsbarnen* [The communion children], Stockholm, 1881. Reissued, 1906. Also published in Swedish in the United States (1891).

Strindberg, August: *Svenska folket i helg och söcken* [The Swedish People on Wednesdays and Sundays], 2 vols, Stockholm, 1881-2. Reissued, 1974, 1978, 1980. Also published in Swedish in the United States (1882, 1910).

Bögh, Erik: *Sanningens vallfärd* [Truth's pilgrimage], Stockholm, 1883. Also published in Denmark (1883), Holland (1891) and Germany (1898).

Nya sagor, Stockholm, 1883.

Djurklou, Nils Gabriel: *Sagor och äfventyr. Berättade på svenska landsmål* [Tales and adventures. Told in Swedish dialects], Stockholm, 1883. Also published in the United States and England (1901).

Fosterländskt Födelsedags-album [National birthday album], Stockholm, 1883.

Ulbach, Louis: *L'espion des écoles*, Paris, 1883.

Wettergrund, Josefina (Lea): *Ur svenska sången* [From the Swedish song], Stockholm, 1883.

Topelius, Zakarias: *Fältskärns berättelser* [Tales of an army doctor], (5 vols. in 3), Stockholm, 1883-4. From 1894 various editions published in Sweden (renewed illustrations, 1890s), Denmark, Finland and the United States.

Hebbe, Wendela (Åstrand): *Nya sannsagor för ungdom* [New true stories for children], Stockholm, 1884.

Från Seinens strand [From the banks of tne Seine], Stockholm, 1884-5 (exhibition catalogue).

Lenngren, Anna Maria: *Samlade skaldeförsök* [Collected attempts at poetry], Stockholm, eleventh edition, 1884. Reissued, 1890, 1903, 1991.

Becker, Hugo von: *Guffars sagor. Gamla och nya historier*, Stockholm, 1885.

Jonason, Aron: 'Genom en Göteborgs-pince-nez' [Through a Gothenburg pince-nez], *Norden*, 1887, 7 pp., unpaginated. Reissued as pamphlet, Gothenburg, 1974.

Snoilsky, Carl: 'Vid Valkiakoski pappersbruk' [By the Valkiakolski paper-mill], *Svea*, vol. 43, 1887, pp. [7]-12.

Strindberg, August: *Hemsöborna* [The People of Hemsö], Stockholm, [1887] (cover illustration).

Strindberg, August: *Skärkarlsliv* [Men of the Skerries], Stockholm, 1881 (cover illustration). Reissue 1888.

Molander, Harald: 'På Hasselbacken', *Norden*, 1889, 6 pp., unpaginated.

Strindberg, August: *I hafsbandet* [In the outer Skerries], Stockholm, [1890?] (cover illustration).

Schiller, Friedrich von: *Kabale und Liebe* [Patience and Love], Berlin, 1891-2. Also published in Leipzig (1890).

Sehlstedt, Elias: *Sånger och visor i urval* [Selected songs and ballads], Stockholm, 1892-3. Reissued, 1915-16.

Rydberg, Viktor: *Singoalla*, Stockholm, 1894. Second edition, 1904. Reissued 1929, 1975, 1985. Also published in the United States (1903) and England (1904).

Halldén, Björn: *Madame Sans-gêne. Polka pour piano (à Madame Hartmann)*, Stockholm, 1895 (sheet music).

Wahlund, C. (trans.): *Sagan om rosen* [The tale of the rose], Stockholm, 1899.

Topelius, Zakarias: *Läsning för barn. Illustrerad af finska och svenska konstnärer* [Reading for children. Illustrated by Finnish and Swedish artists], 4 vols, Stockholm, 1902-3.

Topelius, Zakarias: *Børnenes bog* [The Childrens' Book], Copenhagen, 1907.

Strindberg, August: *Samvetskval* [Pangs of Remorse], Stockholm, 1908 (cover illustration).

Hemmets kokbok [The home's cookery book], Uppsala, 1909. Cover with reproduction of *Martina with the Breakfast Tray*. Many later editions.

Asbjörnsen, Peter Christian and Moe, Jørgen: *Folksagor*, Stockholm, 1927. From original uncut woodblocks of 1877-8. Reissued, 1978. Also published in Norway (1978).

NOTES

ABBREVIATIONS

BA Bonniers Förlag archives, Stockholm
LA Langewiesche-Verlag archives, Frankfurt am Main
NM National Museum of Fine Arts, Stockholm (archives)
NM-L Thorsten Laurin's cuttings collection, National Museum of Fine Arts, Stockholm
UUB Uppsala University Library (Manuscript Department)

INTRODUCTION (pp. 1-9)

1. C. Larsson 1910, p. 3.
2. See Select Bibliography.
3. The Larssons' children were Suzanne (1884-1958), Ulf (1887-1905), Pontus (1888-1984), Lisbeth (1891-1979), Brita (1893-1982), Matts (1894-1895), Kersti (1896-1975) and Esbjörn (1900-1937).
4. Letter to Viktor Rydberg, October 1889 (Royal Library, Stockholm), quoted in Alfons 1952, p. 138. Larsson was travelling with the architect Carl Möller.
5. *The Building News*, 1874, p. 23; quoted in Turner and Ruddick, 1980, p. 14.
6. *The North*, Oct. 11, 1893.

CHAPTER 1 (pp. 10-20)

1. Eriksson 1990; Lundin 1890; see also Medelius and Rentzhog 1991.
2. Sundbärg 1901.
3. Key 1891 1.
4. Nyström and Sörbom 1984.
5. Hult 1989.
6. Nordström 1987.
7. Eriksson 1990.

CHAPTER 2 (pp. 21-52)

1. Strindberg 1884, p. 132.
2. C. Larsson 1899, p. 2.
3. The gallery no longer exists, but some of the fixtures and the triptych, as well as the Fürstenberg art collection, are in the Gothenburg Museum of Art.
4. For *Modern Art*, see Fredlund 1986, pp. 103-13.
5. The artists, together referred to as the Varberg School, were Richard Bergh, Karl Nordström and Nils Kreuger.
6. The pictures are undated. The dates assigned here are based on the childrens' ages, building details and other factors. The editors are indebted to Ulwa Neergaard for her generous assistance in these datings.

7. C. Larsson 1895, 1975 edn, p. 10.
8. C. Larsson 1931, 1953 edn, p. 217.
9. Nordensvan 1920-1, vol. I, p. 177.
10. C. Larsson 1931, 1953 edn, p. 223.
11. *Ibid.*, pp. 223-4. Georg Haupt was the foremost eighteenth-century Swedish cabinetmaker.
12. *Ibid.*, p. 18.
13. *Ibid.*, p. 206.

CHAPTER 3 (pp. 53-73)

1. C. Larsson 1899, p. 3.
2. Key 1899, p. 4.
3. Among the foreign art magazines were *Gazette des Beaux-Arts*, *Art et Décoration*, *Kunst für alle*, *Zeitschrift der bildende Kunst* and *The Studio*.
4. Frick 1978, pp. 117-91.
5. C. Larsson 1910, p. 12.
6. Bergh 1900, p. 133.
7. Grandien 1987, pp. 233 and 289.
8. Berg 1933.
9. C. Larsson 1899, p. 3.
10. Danielson 1991.
11. Estlander 1867, pp. 52-5.
12. Steffen 1888, pp. 865-77.
13. Ruskin 1897.
14. Steffen 1898, p. 292.
15. Stina Bather, née Bergöö, letter to

Karin Larsson, 18 November 1896, UUB.
16. Stavenow-Hidemark 1991.
17. Key 1899, pp. 26 and 5.
18. Acknowledgement to Professor Barbara Miller Lane, Wayne, PA, USA.

CHAPTER 4 (pp. 74-87)

1. Ruskin 1873.
2. Williams 1973.
3. Morris 1902, 'Art, Wealth and Riches', p. 87.
4. Ruskin 1865, vol. 1, no. 68.
5. 'In a properly ordered state of Society', Morris wrote, 'every man willing to work should be ensured: First, Honourable and fitting work; Second, A Healthy and beautiful house; Third, Full leisure for rest of mind and body.' From 'Art and Socialism' in Morris 1902, p. 126.
6. Ruskin 1865, vol. 1, no. 86.
7. In West London. Moncure Daniel Conway described the architects in 1882 as 'building ... an ideal mirage into this dream of old-time homesteads'; Stamp and Goulancourt 1986, p. 206.
8. Creese 1982; Jackson 1985.
9. Muthesius 1902; Eng. trans., 1994.
10. Ibid., pp. 96-7.
11. Muthesius was to promote the

formation of the Deutscher Werkbund in 1907.
12. From the text of a circular promoting the Arts and Crafts Exhibition Society, 1888.
13. The 'examples' presented were historicist, with some designs by Schinkel; see Snodin, ed., 1991, passim and p. 187.
14. Volkov 1978, passim and p. 326.
15. For German housing reform and the English influence on German developments, see S. Muthesius 1974; see also Gunther 1984 and Siepmann, ed., 1978.
16. The Munich-based Vereinigte Werkstätte für Kunst in Handwerk and the Werkstatte für Wohnungsrichten amalgamated with the Dresden Werkstätte für Kunst in Handwerk in 1907; see Heskett 1986 and Wichmann 1992.
17. The Bund für Heimatschutz was an offshoot of the Dürerbund, dedicated to the promotion of art in everyday life; see Stern 1965, and Heskett 1986.
18. Heskett 1986, p. 74.
19. Siepmann, ed., 1978, p. 217.
20. Brunhammer and Tise, eds, 1990, p. 22.
21. Quoted in T. and C. Benton, eds, 1975, p. 35.
22. Bowe, ed., 1993.
23. Crowley 1992 and Omilanowska, 1993, pp. 102–4.
24. Bowe, ed., 1993, pp. 120–4 and passim. 'They [young architects] are all wandering around the country and all returned again and again to Körösfö in the Kalotaszeg region. They kept drawing houses, rooms, gates, tomb headboards and embroideries but most often the Körösfö steeple. So much so that its sensitive contours with its four turrets was imprinted on their soul.'; from Magyar Iparmüvészet (Hungarian Applied Art), 1908, in Bowe, ed., 1993, p. 125.
25. Wickman, ed., 1995.
26. Frykholm 1904, pp. 298–303.
27. C. Larsson 1931; quoted from Eng. trans., 1992, p. 85.
28. Bröchner 1906, p. 222.
29. C. Larsson 1899; quoted from Cavalli-Björkman and Lindwall, 1989, p. 147.
30. Quoted in Dal Co 1990, p. 181.
31. Quoted in Dal Co 1990, p. 302.

CHAPTER 5 (pp. 88-159)
1. Lilla Hyttnäs and the adjacent and leading property, Stora (Big) Hyttnäs, occupied the same point of land. The power-station water channel which now separates them was built by 1904.
2. In 1830 the properties at Hyttnäs (Tax census, State Archives, Stockholm), included one large (Stora Hyttnäs) and one middling (Lilla Hyttnäs), occupied by a clergyman's widow. By 1840 it belonged to Granholm, a miller.
3. The original cottage was probably of sidokammare type, with the present kitchen and dining-room (as a living-room) only, with perhaps a bedroom in the low loft. Perhaps by 1830 (see note 2) the present drawing-room had been added (as a bedroom). Probably at the same time the roof was raised to accommodate more rooms and a fore-building, with stairs, added to the front.
4. Inaugurated on Carl's nameday on 28th January. Letter from Karin to Carl's mother, 26 January 1890, UUB. There are apparently references in autumn 1890 to setting up the wall boarding (Frieberg 1967, p. 139).

5. Karin's father died in May 1890, leaving a small bequest which went towards the building work. The idea of the studio apparently came from him (letter from Karin to her mother, 9 December 1890, UUB).
6. Carl was shocked to discover that the painters had realistically grained like stylized wooden ornament like benches in public walks (Carl to Karin, summer 1890, UUB 90.6).
7. cf. also Larsson's cover to Atelier Wandringar af Svenska Norska och Danska Konstnärer, 1885.
8. cf. frontispiece and fig. 6.
9. Arrows also appear at the Gothenburg school.
10. The so-called crown chimney (kron skorsten). Changes since the 1890s have made it seem closer to the traditional model.
11. Grandien 1987, fig. 51.
12. The building is of frame construction.
13. The familiar form 'du' (for 'you') was famously used in Dalarna regardless of a person's rank.
14. Traces in the dining-room and Carl and Karin's bedrooms.
15. Early in 1889.
16. E.g. in Carl Curman's villa in Lysekil, which also abounds in painted inscriptions.
17. Adapted from John, ch. 13, v. 34.
18. At the New Elementary Grammar School for Girls, Gothenburg, a photograph of a print of Gustav Vasa.
19. This type of table, common also in Germany, was illustrated by C.L. Eastlake (Hints on Household Taste, 1868).
20. Cf. a cupboard in a cottage in Uppland, interestingly with modern boarded walls (ill. Fredlund, 1977, pp. 102-3).
21. Made possible after a scullery was built in 1901 between the west wall of the kitchen and the new studio; henceforth the back door to the west became the indoor entrance to the kitchen.
22. Made of painted paper attached to the bulb socket ring by brass paper clips.
23. Hvar 8 dag, vol. 4, no. 35, May 1903, p. 554, shows the shades but the old sofa.
24. The new drawing-room first appears in Larsson's paintings in 1893.
25. The book contains designs both neo-classical and rococo.
26. See p. 71.
27. cf. Hökby and Topelius 1987, pp. 47, 9.
28. The rail also relates to elements in the sofa on the platform.
29. Especially by C.F.A. Voysey.
30. C. Larsson 1899, p. 11.
31. Bergström.
32. Grandien 1987, p. 226, fig. 79.
33. C. Larsson 1899, p. 12.
34. Letter, Karin to Carl, early 1894, concerning windows (UUB).
35. Key 1899, 1913 edn, p. 17; C. Larsson 1899, p. 13.
36. C. Larsson 1899, p. 13.
37. The illusion is created by forming a bay for the window on the outside of the building, undetectable in the room.
38. C. Larsson 1899, p. 13.
39. The Studio, vol. V, 1895, p. 190.
40. C. Larsson 1910, 1919 edn, p. 24.
41. Probably identical to that in the earlier studio.
42. C. Larsson 1910, 1919 edn, p. 23.
43. They were designed for silver.
44. Hvar 8 dag, vol. 4, no. 35, May 1903, p. 160.

CHAPTER 6 (pp. 160-183)
1. Elin Wägner (1882-1945) was a well-known Swedish journalist and author. Her book Väckarklocka (Alarm Clock; 1941) is an ecological classic.
2. Wägner 1913.
3. Cavalli-Björkman 1987, p. 40.
4. Letter, Karin to her parents, September 1882. All letters quoted in this chapter are from UUB.
5. C. Larsson 1931 (1953 ed.), p. 167.
6. C. Larsson 1902, p. 8.
7. Carl, letter to Adolf Bergöö, 12 September 1882.
8. Bergöö's reply, 17 September 1882.
9. Karin, undated letter [autumn 1882].
10. Bruccoli 1981.
11. Eva Bonnier, letter home, 24 October 1884.
12. Carl, letter to Hilda Bergöö, 2 September 1888.
13. Frieberg 1967, p. 185.
14. For a more detailed description of the Larsson family's everyday life, see Rydin 1992; see also Rydin 1994.
15. Carl, letter to Pontus Fürstenberg, 20 February 1890.
16. Karin, letter to her mother, 25 December 1892.
17. Strindberg was one of Carl Larsson's close friends for a long time but later turned against the family.
18. Karin, diary, 16 July 1921.
19. Ibid., 28 November 1920.
20. Conversation with Professor Elisabeth Wilson, University of North London, 7 December 1995; see also Wilson 1985.
21. Karin, letter to her mother, 31 March 1894.
22. Karin, letter to her mother, 13 August 1907.
23. See Select Bibliography.
24. Conversation with Professor Edna Martin, artistic director of the Svensk Hemslöjd (1946-51), director of Handarbetets Vänner (1951-77) and head of department at Konstfackskolan (College of Arts, Crafts and Design; 1957-69).

CHAPTER 7 (pp. 184-195)
1. C. Larsson 1899, pp. 2-3.
2. C. Larsson 1916, p. 160.
3. Of which it still smells.
4. C. Larsson 1916, p. 162.

CHAPTER 8 (pp. 196-211)
1. Larsson painted twenty-six subjects, of which twenty-four were reproduced in colour and one in half-tone. The last was not reproduced.
2. Bonnier, letter to Carl, August 1899, BA.
3. Bonnier, 24 August 1899, BA.
4. Carl, August 1899, BA.
5. Carl, letter to Thorsten Laurin, month, 1905, NM.
6. Bonnier, letter to Cassirer, 1 August 1906, BA.
7. Ellen Jungbeck-Grönland, letter to Carl, 5 December 1909, UUB.
8. Ibid.
9. Langewiesche, letter to Bonnier, 30 December 1908, BA.
10. Bonnier, letter to Langewiesche, 19 January 1909, BA.
11. Walter Sensel, kunst für Alle 1907: 22
12. Langewiesche, letter to Carl, 1 November 1909, UUB.
13. Larsson's reply, 12 November 1909, LA.
14. Carl, letter to his family, 24 September 1913, UUB.
15. Nordensvan 1920-1, vol. II, p. 173.
16. Frykholm 1904, pp. 298-303.

17. Laurin, letter to Carl, 9 August 1910, NM.
18. Svenska dagbladet, 13 January 1910, copy in NM-L.
19. Carl to E. Thiel, March 1905 (Thiel Gallery); Carl to Stina Bather, 1905 (UUB) I am grateful to Ulwa Neergaard for these references.
20. The exhibition was held from 22 April to 31 July 1911.
21. Daily Chronicle, 22 April 1911.
22. Stockholms dagblad, 13 October 1911, copy in NM-L.
23. Bonnier, letter to Langewiesche, 19 January 1909, BA.
24. Contract dated 31 March 1909, BA.
25. Carl to Bonnier, 26 January 1911, BA.
26. C. Larsson, letter to Laurin, 1910, NM.

CHAPTER 9 (pp. 212-219)
1. Key 1906, p. 211; Key 1915, pp. 107-9.
2. Romdahl 1913; see also Hjert 1983.
3. Romdahl 1913, p. 55.
4. Laurin 1899.
5. Brunius 1911, p. 155-162.
6. Promostyl 1992-3.

CHAPTER 10 (pp. 220-229)
1. L. Larsson 1947, pp. 11, 13.
2. C. Larsson 1931 (1953 ed.), pp. 55, 74.
3. Ibid., p. 55.
4. C. Larsson 1899, p. 8.
5. It mixes old and new furniture.
6. Kerstin Locrantz, Förklädesboken: gamla och nya förkläden att sy själv, Stockholm, 1981.
7. Letter to Elisabet Stavenow-Hidemark, 14 June 1996.

REFERENCES

Alfons 1952: Harriet Alfons and Sven Alfons: *Carl Larsson. Skildrad av honom själv i text och bilder* [Carl Larsson. Described by himself in text and pictures], Stockholm, 1952.

Andersson 1986: Ingrid Andersson: *Karin Larsson konstnär och konstnärshustru* [Karin Larsson artist and artist's wife], Stockholm, 1986.

Benton 1975: Tim Benton and Charlotte Benton, with Dennis Sharp, eds: *Form and Function*, Milton Keynes, 1975.

Berg 1933: Gösta Berg: *Artur Hazelius. Mannen och hans verk* [Artur Hazelius. The man and his work], Stockholm, 1933.

Bergh 1900: Richard Bergh: 'Svenskt konstnärskynne' [Swedish artistic temperament], *Ord och bild*, vol. 9, 1900, p. 133.

Bowe 1993: Nicola Gordon Bowe, ed.: *Art and the National Dream*, Dublin, 1993.

Bröchner 1906: George Bröchner: 'Some Northern Painters and their Homes', *The Studio*, vol. 38, 1906, pp. 19-24.

Bruccoli 1981: Matthew J. Bruccoli: *Some Sort of Epic Grandeur. The Life of F. Scott Fitzgerald*, New York, 1981.

Brunhammer and Tise 1990: Yvonne Brunhammer and Suzanne Tise, eds: *French Decorative Art. The Société des Artistes Decorateurs, 1990-1942*, Paris, 1990.

Brunius 1911: August Brunius: *Hus och hem. Studier af den svenska villan och villastaden* [House and home. Studies of the Swedish villa and villa district], Stockholm, 1911.

Cavalli-Björkman 1987: Görel Cavalli-Björkman, *Carl Larsson porträttmålaren* [Carl Larsson the portrait painter], Stockholm, 1987.

Cavalli-Björkman and Lindwall 1989: Görel Cavalli-Björkman and Bo Lindwall, *The World of Carl Larsson*, London, 1989.

Crane 1888: Walter Crane: circular promoting the Arts and Crafts Exhibition Society, 1888.

Creese 1982: Walter Creese: *The Search for the Environment. The Garden City, Before and After*, New Haven and London, 1982.

Crowley 1992: David Crowley: *National Style and Nation-State. Design in Poland from the Vernacular Revival to the International Style*, Manchester, 1992.

Dal Co 1990: Francesco Dal Co: *Figures of Architecture and Thought. German Architectural Culture 1880-1920*, New York, 1990.

Danielson 1991: Sofia Danielson: *Den goda smaken och samhällsnyttan* [Good taste and social welfare], Stockholm, 1991.

Eastlake 1868: C.L. Eastlake: *Hints on Household Taste*, London, 1868.

Eriksson 1990: Eva Eriksson: *Den moderna stadens födelse. Svenska arkitektur 1890-1920.* [The birth of the modern town], Stockholm, 1990.

Estlander 1867: Carl Gustaf Estlander: *De bildande konsternas historia*, Stockholm, 1867.

Fredlund 1977: Jane Fredlund: *Målade allmogemöbler*, Västerås, 1977.

Fredlund 1986: Björn Fredlund, 'Nutida konst av Carl Larsson', *Konsthistoriska studier* [Essays on the history of art], Helsinki, 1986, pp. 103-13.

Frick 1978: Gunilla Frick: *Svenska slöjdföreningen och konstindustrin före 1905* [The Swedish Society of Crafts and Design before 1905], Stockholm, 1978, pp. 117-91.

Frieberg 1967: Axel Frieberg, *Karin*, Stockholm, 1967.

Frykholm 1904: Sunny Frykholm, 'The Imaginative and Realistic Art of Carl Larsson', *The Studio*, vol. 32, 1904, pp. 298-303.

Geller 1993: Katalin Geller: 'Romantic Elements in Hungarian Art Nouveau', in Bowe 1993, pp. 117-126.

Grandien 1987: Bo Grandien: *Rönndruvans glöd* [The rowanberry's glow], Stockholm, 1987.

Gunther 1984: Sonja Gunther: 'Das deutsche Heim. Luxusinterieurs und Arbeitermöbel von der Gründerzeit bis zum Dritten Reich', Giessen, 1984.

Heskett 1986: *Design in Germany, 1870-1918*, London, 1986.

Hjert 1983: Bertil, Gunnel and Svenolof Hjert: *Carl Larsson. Grafiska verk. En komplett katalog*, Uppsala, 1983.

Hult 1989: Jan Hult: 'Bondeland blir industriland. 1870-1914' [From peasant society to industrial nation. 1870-1914], *Svensk teknikhistoria*, ed. Sven Rydberg, Hedemora, 1989.

Hökby and Topelius 1987: Nils-Göran Hökby and Ann-Sofi Topelius (eds): *Hemma i konsten*, Stockholm, 1987.

Jackson 1985: Frank Jackson: *Sir Raymond Unwin, Architect, Planner, Visionary*, London, 1985.

Key 1897: Ellen Key: 'Skönhet i hemmen' [Beauty in homes], Idun, no. 50, 1897, p. 4 et seq.

Key 1897 I: Ellen Key: 'Om patriotismen: öppet bref till min vän Verner von Heidenstam', *Vintergatan*, vol. 4, 1897, pp. 89-92.

Key 1899: Ellen Key: *Skönhet för alla* [Beauty for everyone], Uppsala, 1899.

Key 1906/1915: Ellen Key 1906/1915: *Folkbildningsarbetet särskildt med hänsyn till skönhetssinnets odling* [Adult education and the cultivation of a sense of beauty], Uppsala, 1906. Second ed. 1915.

C. Larsson 1895: Carl Larsson: *De mina* [My loved ones], Stockholm, 1895. Reissued, Gothenburg, 1975.

C. Larsson 1899: Carl Larsson: *Ett hem* [A home], Stockholm, 1899.

C. Larsson 1902: Carl Larsson: *Larssons* [The Larssons], Stockholm, 1902.

C. Larsson 1910: Carl Larsson: *Åt solsidan* [On the sunny side], Stockholm, 1910.

C. Larsson 1916: Carl Larsson: 'Carl Larssons hem i Sundborn skildrat af honom själf', *Svenska hem i ord och bilder*, vol. 8, 1916, pp. 155-65.

C. Larsson 1931: Carl Larsson: *Jag* [Myself], Stockholm, 1931. Second edition 1953.

Larsson and Svedberg 1947: Lena Larsson and Elias Svedberg: *Heminredning* [Interior decoration], Stockholm, 1947.

Laurin 1899: Carl G. Laurin: *Konsten i skolan och konsten i hemmet* [Art in the school and home], Stockholm, 1899.

Lundin 1890: Claes Lundin: *Nya Stockholm* [New Stockholm], Stockholm, 1890.

Medelius and Rentzhog 1991: Hans Medelius and Sten Rentzhog: '90-tal, Visioner och vägval' [The 1890s. Visions and choices], Nordic Museum and Skansen Yearbook, *Fataburen*, 1991.

Morris 1902: William Morris: 'Art, Wealth and Riches' (address at the Royal Institution, Manchester, 1883) and 'Art and Socialism' (lecture to the Secular Society of Leicester, 1884), in *Architecture, Industry and Wealth: Collected Papers*, London, 1902, pp. 80-104 and 105-132.

H. Muthesius 1902: Hermann Muthesius: *Stilarchitektur und Baukunst*, Mülheim-Ruhr, 1902. English translation by Stanford Anderson, Malibu, 1994.

S. Muthesius 1974: Stefan Muthesius: *Das englische Vorbild*, Munich, 1974.

Nordensvan 1920-1: Georg Nordensvan, *Carl Larsson*, 2 vols, Stockholm, 1920-1.

Nyström and Sörbom 1984: Bengt Nyström and Per Sörbom (eds): 'När elektriciteten kom' [The arrival of electricity], Technical Museum Yearbook, *Daedalus*, 1984.

Nördström 1987: Alf Nördström: *Bergsmän och brukspatroner* [Mine shareholders and ironmasters], Stockholm, 1987.

Omilanowska 1993: M. Omilanowska: *Searching for a National Style in Polish Architecture at the End of the 19th and the Beginning of the 20th Century*, in Bowe 1993, pp.99-116

Romdahl 1913: Axel L. Romdahl: 'Carl Larsson som etsare', [Carl Larsson as an etcher], Stockholm, 1913.

Ruskin 1865: John Ruskin: *Sesame and Lilies*, vol. 1, no. 68, 1865.

Ruskin 1873: John Ruskin: *Fors Clavigera*, vol. 11, letter XXIX, 2 April 1873.

Ruskin 1897: John Ruskin: *Huru vi skola arbeta och hushålla. Tankar om nationalekonomiens första grundar*, Stockholm, 1897.

Rydin 1992: Lena Rydin: *Den lustfyllda vardagen* [The joys of everyday life], Stockholm, 1992.

Rydin 1994: Lena Rydin: *Carl Larsson-gården. Ett hem/A Home/Ein Heim*, Malung, 1994.

Siepmann 1978: Ekhard Siepmann: 'Kunst und Alltag um 1900', Giessen, 1978.

Snodin 1991: Michael Snodin, ed.: *Karl Friedrich Schinkel. A Universal Man*, New Haven and London, 1991.

Stamp and Goulancourt 1986: Gavin Stamp and André Goulancourt: *The English House 1860-1914*, London, 1986.

Stavenow-Hidemark 1991: Elisabet Stavenow-Hidemark: *Sub Rosa. När skönheten kom från England* [Sub Rosa. When beauty came from England], Stockholm and Helsingborg, 1991.

Steffen 1888: Gustaf F. Steffen: 'John Ruskin. En engelsk nutidskaraktär' [John Ruskin. A modern English personality], *Ur dagens krönika*, no. 188, 1888, pp. 865-77.

Steffen 1898: Gustaf F. Steffen: *England som världsmakt och kulturstat* [England as a world power and civilized nation], Stockholm, 1898.

Stern 1965: F. Stern: *The Politics for Cultural Despair*, New York, 1965.

Strindberg 1884: August Strindberg: 'Carl Larsson. Ett svenskt porträtt med fransk bakgrund', *Svea*, vol. 40, 1884, p. 130-45.

Sundbärg 1901: Gustav Sundbärg: 'Ett rum och kök' [One room and kitchen], *Social tidskrift*, vol. 1, 1901.

Turner and Ruddick 1980: Mark Turner and William Ruddick: *A London Design Studio 1880-1963: The Silver Studio Collection*, London, 1980.

Volkov 1978: Shulamit Volkov: *The Rise of Popular Anti-Modernism in Germany. The Urban Master Artisans, 1873-1896*, Princeton, 1978.

Wägner 1913: Elin Wägner: 'Till fru Karin Larsson', Idun, no. 21, 25 May 1913, p. 344.

Wichmann 1992: H. Wichmann: *Deutsche Werkstatten und WK-Verband 1898-1990. Aufbruch zum neuen Wohnen*, Munich, 1992.

Wickman 1995: Kerstin Wickman, ed.: *Formens rörelse Svensk Form genom 150 år*, Stockholm, 1995.

Williams 1973: Raymond Williams: *The Country and the City*, London, 1973.

Wilson 1985: Elisabeth Wilson: *Adorned in Dreams: Fashion and Modernity*, London 1985. Swedish translation, 1985.

Zweigbergk 1968: Eva von Zweigbergk: *Hemma hos Carl Larssons* [At home with the Larssons], Stockholm, 1968.

LIST OF EXHIBITS

Shown at the *Carl and Karin Larsson* exhibition, Victoria and Albert Museum, October 23, 1997 to January 18, 1998, curated by Michael Snodin and Elisabet Stavenow-Hidemark. The list was prepared before the final form of the exhibition was known; this applies especially to the final section , guest-curated by Denise Hagströmer.

INTRODUCTION

1. Carl Larsson
Before the Mirror (Self-portrait in a Red Dressing-gown) 1900
Oil on canvas. 2410 x 990 mm
(Gothenburg Museum of Art; GKM F80)

2. Carl Larsson
De mina (My Loved Ones) 1892
Oil on canvas. 3600 x 2630 mm
(Private collection)

LIFE AND ART

3. Hans Christian Andersen
Sagor och berättelser af H.K. Andersen (Tales and Stories), Stockholm, 1877
Wood engraving. With illustrations by Carl Larsson
(Private collection)

4. *Palettskrap,*1879
Lithograph. With text and illustrations by Carl Larsson
(The Carl Larsson House, Sundborn)

5. John Olof Wallin
Dödens ängel (The Angel of Death), Stockholm, 1880
With illustrations and cover by Carl Larsson (The Carl Larsson House, Sundborn)

6. John Olof Wallin
Des Engel des Todes (The Angel of Death) Undated German edition. With illustrations by Carl Larsson (Victoria and Albert Museum, National Art Library)

7. Zakarias Topelius
Fältskärns berättelser (Tales of an Army Doctor), Stockholm, 1883-4 With illustrations by Carl Larsson (The Carl Larsson House, Sundborn)

8. Engraved woodblock for illustration to Topelius's *Fältskärns berättelser*
(Private collection)

9. Exhibition catalogue, *Från Seinens strand* (From the Banks of the Seine), 1884
Title page by Carl Larsson (The Carl Larsson House, Sundborn)

10. Peter Severin Krøyer *The Artists' Breakfast at Grez* 1884
Pastel. 490 x 640 mm
(Prince Eugen's Waldemarsudde, Stockholm; W1487)

11. Carl Larsson
In the Kitchen Garden 1883
Watercolour. 930 x 610 mm
(The Nationalmuseum, Stockholm; NMB 165)

12. Carl Larsson
The Toy Corner 1887
Watercolour. 910 x 585 mm
(Pro Arte Foundation, Stockholm)

13. Carl Larsson
Drawing of the Fürstenberg triptych. c. 1895?

Pen and ink and wash and Chinese white. 220 x 190 mm, 290 x 380 mm, 220 x 190 mm
(Private collection)

14. Carl Larsson
Profiles 1888
Etching. 238 x 157 mm
(British Museum; 1949-4-11-4)

15. Carl Larsson
Svenska kvinnan genom seklen (Swedish Womanhood through the Centuries), supplement to *Idun,* 1907
(The Carl Larsson House, Sundborn)

16. Carl Larsson
Gustav Vasa's Triumphal Entry into Stockholm 1891
Oil on canvas. 760 x 1360 mm
(Private collection)

17. Carl Larsson
Portrait of Gustaf Upmark 1894
Watercolour. 490 x 360 mm
(The National Art Museums, Gripsholm Castle, Mariefred; Grh 2389)

18. Carl Larsson
The Princess and the Shepherd Boy: A Swedish Fairy Story 1893
Oil on canvas and gilt wood. 1640 x 1643 mm
(The Nationalmuseum, Stockholm; NM 6840)

19. Carl Larsson
The Artist's Wife, Children and Birds' Wings 1890
Pen and wash. 252 x 337 mm
(The Nationalmuseum, Stockholm; NMH 32/1908)

20. Carl Larsson
Nameday Picture for Karin Larsson 1894
Pen, ink and watercolour. 505 x 754 mm
(Gothenburg Museum of Art; T 35/1905)

21. Carl Larsson
Suzanne 1894
Watercolour. 455 x 285 mm
(Gothenburg Museum of Art; GKM F73)

22. Carl Larsson
Lisbeth 1894
Watercolour. 475 x 270 mm
(Gothenburg Museum of Art; GKM F75)

23. Carl Larsson
On Christmas-Day Morning 1895
Watercolour. 600 x 430 mm
(Stiftelsen SAF)

24. Carl Larsson
Brita and I 1895
Watercolour. 630 x 270 mm
(Gothenburg Museum of Art; GKM F72)

25. Carl Larsson
Karin and Kersti 1898
Watercolour. 620 x 250 mm
(Gothenburg Museum of Art; GKM F78)

26. Carl Larsson
The Strangers from Egypt (illustration for Victor Rydberg,

Singoalla) 1894
Ink and wash. 420 x 240 mm
(Gothenburg Museum of Art; GKM T552)

27. Carl Larsson
Rider and Horse (illustration for Victor Rydberg, Singoalla) 1894
Ink and wash. 423 x 240 mm
(Gothenburg Museum of Art; GKM T559)

28. Victor Rydberg
Singoalla, Stockholm, 1894
With cover and illustrations by Carl Larsson (The Carl Larsson House, Sundborn)

29. Carl Larsson
The Singer Anna Pettersson-Norrie 1895
Watercolour. 450 x 610 mm
(The National Art Museums, Harpsund; Hpd 123)

30. Carl Larsson
Portrait of August Strindberg 1899. Charcoal and oil on canvas. 560 x 390 mm
(The Nationalmuseum, Stockholm; NMB 398)

31. August Strindberg
I Hafsbandet (In the outer Skerries), Stockholm, 1890?
With title-page by Carl Larsson (The Carl Larsson House, Sundborn)

32. Carl Larsson
Convalescence 1899
Watercolour. 529 x 660 mm
(The Nationalmuseum, Stockholm; NMB 505)

33. Carl Larsson
Portrait of Oscar Levertin 1906
Oil on canvas. 700 x 925 mm
(The Bonniers' Portrait Collection, Nedre Manilla, Stockholm)

34. Carl Larsson
On the Model Table 1906
Watercolour. 570 x 775 mm
(Gothenburg Museum of Art; GKM 1235)

35. Carl Larsson
The Carpenter Hans Arnbom 1915.
Oil on canvas. 1255 x 1005 mm
(Falu Kommun)

36. Carl Larsson
Self-portrait 1916
Oil on canvas. 730 x 540 mm
(Falu Kommun)

37. Carl Larsson
Portrait of Selma Lagerlöf 1908
Oil on canvas. 1480 x 1100 mm
(The Bonniers' Portrait Collection, Nedre Manilla, Stockholm)

38. Hat
Belonged to Carl Larsson (The Carl Larsson House, Sundborn)

39. Artist's smock
Belonged to Carl Larsson (The Carl Larsson House, Sundborn)

40. Clown doll
Belonged to Carl Larsson (The

Carl Larsson House, Sundborn)

41. Carl Larsson
Saint George and the Princess 1896. Colour lithograph. 474 x 625 mm
(The Carl Larsson House, Sundborn)

42. Carl Larsson
Design for title-page of *Ett hem* 1899
Pen and ink and wash. 290 x 465 mm
(Private collection)

43. Carl Larsson
Kersti (Vignette for *Ett hem*) 1899
Pen and ink. 324 x 257 mm
(Private collection)

44. Carl Larsson
Brita as Idun 1900
Watercolour. 500 x 320 mm
(Private collection)

45. Carl Larsson
Design for title-page of *Spadarvet* c. 1906
Pen and ink and watercolour. 330 x 490 mm
(The Bonniers' Portrait Collection, Nedre Manilla, Stockholm)

46. Carl Larsson
Design for endpapers of *Spadarvet* c. 1906
Pen and ink. 360 x 510 mm
(Private collection)

47. Postcard
Colour lithograph After Carl Larsson, 1909
(Private collection)

48. Carl Larsson
De mina. Gammalt krafs af C.L. (My Loved Ones. Old Scrawls by C.L.), Stockholm, 1895
(The Carl Larsson House, Sundborn)

49. Carl Larsson
Ett hem (A Home), Stockholm, 1899. (Victoria and Albert Museum, National Art Library)

50. *Idun,* Christmas issue, 1901.
(The Carl Larsson House, Sundborn, not exhibited)

51. Carl Larsson
Larssons (The Larssons), Stockholm, 1902
(Private collection)

52. Carl Larsson
Spadarfvet, mitt lilla landtbruk (modern form: Spadarvet, mitt lilla lantbruk), (Spadarvet My Little Farm), Stockholm, 1906
(Private collection)

53. Carl Larsson
Åt solsidan (On the Sunny Side), Stockholm, 1910
(The Carl Larsson House, Sundborn)

54. Carl Larsson
Esbjörn is fishing, 1903
Pen and ink and watercolour. 425 x 320 mm
(Private collection)

Idun, Carl Larsson issue, 1913
(The Carl Larsson House, Sundborn)

56. Carl Larsson
De mina och annat gammalt krafs av C. L. (My Loved Ones and other Old Scrawls by C. L.), Stockholm, 1919
(Private collection)

57. Carl Larsson
Åt solsidan (On the Sunny Side), Stockholm, second edition, 1917
(Private collection)

58. Carl Larsson
Larssons (The Larssons), Stockholm, 1902
(Private collection)

59. Carl Larsson
Åt solsidan (On the Sunny Side), Stockholm, 1910
(Private collection)

60. Carl Larsson
Das Haus in der Sonne (The House in the Sun), Düsseldorf and Leipzig, 1909
(Private collection)

ART, NATURE AND NATURALISM

61. Eugène Jansson (1862-1915)
Riddarfjärden in Stockholm 1898
Oil on canvas. 1150 x 1350 mm
(The Nationalmuseum, Stockholm; NM 1699)

62. Prince Eugen (1865-1947)
The Cloud 1896
Oil on canvas. 1120 x 1030 mm
(Prince Eugen's Waldemarsudde)

63. Carl Wilhelmson
(1866-1928) *Daughter of the Farm* 1902.
Oil on canvas. 1300 x 900 mm
(Gothenburg Museum of Art)

64. Anders Zorn (1860-1920)
Midsummer Dance 1903
Oil on canvas. 1175 x 900 mm
(Private collection)

65. Gustav Fjæstad (1868-1948)
Winter Moonlight 1895
Oil on canvas. 1000 x 1340 mm
(The Nationalmuseum, Stockholm; NM 1628)

SOURCES FOR SUNDBORN: OLD NORSE STYLE

66. Oak chair
Designed by August Malmström (1829-1901) for Axel Key's Villa, Bråvalla c. 1870
(The Nordic Museum, Stockholm; 272 189)

67. Johann Wolfgang von Goethe
Goethes ballader, (trans. Carl Snoilsky), Stockholm, 1876
With illustrations by Carl Larsson (The Carl Larsson House, Sundborn)

SOURCES FOR SUNDBORN: FOLK ART

68. Amalia Lindegren (1814-1891)
Sunday Evening in a Cottage in Dalarna 1860
Oil on canvas. 870 x 1160 mm
(The Nationalmuseum, Stockholm; NM 992)

69. Carl Larsson
The Winter Cottage 1890
Watercolour. 650 x 980 mm
(The National Art Museums, Harpsund; Hpd 124)

70. Corner cupboard
Painted pine 1796
From Folkärna parish in Dalarna (The Nordic Museum, Stockholm; NoM 177 226)

71. Painted wall hanging
The Marriage Feast at Cana and Jesus entering Jerusalem 1781
Painted textile, Southern Swedish (The Nordic Museum, Stockholm; 59.608)

72. Carriage seat cushion Late 18th or early 19th century
From the province of Skåne
Wool tapestry weave (The Carl Larsson House, Sundborn)

SOURCES FOR SUNDBORN: IDEAS FROM ABROAD

73. *Palettskrap*, 1882
With illustrations by Carl Larsson showing Julia Beck and Karin Bergöö (The Carl Larsson House, Sundborn)

74. Utagawa Kunisada (1786-1864) *View of Hakone* from the series *Fifty-three Stations of the Tokaido* c. 1840
Colour print from wood blocks (The Carl Larsson House, Sundborn)

75. Japanese female theatrical mask
Probably 19th century (The Carl Larsson House, Sundborn)

76. Elias Sehlstedt
Sånger och visor i urval (Selected Songs and Ballads), Stockholm, 1893
With illustrations by Carl Larsson (The Carl Larsson House, Sundborn)

77. Issues of *Deutsche Kunst und Dekoration, Art et Décoration,* and *The Studio* from the house library (The Carl Larsson House, Sundborn)

78. Jacob von Falke
Die Kunst im Hause, Vienna, 1874
(Victoria and Albert Museum, National Art Library)

SOURCES FOR SUNDBORN: OLD SWEDEN

79. Carl Larsson
A Door at Gripsholm 1874
Watercolour. 270 x 280 mm
(The Nationalmuseum, Stockholm; NMH 1/1908)

80. Carl Larsson
The Journey to the Bridal Bath 1881-2. Pen and ink and wash
Illustration to August

Strindberg's *Svenska folket i helg och söcken* (The Swedish People on Weekdays and Sundays) (The Nationalmuseum, Stockholm; NMH 148/1933)

81. Chair 1760s
Painted softwood (The Nordic Museum, Stockholm; 92055 a)

82. Carl Larsson
Grandmother's Room
Illustration for the poem 'Gammalstämning' (The Good Old Days) for *Svea*, 1890.
Pen and ink. 240 x 90 mm
(Private collection)

83. Carl Larsson
The Skipper and the Shipowner
Illustrations for Anna Maria Lenngren's *Samlade skaldeförsök* (Collected Attempts at Poetry), Stockholm, 1884
Pen and ink and wash. 260 x 210 mm
(Private collection)

84. Kate Greenaway
Smått folk. Bilder från barnvärlden, Stockholm, 1882
A translation of *Under the Window*, London, 1878
(The Carl Larsson House, Sundborn)

85. Anna Maria Lenngren
Samlade skaldeförsök (Collected Attempts at Poetry), Stockholm, 1884
With illustrations by Carl Larsson (The Carl Larsson House, Sundborn)

86. Johan Fredrik Krouthén (1858-1932)
The Home of the Goldsmith Sam Pettersson 1895
Oil on canvas. 570 x 760 mm
(Östergötland County Museum, Linköping; B.2947)

87. Fanny Brate (1861-1940)
Nameday 1902
Oil on canvas. 880 x 1100 mm
(The Nationalmuseum, Stockholm; NM 1605)

88. Chair c. 1800
Painted softwood Made by Carl-Johan Wadström of Stockholm (The Nordic Museum, Stockholm; 131.409)

WELCOME TO SUNDBORN

89. Model of Lilla Hyttnäs 1996. Softwood. Made by Jacob Hidemark and Martin Stintzing

90. Carl Larsson
A View of Bondesgården, Sundborn 1885
Pencil and pen and wash. 275 x 240 mm
(The Nationalmuseum, Stockholm; NMH 13/1908)

91. Carl Larsson
The Place in its Rural Plainness c. 1899
Pen and ink.
(Private collection)

92. Carl Larsson
Ulf in the Front of the Cottage 1890. Pen and ink and watercolour. 105 x 174 mm

(Gothenburg Museum of Art; GKM 578)

93. Letter from Carl Larsson to Pontus Fürstenberg, July 1890.
Pen and ink (Gothenburg University Library)

94. Carl Larsson
In the Country c. 1890
Pen and ink and watercolour
Illustration to Elias Sehlstedt's *Sånger och visor i urval* (Selected Songs and Ballads) 325 x 235 mm (Private collection)

95. Carl Larsson
The Cottage (*Ett hem* series) 1894-5
Watercolour. c. 320 x 430 mm
(The Nationalmuseum, Stockholm; NMB 261)

96. Carl Larsson
The Veranda (*Ett hem* series) 1896-7.
Watercolour. c. 320 x 430 mm
(The Nationalmuseum, Stockholm; NMB 262)

96a. Carl Larsson
Raking 1900
Watercolour.
(Private collection)

97. Carl Larsson
Breakfast under the Big Birch (*Ett hem* series) 1896
Watercolour. c. 320 x 430 mm
(The Nationalmuseum, Stockholm; NMB 279)

98. Carl Larsson
Crayfishing (*Ett hem* series) 1897.
Watercolour. c. 320 x 430 mm
(The Nationalmuseum, Stockholm; NMB 278)

99. Carl Larsson
The Front Yard and the Wash-house (*Ett hem* series) 1897
Watercolour. c. 320 x 430 mm
(The Nationalmuseum, Stockholm; NMB 276)

100. Carl Larsson
Breakfast Out of Doors 1910
Watercolour. 650 x 980mm
(Private collection)

101. Carl Larsson
Viking Raid in Dalarna 1900
Watercolour. 610 x 1030 mm
(Stiftelsen SAF)

102. Carl Larsson
In Front of My House 1905
Watercolour. l630 x 970 mm
(Private collection)

103. Carl Larsson
Late Summer 1908
Watercolour. 524 x 745 mm
(Malmö Museum of Art; MM 6803)

104. Carl Larsson
Suzanne on the Porch 1910
Watercolour. 530 x 740 mm
(Private collection)

105. Carl Larsson
In the Snow 1904
Watercolour. 670 x 1000 mm
(Private collection, not exhibited)

106. Carl Larsson
The Porch: Suzanne, Ulf, Pontus and Lisbeth (Vignette for *Ett hem*) 1899
Pen and ink. 465 x 290 mm
(Private collection)

AT HOME WITH THE LARSSONS: THE DINING-ROOM

107. Carl Larsson
When the Children have Gone to Bed (*Ett hem* series) 1894-7
Watercolour. c. 320 x 430 mm
(The Nationalmuseum, Stockholm; NMB 266)

108. Carl Larsson
Between Christmas and New Year (*Ett hem* series) 1896
Watercolour. c. 320 x 430 mm
(The Nationalmuseum, Stockholm; NMB 265)

109. Carl Larsson
For a Little Card Party 1901
Oil on canvas. 680 x 920 mm
(The Nationalmuseum, Stockholm; NM 1961)

110. Carl Larsson
Karin is Reading 1904
Watercolour. 460 x 650 mm
(The Zorn Collections, Mora, Sweden)

111. Carl Larsson
Version of the painting on the dining-room window 1905
Watercolour. 750 x 1210 mm
(The Carl Larsson House, Sundborn)

112. Carl Larsson
Mother, Father and Child
Illustration in *Jultomten*, 1910
330 x 270 mm (The Carl Larsson House, Sundborn)

113. Cupboard
Painted softwood. With decorations by Carl Larsson, dated 1891
(The Carl Larsson House, Sundborn)

114. Chair 1901
Painted softwood with leather seat-cover. Made by Hans Arnbom, Sundborn (The Carl Larsson House, Sundborn)

115. Six plates. Porcelain.
Decorated by Carl and Karin Larsson (The Carl Larsson House, Sundborn)

116. Mug
Made by Villeroy and Boche 1890-1897
(The Carl Larsson House, Sundborn, not exhibited)

117. Door between the dining-room and drawing-room With painted decorations by Carl Larsson Dated 1891 and 1900
(The Carl Larsson House, Sundborn)

AT HOME WITH THE LARSSONS: THE DRAWING-ROOM

118. Carl Larsson
A Woman in an Interior 1885
Oil on canvas. 451 x 540 mm
(Private collection)

119. Carl Larsson
Pontus 1890
Oil on canvas. 1250 x 1000 mm
(The Nationalmuseum, Stockholm; NM 2343)

120. Elias Sehlstedt
Sånger och visor i urval (Selected Songs and Ballads),

Stockholm, 1892-3
With illustrations by Carl Larsson (The Nordic Museum, Stockholm)

121. Anonymous artist
Pattern book of room decorations c. 1780
Watercolour. (The Carl Larsson House, Sundborn)

122. Carl Larsson
The Flower Window (*Ett hem* series) 1894
Watercolour. c. 320 x 430 mm
(The Nationalmuseum, Stockholm; NMB 268)

123. Carl Larsson
Holiday Reading (Illustration for *Ett hem*) 1899
Pen and ink. 315 x 465 mm
(Private collection)

124. Carl Larsson *The Evening before the Journey to England* 1909
Watercolour. 510 x 730 mm
(Private collection)

AT HOME WITH THE LARSSONS: THE WORKSHOP

125. Carl Larsson
The Studio, the Other Half (*Ett hem* series) 1894-5
Watercolour. c. 320 x 430 mm
(The Nationalmuseum, Stockholm; NMB 272)

126. Carl Larsson
Lisbeth is Reading 1904
Watercolour. 600 x 760 mm
(The Nationalmuseum, Stockholm; NMB 2342)

127. Carl Larsson
Interior with Cactus 1914
Watercolour. 700 x 920 mm
(Helsingborg Museum; 569-54)

128. Carl Larsson
The Workshop 1908
Watercolour. 520 x 730 mm
(Private collection, not exhibited)

AT HOME WITH THE LARSSONS: THE BIG STUDIO

129. Carl Larsson *The Carpenter's Shop, Winnowing and Christmas Eve* (Three drawings in one frame for *Spadarvet*) c. 1905
Watercolour. 330 x 490 mm
(The Bonniers' Portrait Collection, Nedre Manilla, Stockholm)

130. Carl Larsson
Shelling Peas 1908
Watercolour. 530 x 775 mm
(Private collection, not exhibited)

131. Carl Larsson
After the Ball in the Studio 1908
Watercolour. 528 x 746 mm
(Malmö Museum of Art; MM 6804)

132. Carl Larsson
Self-portrait 1912
Watercolour. 535 x 753 mm
(Malmö Museum of Art; MM 6802)

133. Carl Larsson
Design for the installation of

the panelling in the big studio
c. 1899
Pencil and oil on canvas.
610 x 910 mm
(The Carl Larsson House,
Sundborn)

134. Settle
Late 18th century, early 19th
century. Painted softwood (The
Carl Larsson House, Sundborn)

135. Table. Painted softwood
18th century
(The Carl Larsson House,
Sundborn)

136. Two chairs
c. 1780
Painted softwood with a
woven linen and wool seat
(The Carl Larsson House,
Sundborn)

137. Tablecloth
Embroidered linen. Copy of
original by Karin Larsson
(The Carl Larsson House,
Sundborn)

138. Carl Larsson
Life's Mystery 1911
Oil on canvas. 1560 x 2150 mm
(The Carl Larsson House,
Sundborn)

139. A pair of sconces, 18th
century. Brass
(The Carl Larsson House,
Sundborn)

140. Carl Larsson
Esbjörn 1917
Watercolour. 1155 x 815 mm
(The Carl Larsson House,
Sundborn)

141. Chair with arms
c. 1760
Painted softwood
(The Carl Larsson House,
Sundborn)

142. Table. Painted softwood.
Designed by Karin Larsson
before 1909
(The Carl Larsson House,
Sundborn)

143. Pair of candelabra, 18th
century. Brass (The Carl Larsson
House, Sundborn)

144. Carl Larsson
Hilda 1911
Watercolour. 670 x 1010 mm
(Private collection)

**AT HOME WITH THE
LARSSONS: KARIN'S
WRITING-ROOM**

145. Carl Larsson
Letter Writing 1912
Watercolour. 520 x 740 mm
(The Nationalmuseum,
Stockholm; NMB 1438)

146. Textile pelmet
From Karin Larsson's writing-
room. Embroidered linen. Copy
of original by Karin Larsson
(The Carl Larsson House,
Sundborn)

**AT HOME WITH THE
LARSSONS: CARL'S
BEDROOM**

147. Carl Larsson
Father's Room (Ett hem series)
1894-7

Watercolour. c. 320 x 430 mm
(The Nationalmuseum,
Stockholm; NMB 273)

148. Cupboard
Softwood. Swedish. Dated 1694
(The Carl Larsson House,
Sundborn)

149. Bed hangings
From Carl Larsson's bedroom
Embroidered linen. Copies of
originals by Karin Larsson
(The Carl Larsson House,
Sundborn)

150. Toilet table. From Carl
Larsson's bedroom c. 1893
Painted softwood (The Carl
Larsson House, Sundborn)

151. Cloth on toilet table
Linen. Copy of original
(The Carl Larsson House,
Sundborn)

152. Portière. From Carl
Larsson's bedroom. Macramé
and flatweave. Copy of original
by Karin Larsson (The Carl
Larsson House, Sundborn)

153. Hanging cupboard.
From Carl Larsson's bedroom
18th century, with 19th century
lock (The Carl Larsson House,
Sundborn)

154. Blanket. Cotton and wool
flatweave. Designed by Karin
Larsson in 1901
Made in 1921. (The Carl
Larsson House, Sundborn;
CL 20)

**AT HOME WITH THE
LARSSONS: THE LIBRARY**

155. Carl Larsson
The Small Studio (Illustration
for *Ett hem*) 1899
Pen and ink. 315 x 460 mm
(Private collection)

156. Frame of cuttings from
medieval manuscripts
(The Carl Larsson House,
Sundborn)

157. Tablecloth. Wool tapestry
weaving. Copy of cloth
designed and made by Karin
Larsson 1906-9
(The Carl Larsson House,
Sundborn; CL 2)

158. Books from the library at
Lilla Hyttnäs
(The Carl Larsson House,
Sundbourn)

**AT HOME WITH THE
LARSSONS: KARIN'S AND
THE CHILDREN'S BEDROOM**

159. Carl Larsson
*Mother's and the Little Girl's
Room (Ett hem* series) 1897
Watercolour. 320 x 430 mm
(The Nationalmuseum;
NMB 274)

160. Carl Larsson
The Guardian Angel 1898
Etching. 154 x 197 mm
(British Museum; 1949-4-11-4)

161. Carl Larsson
Nameday Congratulation 1900
Watercolour. 450 x 630 mm
(The Carl Larsson House,
Sundborn)

162. Carl Larsson
The Home's Good Angel 1909
Watercolour. 520 x 740 mm
(Gothenburg University)

**AT HOME WITH THE
LARSSONS: THE OLD ROOM**

163. Carl Larsson
*Morning Serenade for Prince
Eugen in Sundborn* 1902
Pen and ink and wash.
630 x 450 mm (Prince Eugen's
Waldemarsudde, Stockholm)

164. Carl Larsson
The Old Room 1909
Watercolour. 510 x 730 mm
(Private collection)

165. Hanging cupboard
17th century Painted softwood
Decorated by Carl Larsson,
dated 1894 (The Carl Larsson
House, Sundborn)

165a. Carl Larsson
Karin by the Linen Cupboard
1906
Watercolour. 615 x 950 mm
(Private collection)

**AT HOME WITH THE
LARSSONS: SUZANNE'S
ROOM AND THE BATHROOM**

166. Carl Larsson
Suzanne and Another 1901
Watercolour. 940 x 625 mm
(Private collection)

166a. Carl Larsson
Lisbeth (The Bathroom) 1909
Watercolour
(Private collection)

**AT HOME WITH THE
LARSSONS: THE KITCHEN**

167. Carl Larsson
The Kitchen (Ett hem series)
1898
Watercolour. c. 320 x 430 mm
(The Nationalmuseum,
Stockholm; NMB 270)

KARIN'S CONTRIBUTION

168. Karin Larsson
Professor Malmström's Studio
c. 1882
Oil on canvas. 710 x 530 mm
(The Carl Larsson House,
Sundborn)

169. Carl Larsson
Sunday Rest 1900
Watercolour. 680 x 1040 mm
(The Nationalmuseum,
Stockholm; NMB 376)

170. Child's bed c. 1901
Painted softwood and roof
shingles. Designed by Karin
Larsson (The Carl Larsson
House, Sundborn)

171. Chair. Early 18th century.
Painted wood.
Copy of seat cover, woven and
embroidered and designed by
Karin Larsson (The Carl Larsson
House, Sundborn)

172. Chair with arms
Early 18th century. Painted
wood. Copy of seat cover,
woven and embroidered by
Karin Larsson and

perhaps Carl Larsson (The Carl
Larsson House, Sundborn)

173. Carl Larsson
*Caricature Portrait of Karin
Larsson* Probably 1905
Charcoal and pastel.
302 x 278 mm
(The Nationalmuseum,
Stockholm; NMH 204/1908)

174. Karin Larsson
Interior at Grez 1884
Oil on canvas. 545 x 465 mm
(The Carl Larsson House,
Sundborn)

175. Cover of Christmas
magazine of 1895 for
Konstnärs Klubben (The Artists'
Club) Designed by Karin
Larsson (The Carl Larsson
House, Sundborn)

176. Carl Larsson
Karin and Esbjörn 1904
Etching. 178 x 250 mm
(British Museum; 1949-4-11-4)

177. Carl Larsson
Karin and Kersti 1904
Etching. 265 x 182 mm
(British Museum; 1906-4-19-3)

178. Carl Larsson
Karin and Esbjörn 1909
Oil on canvas. 940 x 1220 mm
(Private collection, not
exhibited)

179. Carl Larsson
Karin and Brita in the Garden
1911
Watercolour. 860 x 1200 mm
(Private collection)

179a. Carl Larsson
Kersti's Birthday, 1909
Watercolour 500 x 715mm
(Private collection)

180. Tapestry partially finished.
Flatweave technique. Copy of
'Four Elements' tapestry begun
in 1903. This copy in progress
in 1906 by Karin Larsson (The
Carl Larsson House, Sundborn;
CL 232)

181. Tablecloth. Embroidered
linen. Copy of cloth designed
and made by Karin Larsson in
1897.
(The Carl Larsson House,
Sundborn; CL 35)

182. Ceiling hanging
Embroidered cotton.
Copy of original designed and
made by Karin Larsson in 1893.
(The Carl Larsson House,
Sundborn; CL 42)

183. Cushion cover 1905
Embroidered. Designed
and made by Karin Larsson
(The Carl Larsson House,
Sundborn, CL 5)

184. Cushion cover
Embroidered in
commemoration of the First
World War in 1918.
Designed and embroidered by
Karin Larsson and her
daughters Lisbeth, Brita and
Kersti (The Carl Larsson House,
Sundborn; CL 4)

185. Chair seat cover After
1901
Flatweave tapestry.
Designed by Carl and Karin

Larsson Made by Karin Larsson
(The Carl Larsson House,
Sundborn; CL 248)

186. Chair back.
After 1901. Flatweave tapestry
Designed by Carl and Karin
Larsson. Made by Karin Larsson
(The Carl Larsson House,
Sundborn; CL 248)

187. Chair back, After 1901.
Flatweave tapestry
Designed by Carl and Karin
Larsson, Made by Karin Larsson
(The Carl Larsson House,
Sundborn)

188. Bedspread 1890s
Woven with rag inserts.
Designed by Karin Larsson
(The Carl Larsson House,
Sundborn; CL 20)

189. 'Pegasus' tapestry 1910.
Designed and made by Carl
and Karin Larsson. (The Carl
Larsson House, Sundborn; CL
259)

190. Rocking-chair 1906
Painted wood with leather seat
Designed by Karin Larsson
Made by Hans Arnbom (The
Carl Larsson House, Sundborn)

191. Carl Larsson
Girl with Rocking-chair 1907
Watercolour. 720 x 510 mm
(Malmö Museum of Art;
MMK 33)

192. Chandelier.
Made by 1908. Wrought iron.
Designed by Karin Larsson (The
Carl Larsson House, Sundborn)

**A HUNDRED YEARS OF THE
LARSSON IDEAL**

193. Carl Larsson
Hide-and-Seek 1901
Coloured lithograph
475 x 675 mm
(The Carl Larsson House,
Sundborn)

194. Carl Larsson
*You Know What? Be Good and
Cheerful* 1911
Colour lithograph (Private
collection)

195. Carl Larsson
*You Know What? Be Good and
Cheerful* 1911
Colour lithograph (Private
collection)

196. *Hemmets kokbok* (The
Home's Cookery Book),
Uppsala, 1909
(Private collection)

INDEX

ILLUSTRATION ACKNOWLEDGEMENTS

The Victoria and Albert Museum is indebted to the following for permission to reproduce items in their ownership or care. Illustrations by courtesy of the Trustees of the Museum are as follows: 71-76, 78, 98. All recent photographs of Lilla Hyttnäs have been taken by Nisse Peterson; unless otherwise mentioned they have been commissioned by the Museum. For the owners of illustrations of items shown at the exhibition *Carl and Karin Larsson: Creators of the Swedish Style* (indicated in the captions, by numbers in square brackets) see List of Exhibits, pp. 237-9.

Board of Trustees of the Victoria and Albert Museum 5, 6, 16,71-76, 78, 98, 102, 141, 160, 166, 219, 233, 235, 242, 249

American Swedish Historical Museum, Philadelphia 156

Bonniers Portrait Collection, Nedre Manilla, Stockholm 31, 40, 167

Trustees of the British Museum, London 244

Bukowskis Konsthandel AB, Stockholm 161

Carl Larsson House Sundborn 2, 14, 23, 25, 29, 89, 97, 100, 103, 108, 113, 117, 127, 140, 142, 143, 153, 155, 165, 169, 172, 177, 178, 190-192. The following in the care of Dalarnas Museum, Falun: 89, 95, 96, 110, 146, 157, 168, 185, 189, 195, 216, 248

Gothenburg Art Museum 1, 3, 4, 18, 21, 22, 24, 25, 36, 42, 91, 193, 245

Gothenburg University library 92

Helsingborg Museum 225

H(gan(s Museum 13

IKEA Marketing Services Ltd 255, 257

International Magazine Service AB, Stockholm 186

Kulturen, Lund 47

Malmo Museums 170, 211, 213

Musée Albert Kahn, Boulogne-Billancourt 11

Nationalmuseum, Stockholm 17, 19, 32, 39, 26, 27, 30, 32-34, 37, 38, 44, 49, 50, 59, 68, 80-82, 85-87, 94, 101, 105, 115, 116, 118, 119, 121, 131, 133-135, 138, 139, 145, 147, 150, 152, 158, 176, 188, 197, 258

Nordiska Museet, Stockholm Frontispiece, 10, 12, 45, 53, 55-58, 64, 65, 69, 104, 145, 163, 226, 237, 252, 253

Private Collections 28, 35, 52, 60, 69, 79, 102, 128, 136, 174, 214, 215, 217, 238-241, 243, 252, 253

Reimanns Stillebenfoto AB 256

Royal Collections, Stockholm 62

Royal Institute of British Architects, London 70, 77

Royal Library, Stockholm 54, 254

Stockholm Town Museum 7, 8, 9

Svensk Form, Stockholm 251

Thiels Gallery, Stockholm 51, 114, 187, 228

Uffizi Galleries, Florence 41

Zorn Museum, Mora 122